Springer Studies in the History of Economic Thought

This series offers an outlet for research in the history of economic thought. It features scholarly studies on important theoretical developments and great economic thinkers that have contributed to the evolution of the economic discipline.

Springer Studies in the History of Economic Thought (SSHET) welcomes proposals for research monographs, edited volumes and handbooks from a variety of disciplines that seek to study the history of economic thinking and help to arrive at a better understanding of modern economics. Relevant topics include, but are not limited to, various schools of thought, important pioneers and thinkers, ancient and medieval economic thought, mercantilism, cameralism and physiocracy, classical and neoclassical economics, historical, institutional and evolutionary economics, socialism and Marxism, Keynesian, Sraffian and Austrian economics, econometrics and mathematical studies as well as economic methodology and the link between economic history and history of economic thought.

All titles in this series are peer-reviewed.

For further information on the series and to submit a proposal for consideration, please contact Johannes Glaeser (Senior Editor Economics) Johannes.glaeser@springer.com.

More information about this series at https://link.springer.com/bookseries/16457

Warren Young · Edward W. Fuller

Reinterpreting Mr. Keynes

The IS-LM Enigma Revisited

Springer

Warren Young
Bar Ilan University
Ramat Gan, Israel

Edward W. Fuller
Palo Alto, CA, USA

ISSN 2662-6098 ISSN 2662-6101 (electronic)
Springer Studies in the History of Economic Thought
ISBN 978-3-030-91341-0 ISBN 978-3-030-91342-7 (eBook)
https://doi.org/10.1007/978-3-030-91342-7

This Springer imprint is published by the registered company Springer Nature Switzerland AG
The registered company address is: Gewerbestrasse 11, 6330 Cham, Switzerland

Dedicated to the memories of Marvin Goodfriend, Allan H. Meltzer, Donald Moggridge, Don Patinkin, and Geoff Harcourt

Acknowledgments

This book centers around a document in the *John Maynard Keynes Papers* labeled GTE/5/419. This handwritten document shows that Keynes himself originated the IS-LM approach to his famous work *The General Theory of Employment, Interest and Money*. GTE/5/419 calls for a re-examination of the history of the IS-LM model and, by extension, the early history of macroeconomics.

This work relies heavily on previously unpublished archival material. Thus, we must express our deepest gratitude to all the librarians and archivists who facilitated our research. First and foremost, we thank Patricia McGuire of the Archive Centre at King's College, Cambridge, for her assistance with the *Keynes Papers*. We thank Peter Jones for permitting photographic reproduction of documents from the *Keynes Papers*.

In addition to primary materials from Keynes's own papers, this work relies on student notes from Keynes's lectures in the years leading up to the publication of the *General Theory*. We gratefully acknowledge all of the note takers for sharing their notes with posterity. Donald Moggridge and Don Patinkin recognized the value of the student notes in the 1970s. Thomas K. Rymes collected the original student notes, and he produced a comprehensive transcription in the 1980s under the title *Keynes Lectures, 1932–35: Notes of Students*. This seminal yet inaccessible transcription plays a central role in the current book. After much trouble locating Rymes's transcription, Ingo Barens graciously provided a copy.

Locating the original student notes also proved difficult. Several librarians and archivists were integral in our search. First, we thank Simon Frost and Clare Trowell of the Marshall Library for assistance with the papers of Thomas K. Rymes. We thank Elizabeth Dunn of Rubenstein Library for assistance with the papers of Don Patinkin. Finally, we thank Lloyd K. Keane of MacOdrum Library for assistance with the notes of Robert Bryce.

The doctoral dissertations of Paul Samuelson, Franco Modigliani, and Lawrence Klein played a significant role in the Keynesian Revolution and the Neoclassical Synthesis. While Klein's dissertation is widely available, several librarians helped us obtain copies of the dissertations of Samuelson and Modigliani. We thank Harvard

University Archives for providing Samuelson's dissertation and The New School Libraries and Archives for that of Modigliani.

This book is dedicated to the memories of five great economists and good friends: four Keynes scholars, Allan H. Meltzer, Donald Moggridge, Don Patinkin, and Geoff Harcourt, and someone who "never taught IS-LM," Marvin Goodfriend.

Contents

Chapter 1
Introduction, Keynes's Own IS-LM Approach

In 1987—fifty years after the publication of papers presenting the IS-LM model by Roy Harrod, James Meade, and John R. Hicks, respectively—two works appeared dealing with the model and its legacy. The first dealt with the "enigma" surrounding its origins.[1] The second presented a "defense" against attacks on it as the representation of Keynes's *General Theory* system.[2]

In his 1987 book *Interpreting Mr Keynes: The IS-LM Enigma*, one of the present authors undertook a quest after what, at the time, appeared to be the actual origins of the IS-LM model. He described the model in terms of "sequential cross-fertilization" between a series of interpreters of Keynes's approach from mid-1936 onwards.[3] This cross-fertilization culminated in the IS-LM papers delivered by Harrod, Meade, and Hicks at the September 1936 Oxford Econometric Society meeting.[4] The intricacies of the evolution and dissemination of the IS-LM model, ostensibly with a linkage dating back to Keynes's 1933 lectures, were the focus of Warren Young's 1987 book.

On the other hand, Don Patinkin's 1987 paper "In Defense of IS-LM"—presented at the conference on "50 Years of IS-LM"—focused upon how the model acquired a separate existence and the implications of this for macroeconomics. He posed two questions in this regard. The first was whether IS-LM was "a valid representation" of Keynes's *General Theory*. The second was whether it was "a valid and useful analytical construct."[5]

According to Patinkin, the answer to the first question was that Keynes himself accepted it as being valid.[6] Although he conflated the diagram and equations in his

---

1 Young (1987).

2 Patinkin (1987). The 1987 working paper was revised in 1988 and later published in *Banca Nazionale del Lavoro Quarterly Review* (Patinkin 1990).

3 Young (1987, 3).

4 See Harrod (1937), Hicks (1937), and Meade (1937).

5 Patinkin (1987, 2; 1990, 120).

6 Patinkin (1987, 2; 1990, 120).

W. Young and E. W. Fuller, *Reinterpreting Mr. Keynes*,
Springer Studies in the History of Economic Thought,
https://doi.org/10.1007/978-3-030-91342-7_1

subsequent discussion of Hicks's actual contribution, Patinkin maintained that the IS-LM diagram—first presented by Hicks as CC-LL, and in his 1937 *Econometrica* paper as SI-LL—became the accepted diagrammatic representation of Keyne's system.[7] Patinkin's answer to the second question was based on its later extension of the model to a variety of issues of theory and policy, ranging from prices and inflation to international economics to aggregate supply and demand.[8]

A decade later, in a panel discussion at the *AEA* meeting in January 1997 entitled "Is There a Core of Practical Macroeconomics That We Should all Believe?," economists such as Robert Solow, John B. Taylor, Martin Eichenbaum, Alan Blinder, and Olivier Blanchard were still dealing with the relevance of IS-LM.[9] And again, some five years after the *AEA* panel discussion, at the *HOPE* conference in April 2003, papers were presented exploring what was described as the "Rise, Fall and Strange Persistence" of the IS-LM model, persistence being the operative term.[10]

Both Patinkin and Young reported that student notes of his 1933 lectures showed that Keynes presented a simultaneous equations approach somewhat similar to the IS-LM approach.[11] The problem with the earlier narratives of both Young and Patinkin regarding the origins, evolution, and dissemination of IS-LM, however, lies in the fact that there was no textual evidence provided by them directly linking Keynes to IS-LM.

Today, the conventional account of the origins of IS-LM is a virtual urban legend, a modern tale thought to be true. Indeed, while over three decades ago, a reconstruction of the approach was attempted, which showed that the model ostensibly evolved via cross-fertilization between economists—Harrod, Meade, and Hicks, among others—the story still being told in the textbooks is that it was "introduced" by Hicks and "extended" and "popularized" by Alvin Hansen.[12]

In his 1987 book, *Interpreting Mr Keynes*, one of the authors of the present volume mentioned the fact that Keynes presented IS-LM-type equations to his students in his lecture of December 4, 1933.[13] This was noted earlier by Patinkin.[14] In 1988, Robert W. Dimand also presented this equation system recorded in student notes from December 1933.[15] Thomas K. Rymes reported these equations in his 1989 compilation of student notes from Keynes's lectures over the period 1932–1935.[16] Keynes's 1933 equation system as recorded by students, however, did not appear in

---

[7] See Hicks (1937) on the SI-LL diagram. See Young (1987, 45) on the CC-LL diagram.

[8] Patinkin (1987, 7–14; 1990, 125–130).

[9] See Blanchard (1997), Blinder (1997), Eichenbaum (1997), Solow (1997), and Taylor (1997).

[10] See de Vroey and Hoover (2004).

[11] Patinkin (1976, 79n22; 1982, 23) and Young (1987, 12–13, 33).

[12] For example, see Krugman (2000, 34), Abel and Bernanke (2005, 308), Dornbusch et al. (2008, 223n1), Blanchard (2017, 89, 499), and Mankiw (2019, 289). See Young (1987) on the role of Harrod, Meade, and Hicks in the early history of the IS-LM model.

[13] Young (1987, 12–13, 33).

[14] See Patinkin (1976, 79).

[15] Dimand (1988, 181).

[16] Rymes (1989, 125).

his *General Theory*. At the time Young was researching, and writing his 1987 book, he did not pose the questions:

1. What was the basis for the IS-LM-type equations Keynes presented to his students on December 4, 1933?
2. Did the various student lecture notes have the same equations or were there differences in what they recorded? And if so, what may have brought this about?
3. What was the connection between Keynes's lecture of December 4, 1933, his previous approach, and his subsequent approach in the *General Theory*?

These crucial questions remained unanswered until the coauthor of the present work found a page of Keynes's own notes for his December 4, 1933 lecture in the *Keynes Papers*. This page has been ostensibly overlooked until now. This page of equations and the text explaining them formed the core of his December 4, 1933 lecture, and it includes the partial IS-LM-type equational approach recorded in the student lecture notes. Significantly, the page contained two additional equations describing equilibrium in the goods and money markets. In other words, in the preparatory material for his December 4, 1933, lecture, Keynes set out a complete system of IS-LM equations.

This volume, therefore, is about that sheet of paper and its role in the development of IS-LM. The document, found in the *Keynes Papers*, has never be published or discussed by economists or historians of economic thought, nor did it appear in Keynes's *Collected Writings*. Patinkin recognized as early as 1975 that materials included in Keynes's *Collected Writings* were subject to "editorial decisions."[17] However, it is not known why the document has never appeared in the literature regarding the development of Keynes's approach to economics. Moreover, we cannot explain if this was the result of deliberate omission from Keynes's *Collected Writings* based upon "editorial decisions," or if it was simply "overlooked" by the team of Keynes scholars that edited his *Collected Writings*.

While it is indeed puzzling that the document that forms the core of the present work has remained in obscurity, the question is not necessarily why it did not appear as part of the *Collected Writings*. Rather, the question could be posed: what would have been the reaction to its publication as part of the early volumes of the *Collected Writings*?

In our view, this page of IS-LM-type equations—in effect the complete equational model later set out and applied by Harrod, Meade, and Hicks, among others—and the text written down by Keynes in December 1933 to explain the equations, necessitates a significant revision of the narrative provided by Young in his 1987 account of the history of IS-LM.

Now, from his equational epiphany in December 1933 onwards, as will be seen, Keynes consistently verbally expressed his approach in simultaneous terms. And, while in his 1987 book, Young noted that all the early "interpreters" presented simultaneous IS-LM-type models of what they saw as the structure of Keynes's

[17] Patinkin (1975, 253). Also, see O'Donnell (1995) for a detailed discussion of the editorial decisions made when preparing Keynes's *Collected Writings*.

approach, none were based directly upon Keynes's own representation, as manifest in the document he prepared as the basis for his lecture of December 4, 1933.[18] Furthermore, as will be seen, the student notes do not include all the equations that appear in the Keynes document. While seemingly an anomaly, the equation system in the December 1933 document, again, as will be seen, is of a level of sophistication that Keynes may have deemed somewhat above the ability of his undergraduate students to master. Consequently, he presented a simplified form of the model he had set out in the document.

After the *General Theory* was published, the IS-LM model became the "standard representation" of the Keynesian system and, more importantly, the core of macroeconomics. Indeed, James Tobin and Robert Solow described the IS-LM model as "the trained intuition of economists."[19] No doubt, Harrod, Meade, Hicks, Lange, and others played a central role in establishing IS-LM at the core of macroeconomics. Still, Keynes's December 1933 IS-LM document shows that he was the true originator of what became the trained intuition of economists.

Keynes's document of December 1933 necessitates the reinterpreting of Mr. Keynes. Let us now turn to our revised story of the origins, development, evolution, and dissemination of IS-LM.

References

Abel, A. B., & Bernanke, B. (2005). *Macroeconomics*. Pearson/Addison Wesley.

Blanchard, O. (1997). Is there a core of usable macroeconomics? *The American Economic Review, 87*(2), 244–246.

Blanchard, O. (2017). *Macroeconomics*. Pearson.

Blinder, A. (1997). Is there a core of practical macroeconomics that we should all believe? *The American Economic Review, 87*(2), 240–243.

Champernowne, D. G. (1936). Unemployment, basic and monetary: The classical analysis and the Keynesian. *The Review of Economic Studies, 3*(3), 201–216.

De Vroey, M., & Hoover, K. D. (2004). *The IS-LM model: Its rise, fall, and strange persistence.* Duke University Press.

Dimand, R. W. (1988). *The origins of the Keynesian revolution.* Stanford University Press.

Dimand, R. W. (2007). Keynes, IS-LM, and the Marshallian tradition. *History of Political Economy, 39*(1), 81–95.

Dornbusch, R., Fischer, S., & Startz, R. (2008). *Macroeconomics*. McGraw-Hill.

Eichenbaum, M. (1997). Some thoughts on practical stabilization policy. *The American Economic Review, 87*(2), 236–239.

Harrod, R. F. (1937). Mr. Keynes and traditional theory. *Econometrica, 5*(1), 74–86.

Hicks, J. R. (1937). Mr. Keynes and the 'classics'; a suggested interpretation. *Econometrica, 5*(2), 147–159.

Krugman, P. (2000). How complicated does the model have to be? *Oxford Review of Economic Policy, 16*(4), 33–42.

---

[18] As will be discussed later, Champernowne (1936) and Reddaway (1936) published IS-LM papers before Harrod, Meade, and Hicks. Furthermore, their papers are directly traceable to Keynes's lectures and supervisions. See Young (1987, 60, 72–86) and Dimand (2007, 82).

[19] Tobin (1982, 24) and Solow (1984, 14).

Mankiw, N. G. (2019). *Macroeconomics*. Worth Publishers.
Meade, J. E. (1937). A simplified model of Mr. Keynes' system. *The Review of Economic Studies, 4*(2), 98–107.
Patinkin, D. (1975). The collected writings of John Maynard Keynes: From the tract to the general theory. *The Economic Journal, 85*(338), 249–271.
Patinkin, D. (1976). *Keynes' monetary thought: A study of its development*. Duke University Press.
Patinkin, D. (1982). *Anticipations of the general theory?* University of Chicago Press.
Patinkin D (1987) *In defense of IS-LM*. UCLA Economics Working Papers 537.
Patinkin, D. (1990). In defense of IS-LM. *Banca Nazionale Del Lavoro Quarterly Review, 172*, 119–131.
O'Donnell, R. M. (1995). Editing large unpublished writings: the case of J.M. Keynes. *History of Economic Ideas, 3*(2), 89–130.
Reddaway, W. B. (1936). The general theory of employment, interest and money. *Economic Record, 12*, 28–36.
Rymes, T. K. (1989). *Keynes's lectures, 1932–35: Notes of a representative student*. Macmillan.
Solow, R. M. (1984). Mr Hicks and the classics. *Oxford Economic Papers, 36*, 13–25.
Solow, R. M. (1997). Is there a core of usable macroeconomics we should all believe in? *The American Economic Review, 87*(2), 230–232.
Taylor, J. B. (1997). A core of practical macroeconomics. *The American Economic Review, 87*(2), 233–235.
Tobin, J. (1982). Nobel lecture: Money and finance in the macroeconomic process. *Journal of Money, Credit and Banking, 14*(2), 171–204.
Young, W. (1987). *Interpreting Mr. Keynes: The IS-LM enigma*. Polity Press.

Chapter 2
Prolog to Keynes's IS-LM, 1930 to 1932

The story of Keynes's IS-LM approach begins with his 1930 work *A Treatise on Money*. Indeed, his IS-LM approach has its origins in his effort to solve problems in the *Treatise*. In an important sense, then, Keynes's own IS-LM approach was born out of the *Treatise*.[1]

It must be emphasized that *A Treatise on Money* was Keynes's first major theoretical work on economics. Strictly speaking, Keynes was not an academic economist—nor even an academic for that matter.[2] He spent most of the first fifteen years of his professional career as a civil servant in the British government. After studying mathematics at the University of Cambridge, he served as a clerk in the India Office from October 1906 to June 1908. Even when he left his post for a lectureship at Cambridge, he served as an important advisor to the India Office between 1909 and 1914. His work advising the India Office led to his first published book, *Indian Currency and Finance* (1913).[3]

The First World War erupted in August 1914, and, through his connections at the India Office, Keynes landed a job at the British Treasury in January 1915. By the time the war ended in November 1918, he was the third highest ranking official in the British Treasury. He was sent to the Paris Peace Conference as the Treasury's top representative in January 1919. He resigned from the British delegation in June of that year and returned to England, where he wrote his famous work *The Economic Consequences of Peace* (1919).[4] Published in December 1919, this book

[1] Donald Moggridge writes in his editorial introduction to the *General Theory*, "The origins of the *General Theory* lie in Keynes's dissatisfaction with his *Treatise on Money* even at the time of publication" (in Keynes CW 7, xi).

[2] As Don Patinkin notes, "it would be a serious mistake to think of Keynes as devoting his major efforts in the interwar period to writing [theoretical] books in the quiet halls of academe" and "Keynes did not live in the world of academe" (1982, xxii, 204).

[3] See Keynes (CW 1).

[4] See Keynes (CW 2).

W. Young and E. W. Fuller, *Reinterpreting Mr. Keynes*,
Springer Studies in the History of Economic Thought,
https://doi.org/10.1007/978-3-030-91342-7_2

made Keynes an international celebrity and laid the foundation for his massive influence on twentieth-century economics. Thus, it was a polemical work, rather than a scientific work, that made him the world's most famous economist.[5]

The Economic Consequences of the Peace launched Keynes's extraordinarily successful career in journalism. After the great success of his book, news outlets across the globe were eager to publish his views on post-war problems, and he became a regular commentator in the press. By 1923, he purchased a weekly political newspaper called *The Nation*, and for the rest of the decade, he served as chairman of the renamed *Nation and Athenaeum*. He averaged one article per week for the press during the 1920s. In fact, his journalistic activities were his main source of regular income.[6] Also, he penned popular pamphlets on economic policy, including *The Economic Consequences of Mr. Churchill* (1925), *Can Lloyd George Do It?* (1929), and *The Means to Prosperity* (1933).[7] In summary, during the 1920s, he was a journalist first and an economist second. Indeed, he privately described himself as a "propagandist" and "publicist."[8]

Although he was not an academic, Keynes always had grand academic aspirations. After leaving the India Office in June 1908, he was a lecturer in economics at Cambridge from January 1909 until he entered the Treasury in January 1915. But he was never a professor, and he was not a university lecturer after 1914.[9] Still, he always maintained a close connection to academic life at Cambridge. He retained a residence at Cambridge throughout his entire adult life and spent almost every Saturday, Sunday, and Monday there.[10] So what was Keynes's track record in academia before the *Treatise on Money*?

His first major academic work was *A Treatise on Probability* (1921).[11] Although third by publication date, this must be considered his first book, for it is a reworking of his fellowship dissertation submitted in December 1908.[12] In the 1908 dissertation and 1921 book, he advocates the logical theory of probability. It is only a slight

---

[5] Moggridge describes the book as a "classic polemic" and "political tract," and he writes: "The book ranks as one of the finest polemics written in the field of political economy" (1993, vii, 54–55). Also see Harrod (1951, 255).

[6] As Moggridge notes, "Keynes was an extremely successful journalist" (1992, 555). Patinkin writes, "Keynes earned his living from his publicistic writings and from speculation on the stock market" (1982, 204; 1987, 37). Also see Johnson and Johnson (1978, 32).

[7] See Keynes (CW 19, 357–361), Keynes (CW 19, 761–766), and Keynes (CW 9, 335–366).

[8] Keynes (1924a, 223; CW 22, 38). Elizabeth Johnson, an editor of Keynes's *Collected Writings*, observes: "he was also conspicuously and devotedly a journalist and propagandist" and "He acted like a professional propagandist … [A]ll of his writing was journalism of one order or another" (Johnson and Johnson 1978, 9, 30–31). Moggridge acknowledges Keynes's "propagandist proclivities" (1994, 110).

[9] See Moggridge (1976, 62).

[10] See Moggridge (1976, 74), Patinkin (1982, xxii; 1987, 37), and Marcuzzo (2006, 120–121).

[11] See Keynes (CW 8). Moggridge writes, "between 1906 and 1911 Keynes devoted most of his intellectual energy to probability" (1976, 20).

[12] Rod O'Donnell agrees, "Although the *TP* ranks as his third book by date of publication, it was in an important sense the first he wrote" (1989, 17).

exaggeration to say that no one accepts his logical theory today. In short, Keynes's first major theoretical work was not a success in any sense of the word.[13]

As mentioned, Keynes published *Indian Currency and Finance* in June 1913. The book's title is telling, as it foreshadows the essential role money plays in all his economics books. Still, *Indian Currency and Finance* is descriptive rather than theoretical, and his close connection to the India Office in the years surrounding its publication colored his analysis.[14] His next book in economics was *A Tract on Monetary Reform*, published in December 1923.[15] Rather than a theoretical work on economics, however, the *Tract* is a collection of articles he was commissioned to write for the press.[16] It does not constitute evidence of early academic success, and, as will be shown below, Keynes himself largely abandoned the ideas he expounded in the *Tract* after only eighteen months.[17]

Although he became the editor of *The Economic Journal* in October 1911, Keynes did not publish any notable scientific papers until 1929. Most of the early articles he published in academic journals were memoirs, obituaries, or book reviews. Finally, in March 1929, he published a noteworthy theoretical paper, "The German Transfer Problem[18] This paper ignited a controversy with the Swedish economist Bertil Ohlin. Today, even his most ardent defenders admit that Keynes's theoretical analysis was flawed: There is no transfer problem.[19] In summary, despite all his success in government and journalism, academic success eluded Keynes in the years leading up to the publication of *A Treatise on Money*.[20]

---

[13] Lawrence Klein writes, "Keynes's ideas on probability represent a minority position among current workers on the subject and are not those for which we shall long remember his work … He did not make a sensational advance in probability theory" (1951, 446). Jochen Runde admits, "The 'logical' approach to probability he advocates in his *Treatise on Probability* currently occupies what can only be described as a marginal position in the philosophy of probability" (1994, 97). See Gillies (2000, 25–49) for a detailed exposition and critique of Keynes's logical theory of probability.

[14] As Moggridge says, "his writings on India reflected what might be called the India Office view of the world" (1992, 203). Although he provides a sympathetic account of the work, Skidelsky admits Keynes was a "public defender" who used "inside knowledge to defend government performance" (1983, 272, 275).

[15] See Keynes (CW 4).

[16] See Keynes (CW 4, xii), Patinkin (1982, xx), and Moggridge (1992, 434) on the journalistic origins of the *Tract*. Patinkin notes "the limited theoretical discussion" (1982, xx). Klein writes, "By itself it does not create revolutionary ideas" (1951, 446).

[17] See Moggridge (1976, 73).

[18] See Keynes (CW 11, 451–459).

[19] Harry G. Johnson says that Keynes's work on the transfer problem was "technically incompetent" (1975, 30). Similarly, Robert Mundell writes that "Keynes let himself fall victim to such an absurd position" (2002, 245). Robert Skidelsky admits, "If we stick to the pure theory of the matter, Keynes was wrong" (1992, 311).

[20] Austin Robinson writes, "When one thinks of Keynes as the innovator in economic theory it is almost wholly of his work embodied in the *Treatise* and the *General Theory*" (1972, 534). Moggridge summarizes Keynes's work on economics before 1930 as follows: "Prior to the 1930s, Keynes' contributions to economics were noted less for their theoretical innovations than for their realist acumen and their understanding of the working of complex institutions" (1993, 44).

2.1 The Failure of *A Treatise on Money*

Keynes began planning the *Treatise* almost immediately after his *Tract* was published in December 1923. On February 1, 1924, he revealed to his future wife, Lydia Lopokova, that he was planning "a short new book, which would be a sequel to *Monetary Reform*."[21] On May 2, 1924, he wrote to Lopokova: "In making up my lectures, the shape of my new book begins to form in my mind."[22] Keynes prepared his first draft table of contents on July 14, 1924, and he produced an early draft by November 30, 1924.[23] He could write to Kurt Singer on April 23, 1925:

> I am beginning to feel that all comments on my *Tract on Monetary Reform* are dealing with the remarks of some dead person, and not of the present me. The new book on Monetary Theory which I have in preparation will, I am hopeful, throw much new light on my fundamental arguments in favour of the dogmas to which I have rashly given utterance without sufficiently substantiating them.[24]

Keynes fully expected *A Treatise on Money* would be his magnum opus while he was developing and writing the book, and it was highly anticipated in the economics profession.[25] Finally, after six long years in development, *A Treatise on Money* was published on October 31, 1930. The book disappointed expectations.[26] No doubt, Keynes knew the book was a failure before it was even published.[27] He started making significant revisions in summer 1929 and reported to his publisher on August 28: "The rewriting of my book on which I have had to embark turns out-to be somewhat drastic."[28] He groaned in the introduction,

> As I read through the page proofs of this book I am acutely conscious of its defects. It has occupied me for several years, not free from other occupations, during which my ideas have been developing and changing, with the result that its parts are not all entirely harmonious with one another.... I could do it better and much shorter if I were to start over again. I feel like someone who has been forcing his way through a confused jungle.... [I]t represents a collection of material rather than a finished work.[29]

---

[21] Keynes (1924b, 150).

[22] Keynes (1924c, 180–181).

[23] Keynes (CW 13, 15; CW 13, 19).

[24] Keynes (Keynes Papers, NS/1/1/229).

[25] Patinkin observes, "Keynes's regarded the *Treatise* ... as the definitive work on monetary economics for years to come: the *magnum opus* which would bring him worldwide scientific fame ... That Keynes at the time viewed the *Treatise* as his magnum opus is clear from his preface to the book" (1976, 54; 1977, 3–4; 1982, 205). Moggridge also uses the term "magnum opus" in connection with the *Treatise on Money* (1992, 530).

[26] Patinkin notes, "Despite the high hope which Keynes presented his *Treatise* to the profession, it rapidly became clear that the theoretical part of the book was not a success" (1982, xxi).

[27] Robert Dimand reports, "Keynes was already dissatisfied with the *Treatise* when it was published" (1988, 163, 83, 87, 120). Also see Johnson and Johnson (1978, 11), Moggridge (1992, 530) and Laidler (1999, 131n1).

[28] Keynes (CW 13, 117).

[29] Keynes (CW 5, xvii–xviii). Moggridge writes, "Keynes spent six years and two months on the *Treatise*. During this this period his ideas were continually changing and traces of many stages in

Keynes submitted the final version of *A Treatise on Money* to his publisher on September 14, 1930. He wrote to his mother that same day: "Artistically it is a failure—I have changed my mind too much during the course of it for it to be a proper unity."[30] Later, in the *General Theory*, he admitted that the "dynamic development" of the *Treatise* was "extremely confused."[31] Lawrence Klein wrote a few years after Keynes's death:

> The *Treatise on Money* was evidently intended to be a great work of lasting value, but turned out to be a double volume of confusion interspersed with some useful and some superb chapters on a variety of things. If it were not for the fact that this *Treatise* was followed by the *General Theory*, it probably would be of doubtful value today.[32]

Don Patinkin summarized the legacy of the *Treatise* as follows:

> The recent revival of interest in the *Treatise* notwithstanding, I can (from the viewpoint of macroeconomic theory) see little profit (and certainly no pleasure) in reading it today. Indeed, my rereading of it now has only convinced me that the hitherto generally accepted view that it is not a good book is fully justified.[33]

2.2 The *Treatise* and IS-LM: 1930

Although it was a failure, the *Treatise* contains some seeds of the IS-LM model. For context, the following is a standard, four-equation IS-LM model in its simplest form.[34]

$$Y = C + I \tag{2.1}$$

$$C = C(Y) \tag{2.2}$$

$$I = I(r) \tag{2.3}$$

$$M = L(Y, r) \tag{2.4}$$

where Y is income, C is consumption, I is investment, r is the interest rate, M is the quantity of money, and L is liquidity preference (money demand). Equations 2.1–2.3 provide the investment-saving (IS) curve, and Eq. 2.4 provides the liquidity

his development lie in the published version like sloughed-off snakeskins" (1976, 74). Also see Patinkin (1976, 54).

30 Keynes (CW 13, 176).

31 Keynes (CW 7, xxii).

32 Klein (1951, 447).

33 Patinkin (1976, 25).

34 See Hansen for a classic example (1949, 61, 72).

preference–money supply (LM) curve. To be clear, the *Treatise* does not contain any of these four equations in the explicit mathematical form specified above. However, it does contain informal, verbal prototypes of Eqs. 2.3 and 2.4, as will be demonstrated below.

Today, there is near universal agreement that Keynes originated the liquidity-preference theory of the interest rate.[35] Moreover, there is widespread consensus that the *Treatise* contains hints of the liquidity-preference theory.[36] In fact, in a lecture on October 29, 1932, Keynes himself noted that his liquidity-preference theory has its origins in the *Treatise*: "state of liquidity preferences [is] somewhat similar to State of Bearishness."[37] Although it only appears in embryonic form, the groundwork for the liquidity-preference theory is there to be found in the *Treatise.*

The term liquidity preference is the term Keynes uses in the *General Theory* to denote money demand. By 1924, Keynes was already giving priority to the demand for money as opposed to the money supply.[38] This emphasis on money demand was prominent in the *Treatise.* As in the *General Theory*, there are two primary components of money demand in the *Treatise*: cash deposits (k_1) and savings deposits (k_2).[39] Recall Keynes's liquidity-preference function takes the following form in the *General Theory*[40]:

$$M = L_1(Y) + L_2(r) \tag{2.5}$$

which is commonly expressed as $M = L(Y, r)$.[41] While Keynes does not provide a formal, mathematical money-demand function in the *Treatise*, the verbal analysis from the *Treatise* can be formalized.[42]

$$M = k_1 + k_2(r) \tag{2.6}$$

Clearly, the formal version of money-demand function in the *Treatise* (Eq. 2.6) bears resemblance to the liquidity-preference function in the *General Theory* (Eq. 2.5). The essential difference is that income (Y) is missing from the *Treatise* money-demand

---

[35] Patinkin writes, "In the case of the theory of liquidity preference, Keynes was indeed the innovator" (1976, 80).

[36] For examples, see Klein (1947, 16), Harrod (1951, 409), Patinkin (1976, 80–81; 1977, 10), Kahn (1984, 71, 137, 140, 146–147), Dimand (1988, 21, 43), Meltzer (1988, 57, 75), and Laidler (1999, 139; 2006, 47).

[37] Keynes (1932–35, I16, A29).

[38] See Keynes (CW 19, 207).

[39] Keynes (CW 5, 31).

[40] Keynes (CW 7, 199). Also see Dillard (1948, 171) and Patinkin (1990, 223).

[41] For examples, see Hicks (1937, 153, 156), Lange (1938, 12), Samuelson (1941, 114; 1947, 276), Modigliani (1944, 46), Hansen (1949, 56), and Friedman (1997, 9).

[42] See Meltzer (1988, 76).

function.[43] This is because Keynes did not have a theory of output in the *Treatise*, as will be shown below.

Furthermore, Keynes's theory of uncertain expectations in the *General Theory* is on display in the *Treatise*.[44] In the *Treatise*, k_1 is the stable component of money demand, while k_2 is the unstable component. Keynes argues k_2 is unstable because "[A money-holder's] distaste for other securities is not absolute and depends on his expectations of future returns to be obtained from savings deposits and from other securities respectively."[45] To Keynes, an increase in "bullish" expectations causes money to flow out of savings deposits into securities. Conversely, an increase in "bearish" expectations causes money to flow out of securities into savings deposits. Like the *General Theory*, uncertain expectations are featured in the *Treatise*:

> [I]n truth, we know almost nothing about the more remote future.... [T]he vast majority of those who are concerned with the buying and selling of securities know almost nothing whatever about what they are doing. They do not possess even the rudiments of what is required for a valid judgment, and are the prey of hopes and fears easily aroused by transient events and as easily dispelled. This is one of the odd characteristics of the capitalist system under which we live.[46]

Keynes's theory of uncertain expectations has its basis in his early work on probability theory.[47] Although first formulated in a January 1904 paper, "Ethics in Relation to Conduct," his probability theory was fully developed in his 1908 dissertation *Principles of Probability*.[48] Psychological and expectational notions permeate his economic thought by 1910: "[Investment] will often depend upon fashion, upon advertisement, or upon purely irrational waves of optimism or, depression."[49] Keynes published a reworking of his dissertation as *A Treatise on Probability* in August 1921.[50] That same month he wrote, "the psychology and miscalculations of traders

---

[43] As Patinkin notes, "the portfolio choice model of the *Treatise* is effectively a two-asset one: money and equity securities. In contrast, the corresponding model of the *General Theory* is effectively a two-stage three-asset model" (1976, 81). Also see Meltzer (1988, 75).

[44] Meltzer agrees, "Anticipations, or expectations, have a large role in the *General Theory*, but they are present in the *Tract* and become more important in the *Treatise*" (1988, 55). Also see Laidler (2006, 46).

[45] Keynes (CW 5, 137).

[46] Keynes (CW 6, 322–323).

[47] Meltzer agrees, "Keynes's views on probability and uncertainty were not new [in the *Treatise on Money*]. They were first developed in his prize-winning fellowship dissertation of 1908 and revised and published in his [1921 book] *Treatise on Probability*" (1981, 57, 62; 1988, 120, 139, 199). O'Donnell writes, "the *GT*'s treatment of behaviour under uncertainty is significantly based on the conceptual framework of the *TP*" (1989, 248).

[48] O'Donnell agrees, "By January 1904, Keynes had thus essentially formulated the key idea of the *TP*" (1989, 12). Also see Carabelli (1988, 5).

[49] Keynes (CW 15, 46). O'Donnell writes, "The *GT* is not unique among Keynes's writings in referring to expectations; from at least 1910 onwards, he regularly noted the importance of expectations to economic behavior" (1989, 245). Also see Carabelli (1988, 195, 216, 238).

[50] The editorial introduction to *A Treatise on Probability* reads, "Keynes started work on probability in 1906 ... Although much of the *Treatise* was set up in type by August 1914, it was not published until August 1921" (Keynes CW 8, xv). O'Donnell notes, "[*A Treatise on Probability*] is essentially

[investors] … lead to the alteration of boom and depression."[51] His 1926 pamphlet *The End of Laissez-Faire* was based on a November 1924 lecture at Oxford, and it reads: "Many of the greatest economic evils of our time are the fruits of risk, uncertainty, and ignorance."[52] All this shows that uncertain expectations always played a role in Keynes's economic thought, even before the *Treatise on Money* and the *General Theory*.

In addition to the money-demand function, the *Treatise* anticipates the IS-LM investment function. Again, it must be stressed that there is no explicit, formal IS-LM investment function in the *Treatise*. But the basic structure of that function is there. Specifically, in the *Treatise*, Keynes makes investment decisions depend on expected future cash flows (prospective yield) and the interest rate.[53] He writes, "the value of capital goods depends on the rate of interest at which the prospective income from them is capitalised. That is to say, the higher (e.g.) the rate of interest, the lower, other things being equal, will be the value of capital goods."[54] He elaborates,

> Upon what does the demand price of capital goods depend? It depends on two things—on the estimated [expected] net prospective yield from fixed capital (estimated by the opinion of the market after such allowance as they choose to make for the uncertainty of anticipation, etc.), measured in money, and on the rate of interest at which this future yield is capitalised. It follows that the price of such goods can change for either of two reasons—because the prospective yield has changed or because the rate of interest has changed.[55]

These passages anticipate Keynes's theory of investment based on the marginal efficiency of capital.[56] Although he did not formalize his investment theory in mathematical form, the verbal analysis in the *Treatise* can be formalized as follows:

$$I = I(E, r) \tag{2.7}$$

where E is expected cash flow (what Keynes calls prospective yield or quasi-rent) and r is the interest rate. Plainly, the investment function derived from the *Treatise* (Eq. 2.7) closely resembles the IS-LM investment function above (Eq. 2.3). In short, there are hints of the IS-LM investment function in the *Treatise*.

In one sense, the traces of the IS-LM investment function in the *Treatise* seem insignificant. From a strictly technical point of view, the investment function is the least novel element of the IS-LM model. In both the *Treatise* and the *General Theory*,

---

a reworking and expansion of the dissertations of 1907 and 1908. The remarkable thing is the strength of continuity in philosophical thought from 1904 to 1921" (1989, 17).

[51] Keynes (CW 17, 263). Moggridge agrees that here, "Keynes explained fluctuation in terms of the by now conventional model of businessmen's errors of optimism and pessimism" (1976, 67).

[52] Keynes (CW 9, 291).

[53] Dimand agrees, "In *A Treatise on Money*, investment decisions depend on anticipated streams of earnings and on the rate of interest" (1988, 35). Also see Klein (1947, 25).

[54] Keynes (CW 5, 139).

[55] Keynes (CW 5, 180–181).

[56] Meltzer writes that in the *Treatise*, Keynes provides "an early version of the relation between the marginal efficiency of capital and the rate of interest" (1988, 67).

Keynes roots his theory of investment in present-value analysis. Mathematicians and merchants have been making present value calculations since at least the thirteenth century, when Fibonacci published his classic *Liber Abaci*.[57] In January 1909, Keynes lectured on Irving Fisher's 1907 book *The Rate of Interest*, a classic work on present-value analysis.[58] In 1936, he (erroneously) aligns the marginal efficiency of capital with Fisher in the *General Theory*.[59] Finally, he wrote to Fisher in July 1944, "You were one of my earliest teachers."[60]

In another sense, the traces of the IS-LM investment function in the *Treatise* are highly significant. Investment was always Keynes's main concern. He wrote in the *General Theory*, "The weakness of the inducement to invest has been at all times the key to the economic problem."[61] He determined by 1910 that private capital investment was the source of the economic problem facing humankind, and he maintained this early view throughout his entire life.[62] The *Treatise* contains an informal IS-LM investment function with the same basic structure as the one in the *General Theory*, and this is significant because the theory of investment is the essential theory in both works.[63]

In addition to anticipating two of the IS-LM functions, Keynes employs the IS-LM methodology in the *Treatise*. Specifically, the IS-LM model is a general equilibrium, simultaneous equations model. Keynes first adopted the general equilibrium, simultaneous equations approach in the *Treatise*. He writes of "multiple equilibrium" in his chapter on the Fundamental Equations: "we are dealing with a case of multiple equilibrium in which each element affects every other element more or less."[64] Here, "multiple equilibrium" can be understood as "general equilibrium."[65] Thus, even in the *Treatise*, Keynes embraced the general equilibrium, simultaneous equations

---

[57] For notable early examples, see Fibonacci (1202, 384) and Stevin (1582, 107, 111). See Parker (1968), Poitras (2000), Goetzmann (2004, 2016), and Lewin (2019) on the history of compounding and discounting.

[58] Keynes (Keynes Papers, UA/6/1/5/1–25).

[59] Keynes (CW 7, 140–141). He repeats this error in 1937 (Keynes CW 14, 101n2).

[60] Keynes in Dimand (1995, 248). In his review of Fisher's *The Purchasing Power of Money*, Keynes acknowledged he was familiar with Fisher's works:" Professor Fisher's book is marked, as all his books are, by extreme lucidity and brilliance of statement" (CW 11, 376).

[61] Keynes (CW 7, 347–348).

[62] Anna Carabelli agrees, "Keynes's attitude towards investment ... remained substantially unchanged from his early articles written at the beginning of the century to the latest contributions written after *The General Theory*" (1988, 195).

[63] As Moggridge writes, "In the *Treatise* the most important force for change was the level of investment" (1992, 486). Also see Klein (1947, 15), Patinkin (1982, 230–231), Kahn (1984, 70), Meltzer (1988, 113–114), and Laidler (1999, 144–145).

[64] Keynes (CW 5, 129).

[65] Patinkin (1976, 50) agrees "multiple equilibrium" is another way of saying general equilibrium. Meltzer writes, "The *Treatise* advances the analysis by recognizing that the interest rate is determined as part of a simultaneous, general equilibrium, solution" (1988, 111–112). Also see Rymes (1989, 23).

Table 2.1 *Treatise* model

Factor	Change	*Treatise* model		IS-LM model		AS-AD model	
		Price level	Interest rate	Income	Interest rate	Income	Price level
Investment	↑	↑	↑	↑	↑	↑	↑
Saving	↑	↓	↓	↓	↓	↓	↓
Money supply	↑	↑	↓	↑	↓	↑	↑
Money demand	↑	↓	↑	↓	↑	↓	↓

Note Assume the IS, LM, AS, and AD curves are neither perfectly elastic nor perfectly inelastic

approach of IS-LM. Indeed, this approach is perhaps the most enduring mark the *Treatise* has left on economics.[66]

It is beyond the scope of this work to provide a detailed account of Keynes's *Treatise* model. Such an account can be found elsewhere.[67] Still, it is worthwhile to compare and contrast the main results of the *Treatise* model with IS-LM and AS-AD. Such a comparison highlights the major theoretical problem Keynes perceived in the *Treatise*: There is no theory of output. In the preface to the *General Theory*, he acknowledged that the *Treatise* "failed to deal thoroughly with the effects of changes in the level of output."[68] It was this problem that drove Keynes to develop and write the *General Theory*.

To illustrate, Table 2.1 compares the *Treatise* model to the IS-LM model and AS-AD model. For example, consider an increase in investment. According to both the IS-LM model and AS-AD model, an increase in investment raises output (income). Additionally, the IS-LM column shows the interest rate rises, and the AS-AD column shows the price level rises. Now, according to the *Treatise* model, an increase in investment leads to a higher price level and interest rate, and this is consistent with IS-LM and AS-AD. But what about output? As Table 2.1 highlights, the *Treatise* model lacks a theory of output.[69]

Keynes acknowledged that *A Treatise on Money*, his first major theoretical work in economics, was a failure. His *Treatise* did not provide a theory of output, and

---

[66] Meltzer agrees, "Keynes used a model of simultaneous determination in the *Treatise*" (1988, 173n59, 17, 97, 75, 77, 112). And he continues, "Among the many contributions Keynes made to economics, none is more lasting than the stimulus he gave to the development of the theory of output and employment within a general equilibrium framework" (1981, 60; 1988, 196).

[67] For example, see Klein (1947), Patinkin (1976), Kahn (1984), Dimand (1988), Meltzer (1988), and Laidler (1999).

[68] Keynes (CW 7, xvi). Ralph Hawtrey made Keynes aware that he lacked a theory of output before the book was even published (Keynes CW 13, 152–153). But it was too late for Keynes to address the issue. See Dimand (1988, 53, 87) and Moggridge (1992, 533).

[69] Moggridge writes, "the formal logic of the theoretical segments of the book assumed a fixed, 'full-employment' level of output in the economy" (1976, 76, 88–89; 1993, 74). Also see Robinson (1947, 39), Patinkin (1976, 55), Dimand (1988, 26, 142, 188), Meltzer (1988, 77, 103, 106), Rymes (1989, 14), and Laidler (1999, 135, 139, 247).

his goal in the *General Theory* was to solve this problem.[70] The IS-LM equations above (Eqs. 2.1–2.4) suggest the course he would take. He had the rudiments of the investment function (Eq. 2.3) and the liquidity-preference function (Eq. 2.4). In sharp contrast, he had no consumption function (Eq. 2.2). The consumption function is the crucial element of the IS-LM model that is missing in the *Treatise.* Alvin Hansen wrote,

> It has been my conviction for many year that the great contribution of Keynes' *General Theory* was the clear and specific formulation of the consumption function. This is an epoch-making contribution to the tools of economic analysis ... [T]he consumption function was never fashioned into a workmanlike instrument until the *General Theory.* This, I repeat, is Keynes' greatest contribution.[71]

2.3 Back to the Drawing Board: 1931 and 1932

Keynes started reworking his theory by summer 1931, less than a year after publication of the *Treatise.*[72] The key document from this period is a short letter Keynes wrote to Richard Kahn on September 20, 1931. The letter contains two ideas relevant to the history of IS-LM. First, Keynes introduces the key idea of "'long-period unemployment', i.e. an equilibrium position short of full employment."[73] Second, he presents his very first saving function.[74]

$$\frac{S}{E} = F(O) \tag{2.8}$$

where S is saving, E is income, and O is physical output. Recall, the consumption function is the key element of IS-LM not found in the *Treatise.* Although it is a saving function rather than a consumption function, Eq. 2.8 represents an important first step to the consumption function. Saving is defined as income not spent on consumption. Thus, when Keynes explicitly formulated a functional relationship between saving and income, he implicitly formulated a functional relationship between consumption and income. This point was not lost on Keynes: "However we may prefer to define income, the sum of saving and consumption must be taken as equal to income.

---

70 Patinkin writes, "the *Treatise* did not explain the forces which determine by how much output would expand; and this is was the major deficiency which the *General Theory* was designed to correct" (1982, 8). Also see Moggridge (1976, 76).

71 Hansen (1947, 135; 1953, 27). Dimand (1988, 142), Meltzer (1988, 88), and Blaug (1990, 12) agree there is no consumption or saving function in the *Treatise.*

72 As Moggridge observes, "Keynes was remarkably quick in abandoning much of his magnum opus" (1992, 530).

73 Keynes (CW 13, 374). As Eshag notes, "the new technique of analysis ... recognized the possibility of having a stable equilibrium below the level of full employment" (1963, xiv).

74 Keynes (CW 13, 374; Keynes Papers, GTE/1/21). Patinkin agrees this is "the first instance recorded [of] explicit use of a savings function" (1976, 69; Dimand 1988, 137).

Thus it comes essentially to the same thing to take income and consumption as our fundamental quantities, as to take income and saving."[75]

This brings us to Keynes's lectures. As noted above, he was not a professor nor a university lecturer after the First World War. Still, every year he gave a series of eight lectures at Cambridge, typically in Michaelmas term (autumn). It is significant to note that he dedicated each lecture series to the book he was writing at the time. This means all his lectures from 1932 to 1935 relate to the *General Theory*. Notes from his 1932–35 lectures represent a record of the progress he was making on the *General Theory* from year to year. Austin Robinson wrote,

> In the years following the publication of the *Treatise* Keynes continued his practice of giving eight lectures annually, usually in the Michaelmas Term. Each year he gave us the development of his ideas to date. And these lectures became something wholly unlike anything else that I have ever known in Cambridge lectures. Apart from the third-year undergraduates, to whom officially the course was addressed, there were to be found there the whole body of research students, at least half the members of the Faculty, a visiting Professor or two from America, Australia or where you will, and on occasion a few spies (or should they be called in the modern jargon 'members of the fifth column'?) from London, Oxford or elsewhere. Gradually year by year the essential features of the *General Theory* emerged. Thus, when it was finally published in 1936, Cambridge at least knew fairly well what to expect.[76]

Keynes did not lecture in 1930, and his 1931 lectures were postponed to Easter term (spring) 1932. Unfortunately, there are only two fragments of notes from these Easter 1932 lectures, dated April 25 and May 2. First, Keynes uses the term "propensity to save" for the first time on May 2.[77] He had not yet achieved the propensity to consume. But given the mathematical identity between saving and consumption, he implied the propensity to consume on May 2 when he presented the propensity to save.[78]

Moreover, Keynes presented the critical "investment–income relation" underlying the IS-LM model. In the IS-LM framework, there is a strict positive relationship between output and investment. Put differently, according to IS-LM, the amount of consumption always changes in the same direction as investment.[79] Keynes explicitly stated the positive investment–income relation underlying IS-LM on May 2, 1932:

---

[75] Keynes (CW 13, 436). Klein writes, "Once we have recognized the relationship between consumption and income, we can pass by means of a mathematical identity to the savings-income function" (1947, 37). Also see Robinson (1947, 44n1).

[76] Robinson (1947, 40). Klein writes, "As in the case of the *Treatise*, the appearance of the *General Theory* was well advertised in advance. We know that, for some time, Keynes was lecturing at Cambridge on the theory of employment and output according to the doctrine latter written down in the *General Theory*" (1947, 42). See Dimand (1988, 125, 146) for a description of Keynes's lectures.

[77] Keynes (CW 29, 41).

[78] Joan Robinson writes, "The propensity to save or thriftiness of the community represents the relationship between the level of real income and rate of saving in real terms. It embodies exactly the same relationship as Mr. Keynes's 'propensity to consume'" (1947, 44n1). Also see Klein (1947, 37).

[79] Meltzer writes, "On Keynes's interpretation, the classical position introduces Say's Law when it claims that an increase in saving leads to an increase in investment at an unchanged equilibrium level of income. If this were so, changes in investment and consumption would be negatively

> ΔI has the same sign as ΔO. That is to say O and I increase together, i.e. the volume of output and the volume of investment go up and down together; or, in more familiar language, the volume of employment directly depends on the amount of investment.... Thus we are left with the remarkable generalization that, in all ordinary circumstances, the volume of employment depends on the amount of investment, and that anything which increases or decreases the latter will increase or decrease the former.[80]

At this point in time, Keynes did not have a formal adjustment mechanism to support his claim that output and investment always increase and decrease together. He merely sensed intuitively that a positive investment-income relation was central to his solution.[81] He argues in the *Treatise* that the amount of economic activity depends on investment. By May 2, he grasped that vindicating the *Treatise* required him to develop a theory with a positive relationship between investment and output.

> The general upshot of this and the previous chapter seems to be that the fluctuations of output and employment for a given community over the short period, within the ranges of fluctuations which certainly occur, depend almost entirely on the amount of current investment.... This is a development of a point made in my *Treatise* that changes in the general situation are most often initiated by changes in the amount of investment.[82]

Around this time, Keynes produced a document called *The Monetary Theory of Production*.[83] Here he introduces his investment-saving relation—the key idea that investment determines saving. The pre-Keynesians argued that saving determines investment. But IS-LM reverses the pre-Keynesian saving-investment causal sequence. As noted, Keynes's positive investment-income relation means an increase in investment increases income. Now he takes the next step: He realizes that a portion of this new income is saved. Thus, contrary to the pre-Keynesians, Keynes argues new investment generates new saving:

> Thus if we regard the response of individual spending to any given conditions of earnings and profits as something which is determined by nature and habit and virtually outside deliberate control at the centre, then the level of output, which will be a stable level, entirely depends on the policy of the authorities as affecting the amount of investment. An active policy of stimulating investment renders a greater volume of saving consistent with a greater volume of output. Thus it might be truer to say that the amount of saving over a period of time depends on the amount of investment, than the other way round.[84]

---

related. In Keynes's theory, a permanent increase in investment triggers the multiplier and raises the equilibrium levels of income and consumption until full employment is reached. Investment and consumption are positively related" (1988, 152–153). Also see Dimand (1988, 149–151) and Garrison (2001, 136).

[80] Keynes (CW 29, 39). Dudley Dillard describes the investment–income relation as Keynes's fundamental position: "Keynes's fundamental position is that income and employment can rise only if investment increases" (1948, 92).

[81] Moggridge writes, "with Keynes intuition represented an early, but essential, stage in the act of creation. Very hard, systematic work then went into developing the scheme of thought" (1976, 32–33).

[82] Keynes (CW 29, 41).

[83] Keynes (CW 13, 381–396).

[84] Keynes (CW 13, 388). James Meade described this investment-saving relation as the "quintessence of Keynes' intellectual innovation," and wrote: "Keynes' intellectual revolution was

Again, at this point in time, he did not have a formalized output-adjustment mechanism to support his investment-saving relation. There is no indication that investment generates saving through the multiplier process. But he intuitively sensed that investment must determine saving rather than the other way around. Over the next year, he would strive to develop a theoretical framework to justify this position. And this investment-saving relation is baked into IS-LM.

The *Keynes Papers* contain a handwritten document entitled *Why Are the Equations for Consumption Goods and Investment Goods Asymmetrical?*[85] Although undated, Keynes likely produced the document in summer 1932.[86] This document is especially significant in the history of IS-LM, for it is the first single document that contains formalized saving, investment, and money-demand functions. As shown above, his first saving function appears in a September 1931 letter to Kahn. Figure 2.1 is a page from *Why Asymmetical?*, and it contains Keynes's second saving function.[87]

$$S = \phi(E, Q, P_1, P_2) \tag{2.9}$$

where S is saving, ϕ is the propensity to save, E is income, Q is profit, P_1 is the price of consumer goods, and P_2 is the price of investment goods. There is one notable feature of the 1932 saving function: It incorporates the propensity to save, denoted by the symbol ϕ. This is the first instance of a saving function that explicitly includes the propensity to save. And given the mathematical identity between saving and consumption, this represents a step toward a consumption function with the propensity to consume.

Next, as Fig. 2.1 shows, *Why Asymmetrical?* contains a formal money-demand function. Of course, Keynes provided an informal money-demand function in the *Treatise*. But here he takes the crucial step of formalizing the function. The following is the 1932 hoarding function.[88]

$$M = \psi'(H, P_2) \tag{2.10}$$

where M is the quantity of money, ψ' is the propensity to hoard, H is hoarding, and P_2 is price of investment goods. Clearly, this is a prototype of the liquidity-preference

---

to shift economists from thinking normally in terms of a model of reality in which a dog called savings wagged his tail labelled investment to thinking in terms of a model in which a dog called investment wagged his tail labelled savings" (1975, 82). Also see Klein (1947, 86), Hansen (1953, 153), Moggridge (1976, 96), Presley (1979, 85–86, 166–167), and Fletcher (1987, 69, 96).

[85] Keynes (Keynes Papers, GTE/1/23–41).

[86] It can be said with confidence that Keynes produced *Why Asymmetrical?* after *The Monetary Theory of Production* but before his Michaelmas 1932 lecture series. The document was written sometime between June and October 1932.

[87] Keynes (Keynes Papers, GTE/1/25). Note Keynes uses the notation Q differently in the *Treatise* and the *General Theory* (Dimand 1988, 25).

[88] Keynes (Keynes Papers, GTE/1/25).

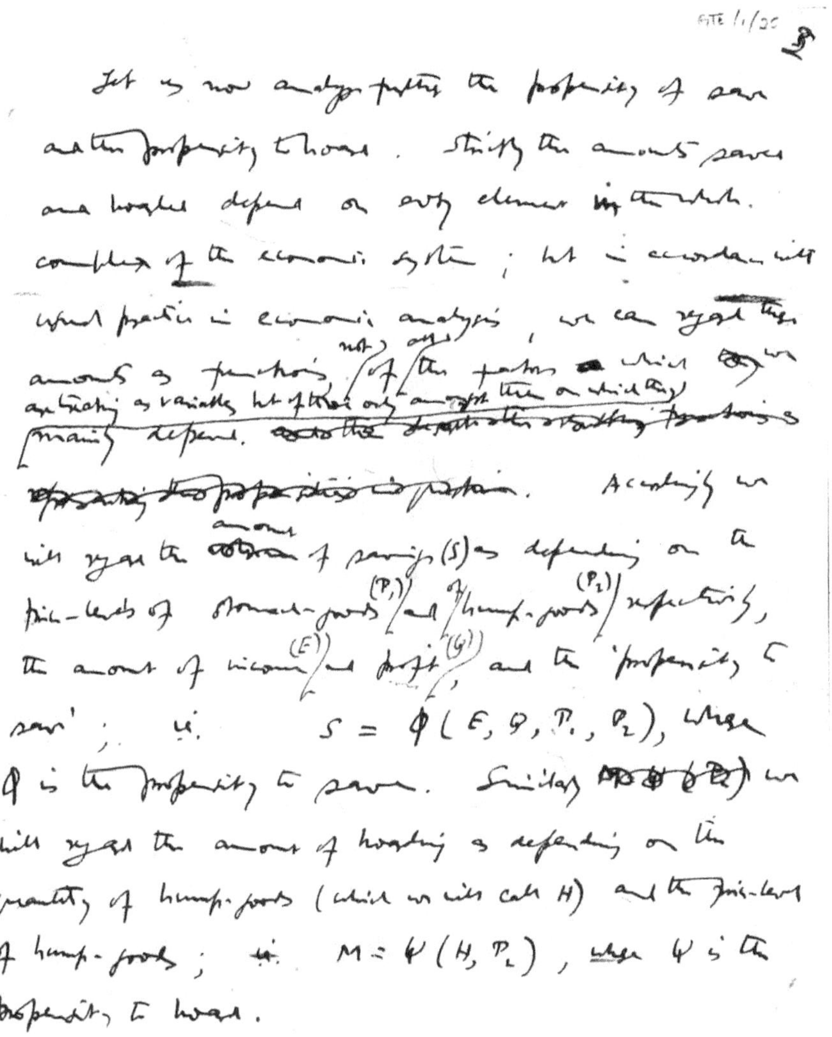

Fig. 2.1 *Why Asymmetrical?* (Keynes Papers, GTE/1/25)

function (Eq. 2.4). The *General Theory* reads, "The concept of hoarding may be regarded as a first approximation to the concept of liquidity-preference."[89]

The *Treatise* only contains an informal, verbal investment function. Figure 2.2 is a page from *Why Asymmetrical?* As it shows, *Why Asymmetrical?* contains Keynes's

[89] Keynes (CW 7, 174). Keynes writes in June 1937, "If we mean by 'hoarding' the holding of idle balances, then my [liquidity preference] theory of the rate of interest might be expressed by saying that the rate of interest serves to equate the demand and supply of hoards" (CW 14, 213). Dillard writes, "Liquidity preference may be defined as the propensity to hoard" (1948, 181). Also see Meltzer (1988, 150) and Dimand (1988, 38).

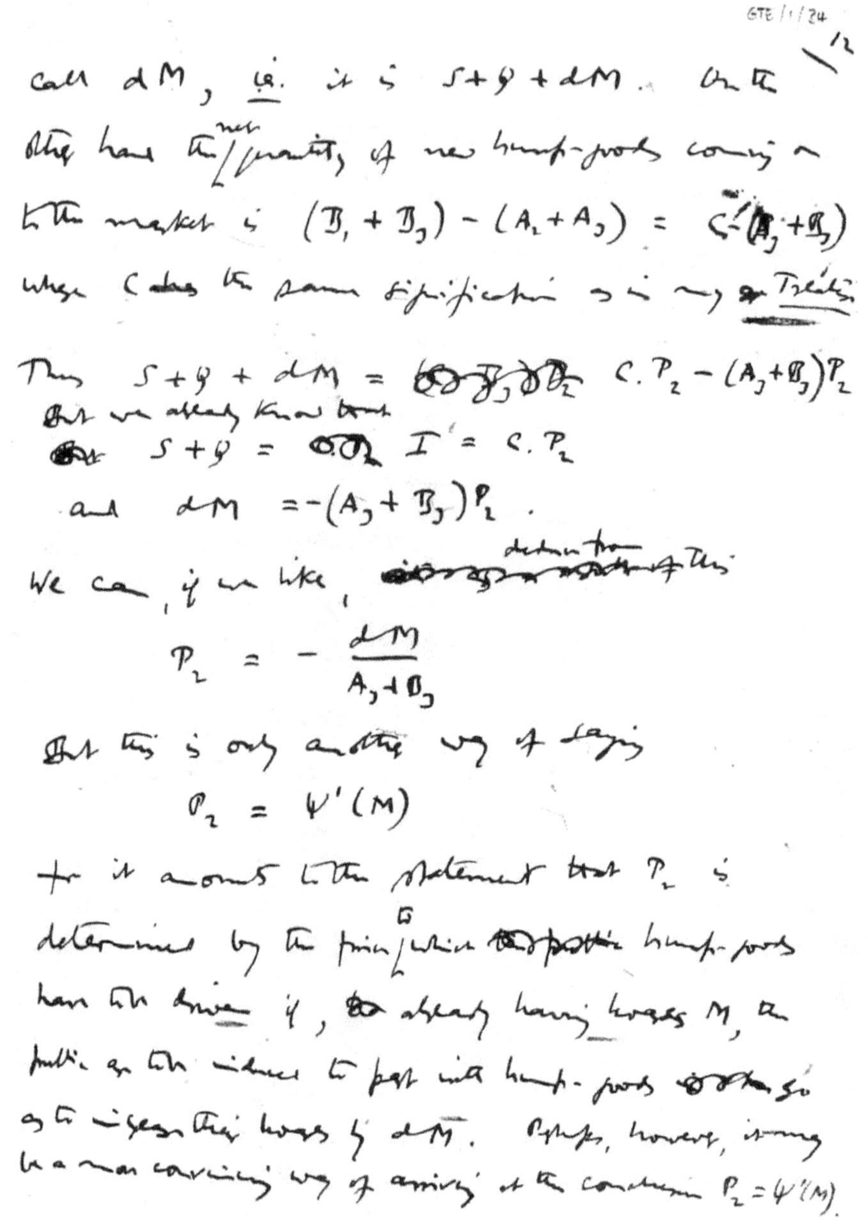
GTE/1/34

12

call dM, i.e. it is $S + Q + dM$. On the other hand the new quantity of new hump-goods coming on to the market is $(B_1 + B_3) - (A_1 + A_3) = C - (A_3 + B_3)$ where C has the same signification as in my Treatise.

Thus $S + Q + dM = C.P_2 - (A_3 + B_3)P_2$

But we already know that

$S + Q = I = C.P_2$

and $dM = -(A_3 + B_3)P_2$.

We can, if we like, deduce from this

$$P_2 = -\frac{dM}{A_3 + B_3}$$

But this is only another way of saying

$$P_2 = \psi'(M)$$

for it amounts to the statement that P_2 is determined by the price to which hump-goods have to be driven if, already having hoards M, the public are to be induced to part with hump-goods so as to increase their hoards by dM. Perhaps, however, it may be a more convincing way of arriving at the conclusion $P_2 = \psi'(M)$.

Fig. 2.2 *Why Asymmetrical?* (Keynes Papers, GTE/1/34)

first attempt at a formalized, mathematical investment function characteristic of IS-LM.[90]

$$P_2 = \psi'(M) \tag{2.11}$$

$$I' = C(P_2) \tag{2.12}$$

where P_2 is the price of investment goods, ψ' is the propensity to hoard, M is the quantity of money, I' is investment, and C is the supply of capital goods. Keynes's use of two functions to characterize his investment theory is somewhat awkward. Still, his function takes the following form if the two functions are condensed.

$$I' = C\left(\psi', M\right) \tag{2.13}$$

Another significant feature of *Why Asymmetrical?* is that it links the goods side of the economy (I') to the money side of the economy (ψ', M). This is the essence of IS-LM.[91] Indeed, the link between the money and goods sides of the economy becomes even more obvious if the notation for the propensity to hoard is changed from ψ' to L. This is not too much of stretch, for Keynes himself used the terms propensity to hoard and liquidity preference interchangeably as late as 1937.[92] With a slight adjustment in notation, his investment function takes the following form:

$$I' = C(L, M) \tag{2.14}$$

Why Asymmetrical? is a key document in the history of Keynes's IS-LM approach. It must be stressed that he did not achieve IS-LM. Still, it is the first contiguous document that contains formal saving, investment, and money-demand functions. Moreover, Keynes links the goods and money sides of the economy. *Why Asymmetrical*? does not contains the IS-LM model, but it represents an important step on the way to IS-LM.

Keynes began drafting the book that became the *General Theory* by late summer 1932. On September 18, 1932, he told his mother that he had written "nearly a third of my new book on monetary theory."[93] The title of his manuscript was *Parameters*

---

[90] Keynes (Keynes Papers, GTE/1/26, GTE/1/32, GTE/1/34). Patinkin writes, "the spirit of IS-LM [is] the determination of the equilibrium level of income by the interaction between the markets for commodities and money" (1990, 224).

[91] This relation is also present in a related document from the same period, entitled *The Determination of Price* (Keynes Papers, GTE/5/473). Also, this document contains hints at a consumption function and an investment function (Keynes Papers, GTE/5/469).

[92] This is clear when he writes, "changes in the propensity to hoard, or in the state of liquidity preference as I have called it, primarily affect, not prices, but the rate of interest" (CW 14, 116).

[93] Keynes (CW 13, 380). In autumn 1931, Meade was "cautiously confident that he took with him back to Oxford most of the essential ingredients of the subsequent system of the *General Theory*"

of a Monetary Economy, and it dates to October and November 1932.[94] Here Keynes uses the term "liquidity preference" for the first time.[95] Beyond that, he expressed a formal liquidity-preference function. Figure 2.3 shows Keynes's 1932 *Parameters* model, and it contains the following liquidity preference function.[96]

$$\rho = A(M) \tag{2.15}$$

where ρ is the interest rate, *A* is liquidity preference, and *M* is the quantity of money. Although the notation is slightly different, this function closely parallels the first liquidity-preference function found in *General Theory*.[97]

$$M = L(r) \tag{2.16}$$

where *M* is the quantity of money, *L* is liquidity preference, and *r* is the interest rate. Thus, by November 1932 at the latest, Keynes had essentially achieved a basic outline of the IS-LM liquidity-preference function.

Figure 2.3 shows that *Parameters* contains a formal investment function. No doubt, this investment function is a refinement of the one found in *Why Asymmetrical?*[98] The following is the *Parameters* investment function as shown in Fig. 2.3.

$$P_2 = B(\rho) \tag{2.17}$$

$$I' = C(P_2) \tag{2.18}$$

where P_2 is the price of investment goods, *B* is the complex of expected quasi-rents, *I'* is investment, and *C* is the supply of capital goods. Again, his use of two functions for his investment theory is cumbersome. The two functions can be combined to yield the following single function.

$$I' = C(B, \rho) \tag{2.19}$$

(in Keynes CW 13, 342). Patinkin (1977, 6) and Dimand (1988, 167) appear correct when they suggest this is not possible.

94 Keynes (CW 13, 396–405; Keynes Papers, GTE/5/59–71).

95 Keynes (CW 13, 397). He also used the term liquidity preference in an early draft table of contents, probably written around this time (CW 29, 50).

96 Keynes (CW 13, 398; Keynes Papers, GTE/5/58 59). Also see Patinkin (1976, 72) and Dimand (1988, 153).

97 Keynes (CW 7, 168).

98 Keynes (CW 13, 398–399).

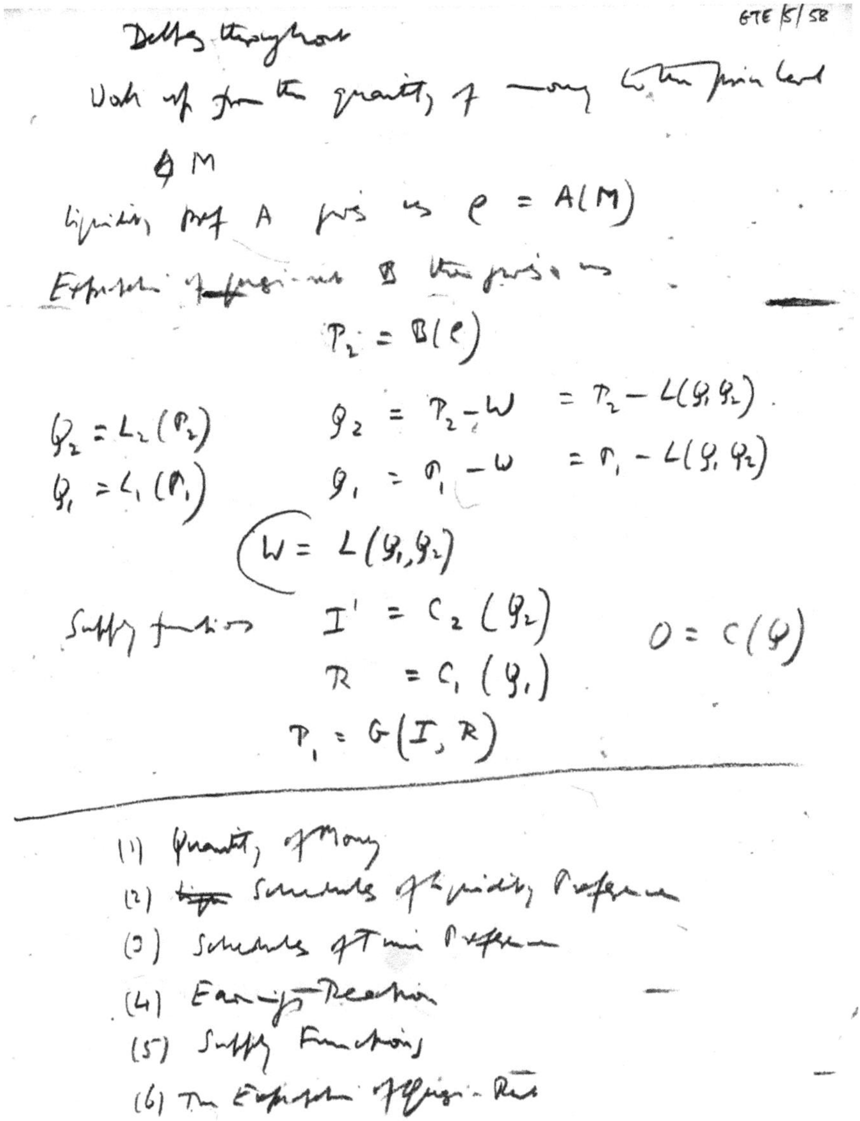

Fig. 2.3 *Parameters of a Monetary Economy* (Keynes Papers, GTE/5/58)

This closely resembles the basic structure of the conventional IS-LM investment function. It is notable that he explicitly includes expectations (B) in the investment function. All this shows that Keynes was laying the foundation for the IS-LM investment function by fall 1932 at the latest.[99]

[99] Patinkin (1976, 72) suggests *Parameters* lacked an investment function. Moggridge agrees with the position taken here when he writes in his editorial commentary on the 1932 lectures: "The

Finally, as Fig. 2.3 shows, *Parameters* contains Keynes's first attempt at the consumption function. To this point, he had formulated saving functions rather than a consumption function. But here Keynes offers a primitive consumption function[100]:

$$R = H(P_1) \tag{2.20}$$

$$P_1 = G(I, H) \tag{2.21}$$

where R is consumption, H is the supply schedule of consumables, P_1 = price of consumables, G is the general state of time preference, and I is investment. These two functions can be condensed as follows.

$$R = H(G, I) \tag{2.22}$$

Parameters indicates that Keynes developed a formal consumption function by late 1932. However, this consumption function is clearly not that of the *General Theory*. Although Kahn had published his famous multiplier article in June 1931, the notion of the multiplier is missing from Keynes's theory in late 1932. The consumption function must be firmly linked to the multiplier for movements in income to equilibrate investment (I) and saving (S).[101] Keynes's 1932 consumption function is not linked to the multiplier, and, consequently, his IS-LM model has not yet been achieved.

There is one final aspect of Keynes's 1932 *Parameters* model that is most significant: It is a general equilibrium, simultaneous equations model. He writes, "we should write in terms of simultaneous equations (just as we should strictly, since all the factors are in some measure interdependent, write the whole of this discussion in terms of multiple simultaneous equations)."[102] He continues,

[*Parameters*] model also had asset values determined by the stream of prospective quasi-rents [cash flows] and the rate of interest, the latter being the upshot of liquidity preference. Thus the volume of investment was a function of prospective quasi-rents, the rate of interest and the cost of production of capital goods" (in Keynes CW 14, 412).

[100] Keynes (CW 13, 403).

[101] Keynes wrote in June 1937, "The novelty in my treatment of saving and investment consists, not in my maintaining their necessary aggregate equality, but in the proposition that it is, not the rate of interest, but the level of incomes which (in conjunction with certain other factors) ensures this equality" (CW 14, 211). Patinkin views the equilibrating role of output (income) as "the major novel feature of the *General Theory* and its central message" (1982, 11). He writes, "the really distinguishing mark of the *General Theory* [is] the crucial role of changes in output as an equilibrating force" and "the theoretical novelty of the book is its theory of effective demand *cum* equilibrating role of changes in output" (1976, 65; 1993, 647). Also see Eshag (1963, 66), Leijonhufvud (1968, 24, 151), Johnson and Johnson (1978, 235), and Presley (1979, 211).

[102] Keynes (CW 13, 403). The early-1933 draft chapters entitled *The Monetary Theory of Employment* have a simultaneous equations approach, continuing the IS-LM vector established from 1932 onwards (Keynes CW 29, 65). Also see Table 5.5.

> The above discussion yields us what I would dub the four parameters of a monetary economy,—namely the quantity of money and the three fundamental factors of market psychology or, if you like, of the prevailing attitude to the future, as expressed in the state of liquidity preference, in the expectation of quasi-rent, and in the rate of time preference. These parameters themselves are not entirely independent of one another and the schedules expressing them should be stated, strictly, in the form of simultaneous equations.[103]

Keynes's Michaelmas 1932 lecture series was titled *The Monetary Theory of Production*. The lecture series was devoted to the *Parameters* model outlined above. Thus, there is no need to analyze each lecture in great detail. For the history of IS-LM, however, a couple of key dates are worth noting. First, he presented a formal liquidity-preference function publically for the first time on October 31.[104]

$$\rho = A(M) \tag{2.23}$$

In addition to the function, Keynes presents a diagram. He says, "This can be represented then by a curve."[105] Keynes's diagram contains a downward sloping A curve relating the interest rate to the quantity of money. He points out that "The curve is generally negatively inclined but not always," and "Curve of liquidity preference may but is unlikely to slope upwards."[106] Although the A curve is not identical to the LM curve, the diagram shows that Keynes was the first to diagram his liquidity-preference theory. This means Keynes himself was the first to diagram elements of the *General Theory*.

Keynes discusses his investment theory on November 7. On that day, he introduces a semiformal investment function that closely parallels the basic structure of the IS-LM investment function. Lorie Tarshis records[107]:

$$\begin{aligned} Volume\ of\ Investment &= f(cost\ of\ production,\ rate\ of\ interest \\ &\quad and\ prospective\ quasi\ rent) \end{aligned}$$

This semiformal investment function bears a closer resemblance to the standard IS-LM investment function than his *Parameters* investment function. This is clear if the semiformal investment function is fully formalized as follows:

$$I = f(P, \rho, E) \tag{2.24}$$

---

103 Keynes (CW 13, 404–405). This passage contradicts interpreters like Luigi Pasinetti when they claim, "Keynes is not thinking in terms of a logical scheme of simultaneous equations" (1974, 46; 1997, 214).

104 Keynes (1932–35, A29, D14, I16). This function received special emphasis from Patinkin (1976, 72).

105 Keynes (1932–35, A29). For the diagram, also see Rymes (1989, 69).

106 Keynes (1932–35, I16, D15).

107 Keynes (1932–35, I17, A32, D16).

where I is investment, P is the cost of production, ρ is the interest rate, and E is prospective quasi-rent. It should be noted that he explicitly includes expectations by including "prospective" quasi-rent. Keynes reverts back to his *Parameters* function in a later lecture. Still, his semiformal investment function of November 7, 1932, represents a notable step toward the IS-LM investment function.

On November 14, he elaborates on his present-value approach to investment. The analysis is similar to the *Treatise*, but his definition of cash flow is different: $(p_r k_r + q_r)$.[108]

$p_r =$ the cost of production of capital assets at time r
$k_r =$ marginal productivity of capital at time r
$q_r =$ profit at time r
$d_r =$ present value of £1 deferred r years
Present value of an asset $= \Sigma(p_r k_r + q_r)d_r$.

This is an early step toward the marginal efficiency of capital. He uses the term "marginal productivity of capital" rather than "marginal efficiency of capital." As will be shown later, however, the marginal efficiency of capital has definite links to his 1932 framework on the marginal productivity of capital.[109]

Keynes repeated the liquidity-preference function on November 14 and 21.[110] His repetition of the function on November 21 is notable, for he presented the *Parameters* investment and consumption functions on the same day.[111] In short, on November 21, he presented the liquidity-preference, consumption, and investment functions in a single, contiguous lecture. In doing so, he pointed the way to IS-LM by linking the goods side of the economy with the money side.

Moreover, Keynes emphasized the simultaneous equations approach to his theory in the 1932 lectures. On November 14, he stressed there is "need in economics of using simultaneous equations" and "All the factors are interdependent and hence simultaneous equations."[112] He re-emphasized on November 21: "everything should be in terms of simultaneous equations"[113] *Parameters of a Monetary Economy* and Keynes's 1932 lectures prove that he took the general equilibrium, simultaneous equations approach to his theory by 1932.

Finally, Keynes highlighted the overwhelming significance of investment. He suggests his investment-income relation on October 17: "Output depends on decisions of individual entrepreneurs [i.e. investors]."[114] He elaborates on November

108 Keynes (1932–35, D17, A37–38, I20–21).

109 Moggridge writes that in late 1932, "he had not, as yet, boiled down the analysis to the sharpness of the marginal efficiency of capital" (1976, 102).

110 Keynes (1932–35, I22, I23).

111 Keynes (1932–35, A41, D19, I23–24).

112 Keynes (1932–35, A38, I21).

113 Keynes (1932–35, A43). These passages contradict interpreters like Athol Fitzgibbons when they insist, "Keynes did not believe that the whole economic system could be represented in principle by a set of simultaneous equations" (1988, 143).

114 Keynes (1932–35, A10, D7).

21, "whether or not output is increasing depends on whether or not investment is increasing."[115] However, he was highly skeptical that investment tends to the optimum level: "There is no inherent tendency for economic system to react back to the optimum output regardless of monetary policy followed—that is even when there is complete fluidity."[116] He proclaims, "whether or not output is increasing depends on whether or not investment is increasing. Then everything is due to the regulation of the problem of investment."[117]

The early origins of Keynes's IS-LM approach trace to his *Treatise on Money*. This work introduces some ideas central to IS-LM. Namely it contains informal, verbal prototypes of the IS-LM liquidity-preference and investment functions. Also, the *Treatise* represents Keynes's first attempt to construct a type of general equilibrium, simultaneous equations model that characterizes IS-LM. As he came to realize, however, the *Treatise* is flawed because it does not have a theory of output. Later, the IS-LM model emerged out of Keynes's efforts to solve the theoretical problems with the *Treatise*.[118]

Keynes's mission to solve the problems with his *Treatise* model began in summer 1931. He introduced his first formal saving function in September 1931, and, although primitive, this represented a first step on the way to the IS-LM consumption function. In mid-1932, he formalized his money demand (hoarding) and investment functions for the first time and took the critical step of using these functions in conjunction with a saving function to summarize his developing theory. By early autumn, he coined the term liquidity preference and formalized a liquidity-preference function. In addition to formulating his first consumption function, he had achieved the basic structure of the IS-LM investment function.

Keynes's 1932 model is clearly not the IS-LM model. Despite his progress toward IS-LM in 1932, he was still missing critical pieces of the puzzle. To start, he had not yet achieved a fully working definition of income. He would attain a usable definition after 1932 with the familiar equation $Y = C + I$.[119] More importantly, the 1932 consumption function is not the IS-LM consumption function. As highlighted, the consumption function is the essential element of IS-LM that is completely absent in the *Treatise*.[120] Keynes had sketched at least three saving and consumption functions in 1931 and 1932. Since they are not underpinned by the multiplier, however, these

[115] Keynes (1932–35, I26).

[116] Keynes (1932–35, I19, A36).

[117] Keynes (1932–35, A47).

[118] Thomas Rymes writes, "The *General Theory* was born out of the *Treatise*" (1989, 5). As Patinkin noticed, "Keynes was so interested in presenting the *General Theory* as a further development of the *Treatise*" (1976, 78).

[119] Moggridge notes, "he had not as yet ... quite evolved a completely useful definition of income" (1973, 80; 1976, 102). Rymes acknowledges "Keynes's great trouble with definitions of income" (1989, 23).

[120] Dimand writes, "the *Treatise* did not contain a theory of output or a saving [consumption] function" (1988, 142). Also see Hansen (1953, 27), Patinkin (1982, 9), and Meltzer (1988, 88).

functions are not those of his IS-LM model.[121] To conclude, while Keynes did not attain IS-LM in 1932, the stage was set for Keynes to achieve IS-LM in 1933.[122]

References

Blaug, M. (1990). *John Maynard Keynes: Life, ideas, legacy*. St. Martin's Press.

Carabelli, A. M. (1988). *On Keynes's method*. Macmillan.

Clarke, P. (1988). *The Keynesian revolution in the making, 1924–1936*. Oxford University Press.

Dillard, D. (1948). *Economics of John Maynard Keynes*. Prentice-Hall.

Dimand, R. W. (1988). *The origins of the Keynesian revolution*. Stanford University Press.

Dimand, R. W. (1995). Irving Fisher, JM Keynes, and the transition to modern macroeconomics. *History of Political Economy, 27*(Supplement), 247–266.

Eshag, E. (1963). *From Marshall to Keynes: An essay on the monetary theory of the Cambridge school*. Basil Blackwell.

Fibonacci. (1202). *Fibonacci's liber abaci*. Springer, 2002.

Fitzgibbons, A. (1988). *Keynes's vision: A new political economy*. Clarendon Press.

Fletcher, G. A. (1987). *The Keynesian revolution and its critics*. Macmillan.

Fletcher, G. A. (2008). *Dennis Robertson*. Palgrave Macmillan.

Friedman, M. (1997). John Maynard Keynes. *Economic Quarterly, 83*(2), 1–23.

Garrison, R. W. (2001). *Time and money: The macroeconomics of capital structure*. Routledge.

Goetzmann, W. N. (2004). *Fibonacci and the financial revolution*. NBER Working Paper 10352.

Goetzmann, W. N. (2016). *Money changes everything: How finance made civilization possible*. Princeton University Press.

Gillies, D. A. (2000). *Philosophical theories of probability*. Routledge.

Hansen, A. H. (1947). The general theory. In S. E. Harris (Ed.), *The new economics: Keynes' influence on theory and public policy* (pp. 133–144). Alfred A. Knopf.

Hansen, A. H. (1949). *Monetary theory and fiscal policy*. McGraw Hill.

Hansen, A. H. (1953). *A guide to Keynes*. McGraw-Hill.

Harrod, R. F. (1951). *The life of John Maynard Keynes*. Macmillan.

Hicks, J. R. (1937). Mr. Keynes and the 'classics'; a suggested interpretation. *Econometrica, 5*(2), 147–159.

[121] Moggridge writes, "He had evolved a view of the relationship between income and consumption in which changes in consumption followed changes in income by a lesser amount but in the same direction. However, he had not, as yet, extracted anything approaching the formal elegance of the multiplier" (1976, 102). But as Johnson notes, "The novel and intriguing element in the theory was the propensity to consume, together with its alter ego, that inexhaustibly versatile mechanical tool. The multiplier" (1961, 11). Klein writes, "the revolution was solely the development of a theory of effective demand" and "The principal difference, then, between Keynes and the classics centers around their theories of savings and investment. The multiplier theory, or the theory of the determination of effective demand, is the Keynesian savings-investment theory" (1947, 56, 82). Also see Patinkin (1976, 65–66).

[122] Peter Clarke maintains, "The evidence thus suggests that the inception of the *General Theory* must be placed firmly in 1932" (1988, 267). Skidelsky (1992, 466) and Fletcher (2008, 198) also suggest 1932 is the key year. Moggridge writes, "Keynes had intuitively grasped most of the essentials of his system as early as 1932" (1976, 32). But he agrees the *General Theory* has not been achieved: "although Keynes was moving forward from the *Treatise* there were many loose ends [in 1932]" (1992, 561). For Patinkin, "Keynes first formulated his theory sometime during 1933" (1982, 22). On 1933 as the key year in the development of the *General Theory*, see Klein (1947, 38), Patinkin (1976, 79; 1982, 81), Dimand (1988, 127, 167), and Moggridge (1992, 564–565).

Johnson, H. G. (1961). The general theory after twenty-five years. *The American Economic Review, 51*(2), 1–17.
Johnson, H. G. (1975). The classical transfer problem: An alternative formulation. *Economica, 42*(165), 20–31.
Johnson, E. S., & Johnson, H. G. (1978). *The shadow of Keynes: Understanding Keynes, Cambridge, and Keynesian economics*. University of Chicago Press.
Kahn, R. F. (1984). *The making of Keynes' general theory*. Cambridge University Press.
Keynes, J. M. (CW). *The collected writings of John Maynard Keynes* (Vols. 1–30). Macmillan and Cambridge University Press for the Royal Economic Society.
Keynes, J. M. (1924). John Maynard Keynes to Lydia Lopokova, 16 June. In P. Hill & R. Keynes (Eds.), *Lydia and Maynard: The letters of Lydia Lopokova and John Maynard Keynes*. Scribner, 1989.
Keynes, J. M. (1924). John Maynard Keynes to Lydia Lopokova, 1 February. In P. Hill & R. Keynes (Eds.), *Lydia and Maynard: The letters of Lydia Lopokova and John Maynard Keynes*. Scribner, 1989.
Keynes, J. M. (1924). John Maynard Keynes to Lydia Lopokova, 2 May. In P. Hill & R. Keynes (Eds.), *Lydia and Maynard: The letters of Lydia Lopokova and John Maynard Keynes*. Scribner, 1989.
Keynes, J. M. (1932–35) Keynes's lectures, 1932–35: notes of students. In T. K. Rymes (Ed.), unpublished typescript. Carleton University, Ottawa, 1988.
Klein, L. R. (1947). *The Keynesian revolution*. Macmillan.
Klein, L. R. (1951). The life of John Maynard Keynes. *Journal of Political Economy, 59*(5), 443–451.
Laidler, D. E. (1999). *Fabricating the Keynesian revolution*. Cambridge University Press.
Laidler, D. E. (2006). Keynes and the birth of modern macroeconomics. In R. E. Backhouse & B. W. Bateman (Eds.), *The Cambridge companion to Keynes* (pp. 39–57). Cambridge University Press.
Lange, O. (1938). The rate of interest and the optimum propensity to consume. *Economica, 5*(17), 12–32.
Leijonhufvud, A. (1968). *On Keynesian economics and the economics of Keynes*. Oxford University Press.
Lewin, C. G. (2019). The emergence of compound interest. *British Actuarial Journal, 24*(e34), 1–27.
Marcuzzo, C. (2006). Keynes and Cambridge. In R. Backhouse & B. W. Bateman (Eds.), *The Cambridge companion to Keynes* (pp. 118–135). Cambridge University Press.
Meade, J. (1975). The Keynesian revolution. In M. Keynes (Ed.), *Essays on John Maynard Keynes* (pp. 82–88). Cambridge University Press.
Meltzer, A. H. (1981). Keynes's general theory: A different perspective. *Journal of Economic Literature, 19*(1), 34–64.
Meltzer, A. H. (1988). *Keynes's monetary theory: A different interpretation*. Cambridge University Press.
Modigliani, F. (1944). Liquidity preference and the theory of interest and money. *Econometrica, 12*(1), 45–88.
Moggridge, D. E. (1973). From the treatise to the general theory: An exercise in chronology. *History of Political Economy, 5*(1), 72–88.
Moggridge, D. E. (1976). *Keynes*. Macmillan.
Moggridge, D. E. (1992). *Maynard Keynes: An economist's biography*. Routledge.
Moggridge, D. E. (1993). *Keynes*. University of Toronto Press.
Moggridge, D. E. (1994). Richard Kahn as an historian of economics. *Cambridge Journal of Economics, 18*(1), 107–116.
Mundell, R. A. (2002). Keynes and Ohlin on the transfer problem. In R. Findlay, L. Jonung, & M. Lundahl (Eds.), *Bertil Ohlin: A centennial celebration, 1899–1999* (pp. 227–262). MIT Press.
O'Donnell, R. M. (1989). *Keynes: Philosophy, economics, and politics*. St. Martin's Press.

Parker, R. H. (1968). Discounted cash flow in historical perspective. *Journal of Accounting Research, 6*(1), 58–71.
Pasinetti, L. L. (1974). *Growth and income distribution: Essays in economic theory*. Cambridge University Press.
Pasinetti, L. L. (1997). The marginal efficiency of investment. In G. C. Harcourt & P. A. Riach (Eds.), *A 'second edition' of the general theory* (pp. 198–218). Routledge.
Patinkin, D. (1976). *Keynes' monetary thought: A study of its development*. Duke University Press.
Patinkin, D. (1977). The process of writing the general theory: A critical survey. In D. Patinkin & J. C. Leith (Eds.), *Keynes, Cambridge and the general theory* (pp. 3–26). Macmillan.
Patinkin, D. (1982). *Anticipations of the general theory?* University of Chicago Press.
Patinkin, D. (1987). Keynes, John Maynard (1883–1946). In J. Eatwell, M. Milgate, & P. Newman (Eds.), *The new Palgrave dictionary of economics* (Vol. 3, pp. 19–41). Palgrave Macmillan.
Patinkin, D. (1990). On different interpretations of the general theory. *Journal of Monetary Economics, 26*, 205–243.
Patinkin, D. (1993). On the chronology of the general theory. *The Economic Journal, 103*(418), 647–663.
Poitras, G. (2000). *The early history of financial economics, 1478–1776: From commercial arithmetic to life annuities and joint stocks*. Edward Elgar.
Presley, J. R. (1979). *Robertsonian economics: an examination of the work of Sir D.H. Robertson on industrial fluctuation*. Holmes and Meier.
Robinson, E. A. G. (1972). John Maynard Keynes: Economist, author, statesman. *The Economic Journal, 82*(326), 531–546.
Robinson, J. V. (1947). *Essays in the theory of employment*. Macmillan.
Runde, J. (1994). Keynes after Ramsey: In defence of a treatise on probability. *Studies in History and Philosophy of Science, 25*(1), 97–121.
Rymes, T. K. (1989). *Keynes's lectures, 1932–35: Notes of a representative student*. Macmillan.
Samuelson, P. A. (1941). The stability of equilibrium: Comparative statics and dynamics. *Econometrica, 9*(2), 97–120.
Samuelson, P. A. (1947). *Foundations of economic analysis*. Harvard University Press.
Skidelsky, R. (1983). *John Maynard Keynes: Hopes betrayed, 1883–1920*. Viking.
Skidelsky, R. (1992). *John Maynard Keynes: The economist as savior, 1920–1937*. Viking.
Stevin, S. (1582). Tables of interest. In D. J. Struik (Ed.), *The principal works of Simon Stevin* (Vol. 2, pp. 25–117). C. V. Swets & Zeitlinger.

Chapter 3
The Advent of Keynes's IS-LM, 1933

The year 1933 saw political sea-change in Europe and the USA, the nadir of the Great Depression, and measures to counter its influence in the USA and elsewhere. Economic policy was changing, with the initiation of Roosevelt's New Deal in the USA. Economic theory in 1933 was also undergoing change, as manifest in Keynes's convergence on his IS-LM approach, to which we now turn.

3.1 GTE/5/423

Document GTE/5/423 found in the *Keynes Papers* is the first piece of evidence from 1933 relevant to the history of IS-LM. Reproduced in Fig. 3.1, GTE/5/423 is single-paged, handwritten note produced by Keynes. It contains three equations: a liquidity-preference function, a saving function, and an investment function. The following is a transcription of GTE/5/423:

> The market rate of interest (ρ) expresses the state of preference (A) for liquid assets against non-liquid; if you like, for money against debts or assets.
>
> Given the state of time preference (B), the market rate of interest determines the rate of saving.
>
> Given the state of production and the state of technique (C) [including in this stock of capital and expectations], the market rate of interest determines the rate of investment.

$$\rho = f_1(M, A)$$

$$S = f_2(\rho, B)$$

$$I = f_3(\rho, C)$$

W. Young and E. W. Fuller, *Reinterpreting Mr. Keynes*,
Springer Studies in the History of Economic Thought,
https://doi.org/10.1007/978-3-030-91342-7_3

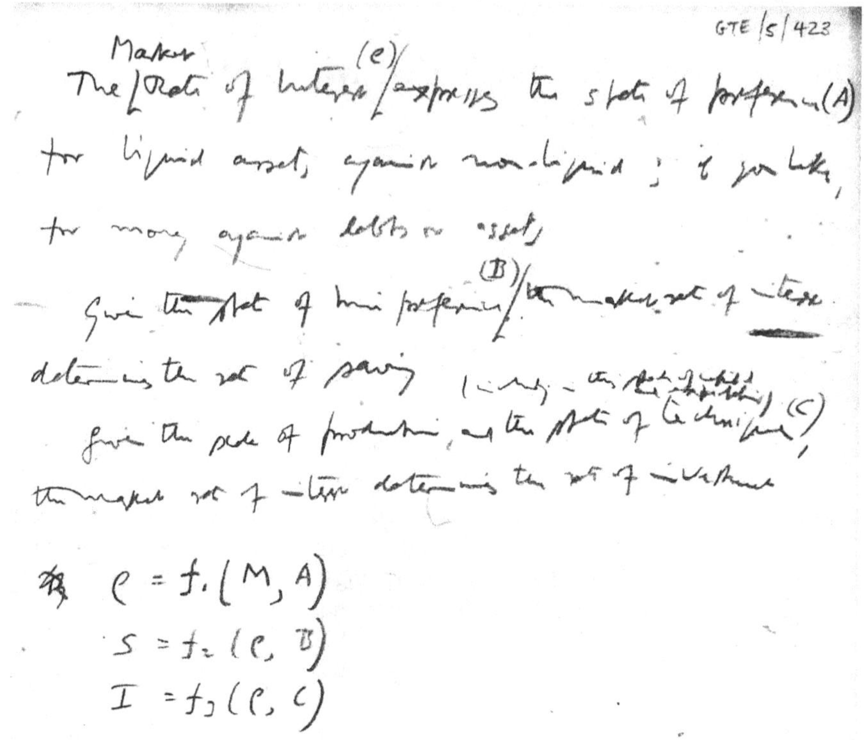

Fig. 3.1 Keynes Papers, GTE/5/423

GTE/5/423 contains elements of a proto IS-LM model. The liquidity-preference function is nearly identical to that of his late-1932 *Parameters* model. But formally, the saving function and the investment function are far more advanced than anything Keynes produced in 1932. First, the form of the investment function is revolutionized. In the *Parameters* model, he expressed his theory of investment with two functions:

$$P_2 = B(\rho) \tag{3.1}$$

$$I' = C(P_2) \tag{3.2}$$

With some manipulation, these can be condensed as follows:

$$I' = C(B, \rho) \tag{3.3}$$

This condensed investment function from *Parameters* approximates the IS-LM investment function. But Keynes did not take this step himself in 1932. By contrast, with GTE/5/423, Keynes takes this step and achieves the basic structure of the IS-LM investment function. The only ambiguity is *C*, or "scale of production and state of technique." This is not carefully defined in this one-page document. In other sources, however, he uses the word "technique" in connection with "capital equipment."[1] Indeed, Keynes scribbles "state of capital and expectations" above the words "state of technique."

Keynes's use of a saving function in GTE/5/423 is noteworthy. There was no saving or consumption function in his 1930 work the *Treatise*.[2] He introduced his first saving function in September 1931, and he was still working with a saving function in mid-1932. But his *Parameters* model of late 1932 featured a consumption function rather than a saving function. Hence, GTE/5/423 shows that he reverted back to a saving function in early 1933 after using a consumption function in late 1932.

This reversion illustrates an important point: Keynes was comfortable expressing his theory with a consumption function or saving function. He wrote, "However we may prefer to define income, the sum of saving and consumption must be taken as equal to income. Thus, it comes essentially to the same thing to take income and consumption as our fundamental quantities, as to take income and saving."[3] His flexibility on this matter is significant, for some IS-LM papers that emerged after the *General Theory* used the saving function while others contained the consumption function.

In form, the saving function in GTE/5/423 represents an advance over the saving and consumption functions of 1932. Still, the saving function in GTE/5/423 does not explicitly include income, and he is still lacking the basic output-adjustment framework found in the *General Theory*. With respect to IS-LM, he has not arrived at the IS-LM saving (consumption) function. Beyond that, Keynes does not include an equation for goods market equilibrium ($S = I$ or $Y = C + I$). GTE/5/423 shows that Keynes was on the verge of IS-LM in early 1933. But there were still a couple critical steps to be taken.

Finally, although GTE/5/423 is undated, it possible to estimate when Keynes produced the document. The inclusion of time preference (*B*) in the document suggests that it dates to early 1933. Recall, Keynes included the "general state of time preference' (*G*) in his *Parameters* model of late 1932.[4] As will be shown below, he dropped the notion of time preference from his 1933 manuscripts of the *General Theory*. Thus, it seems likely that GTE/5/423 was produced after December 1932 but before his first 1933 manuscript.

---

[1] Keynes (CW 13, 444, 480, 516; CW 29, 111).

[2] As Dimand says, "the *Treatise* did not contain a theory of output or a saving [consumption] function" (1988, 142). And Blaug notes the consumption function was "a new and absolutely central concept" (1990, 12). Also see Hansen (1947, 135; 1953, 27) and Meltzer (1988, 88).

[3] Keynes (CW 13, 436).

[4] Keynes (CW 13, 403; 1932–35, A41, D19, I23–24).

3.2 *The Monetary Theory of Employment*

During 1933, Keynes produced three draft tables of contents for his new book on monetary theory. The title of the first draft table of contents is *The Monetary Theory of Employment*.[5] Fragments of chapters from this draft table survive and are reproduced in the Keynes's *Collected Writings*.[6] These chapter fragments contain the following four equations.[7]

$$N = f_1(Q) \tag{3.4}$$

$$E = f_2(N) \tag{3.5}$$

$$C = f_3(D) \tag{3.6}$$

$$D = E + Q = I + C \tag{3.7}$$

where N is employment, f_1 is the supply function, Q is quasi-rent, E is prospective variable cost, f_2 is the cost function, C is consumption, f_3 is the propensity to save, $D =$ aggregate disbursements, and I is investment.

In terms of IS-LM, the consumption function is the most notable feature of *The Monetary Theory of Employment*. After using a saving function in GTE/5/423, Keynes reverts back to a consumption function. Furthermore, *The Monetary Theory of Employment* contains the first instance of the IS-LM consumption function in standard form (Eq. 3.6). Here, consumption is determined by the propensity to save (f_3) and aggregate disbursements (D). Aggregate disbursements are explicitly defined as consumption plus income. This means aggregate disbursements and income are equivalent.

$$D = C + I = Y \tag{3.8}$$

After adjusting for notation, it is clear that the consumption function from *The Monetary Theory of Employment* manuscript is identical in form to the standard IS-LM consumption function:

$$C = f_3(Y) \tag{3.9}$$

---

[5] Keynes (CW 29, 62; Keynes Papers, GTE/5/91).

[6] Keynes (CW 29, 62–66; Keynes Papers, GTE/5/92–98). There are two other draft tables of contents from 1933, both titled *The General Theory of Employment* (CW 29, 63; CW 13, 421–422). Fragments of chapters from these 1933 draft tables of contents are printed in Keynes's *Collected Writings* (CW 29, 66–102).

[7] Keynes (CW 29, 65).

Chapters 8 and 9 of *The Monetary Theory of Employment* draft table of contents are titled "The Factors Governing Investment" and "The Schedules of Liquidity Preference."[8] Unfortunately, these draft chapters did not survive, meaning *The Monetary Theory of Employment* does not contain the liquidity-preference function or the investment function. Still, with only slight adjustments to notation, it is possible to piece together a four-equation IS-LM model from GTE/5/423 and *The Monetary Theory of Employment*.[9]

$$\rho = f_1(M, A) \tag{3.10}$$

$$I = f_2(\rho, E) \tag{3.11}$$

$$C = f_3(Y) \tag{3.12}$$

$$Y = C + I \tag{3.13}$$

where ρ is the interest rate, M is the quantity of money, A is liquidity preference, I is investment, E is state of technique, C is consumption, and Y is income. Finally, Keynes explicitly advocates the simultaneous equations approach to his theory in *The Monetary Theory of Employment*: "the amount of employment will be determined by a set of simultaneous equations."[10]

The second draft table of contents contains material on Keynes's definition of income.[11] Recall, he did not achieve a usable definition of income in the 1932 lectures. Although he was still having trouble defining income in early 1933, his draft chapter "Certain Fundamental Equations" shows meaningful progress.[12]

> Our fundamental equations consist of nothing but the truisms which result from the equality between aggregate Income *(Y)* which is the sum of Earnings *(E)* and Quasi-rents *(Q)*, and aggregate Disbursement *(D)* which is the sum of Consumption-expenditure *(C)* and Investment (*I*), so that we have
>
> $$Y = E + Q = C + I = D$$

---

[8] Keynes (CW 29, 62).

[9] Specifically, Keynes uses the notation C for state of technique in GTE/5/423. This might be confused for consumption in *The Monetary Theory of Employment*. Thus, to avoid confusion, the notation E is used here for state of technique.

[10] Keynes (CW 29, 65). This passage contradicts interpreters like Victoria Chick who claim, "the formal nature of the 'Keynesian Revolution'... involved the complete overthrow of the static method of solving a set of simultaneous equations" (1992, 77).

[11] Keynes (CW 29, 63).

[12] Keynes (CW 29, 68–73). Rymes notes "Keynes's great trouble with definitions of income" (1989, 23).

Furthermore, the second draft table of contents contains material on the positive investment--income relation underlying IS-LM. He writes, "ΔN [change in employment] and ΔQ [change in quasi-rent] have the same sign."[13] Moreover, he stresses that fluctuations in income, and hence employment, are driven primarily by fluctuations in investors' cash flow (quasi-rent) expectations: "fluctuations of aggregate quasi-rent ... lead to fluctuations in employment."[14] He describes the positive investment--income relation as "Our first fundamental proposition," and re-emphasizes: "*N* and *Q* have the same sign ... [T]he quantity of employment and the expectation of quasi-rent during the employment period increase and decrease together."[15]

3.3 Mr. Keynes's Multiplier

As described above, Keynes had already formulated at least five different saving and consumption functions prior to March 1933. But these early functions are not those of the *General Theory* and the IS-LM model. Specifically, these early functions are not underpinned by the multiplier. Although he had developed an informal relationship between income, saving, and consumption, the formal precision of the multiplier was not a feature of his theory in 1932.[16]

The traditional view is that Keynes did not originate the multiplier himself.[17] During the early decades of Keynesian Revolution, it was widely believed that Richard Kahn introduced the multiplier in his classic 1931 article, "The Relation of Home Investment to Unemployment."[18] The view that Kahn introduced the multiplier can be traced to Keynes himself. He states in the *General Theory*, "The conception of the multiplier was first introduced into economic theory by Mr R.F. Kahn."[19]

Today, scholars recognize that the history of the multiplier is more complicated than Keynes suggests in the *General Theory*. Indeed, he certainly knew the history of the multiplier was more nuanced. In 1938, he wrote a short section on "History of the Multiplier Doctrine," and he acknowledges his own role in the development of the multiplier.

> One must distinguish here between some sort of formal statement such as was given in Kahn's *Economic Journal* article and the general notion of there being such a thing as secondary

---

[13] Keynes (CW 29, 70).

[14] Keynes (CW 29, 71).

[15] Keynes (CW 29, 76).

[16] As Moggridge writes, "The consumption function led to the multiplier.... It was through the multiplier, itself a corollary of the propensity to consume, that variations in output become part of the equilibrating mechanism of the *General Theory* and the theory of effective demand was born" (1993, 94). However, Moggridge agrees that in late 1932, "He had not yet extracted the formal elegance of the multiplier relationship" (1976, 102; 1993, 100).

[17] Laidler says, for example, "[Keynes] did not originate the multiplier" (1999, 336).

[18] Kahn (1931).

[19] Keynes (CW 7, 113).

> employment.... The general notion of secondary employment, however, must go back much further. For example, it is clearly explained in *Can Lloyd George Do It?* by Hubert Henderson and myself.[20]

This distinction between a "formal statement" of the multiplier and "the general notion" is significant. No doubt, Keynes formulated the general notion before Kahn.[21] Beyond that, Kahn admits that Keynes's general notion inspired his formal statement: "I began work on my so-called multiplier article in the Austrian Tyrol in August 1930.... I was inspired by *Can Lloyd George Do It?*"[22]

Published in May 1929, *Can Lloyd George Do It?* was co-authored with Hubert Henderson. In the pamphlet, Keynes and Henderson introduce the idea of secondary employment, or "indirect employment," from a government policy of capital-expenditure:

> [T]he indirect employment which schemes of capital expenditure would entail is far larger than the direct employment. This fact is one of the strongest arguments for pressing forward with such schemes; for it means that the greater part of the employment they would provide would be spread far and wide over the industries of the country. But the fact that the indirect employment would be spread far and wide does not mean that it is in the least doubtful or illusory. On the contrary, it is calculable within fairly precise limits.[23]

The idea of direct and indirect employment is suggestive of his later distinction between primary and secondary employment. There is a section on "Cumulative Force of Trade Activity," and it reads: "the greater trade activity would make for further trade activity; for the forces of prosperity, like those of a trade depression, work with a cumulative effect."[24] This "cumulative effect" is the essence of the Keynesian multiplier.[25]

Keynes did not provide a formal statement of the multiplier in his May 1929 pamphlet.[26] And his 1938 distinction between the "general notion" and "formal statement" might suggest he did not attempt a formal statement at that time. But document PS/4/121 in the *Keynes Papers* shows he did. As Richard J. Kent highlights,

---

[20] Keynes (CW 12, 806). Patinkin writes, "Keynes' relation to the multiplier—albeit without the use of that term—dates back at least to the May 1929 pamphlet *Can Lloyd George Do It?*" (1982, 191). Also see Dillard (1948, 310n32) and Laidler (1999, 173). It should be noted that Henderson became a harsh critic of the Keynesian multiplier, and even "denounced the *General Theory* as a hoax" (in Straight, 1983, 57).

[21] Keynes (CW 9, 86–125). The general notion of the multiplier has earlier origins. The general notion can be traced to Walter Bagehot (1873, 125–126). Nicholas Johannsen used the term "multiplying principle" (1908, 43n). Keynes referred to this work in *A Treatise on Money* (CW 6, 90, 90n2). Also see Klein (1947, 143) and Patinkin (1982, 191).

[22] Kahn (1984, 91). Moggridge agrees, "[Kahn was] inspired by *Can Lloyd George Do It?*" (1976, 89).

[23] Keynes (CW 9, 106).

[24] Keynes (CW 9, 106).

[25] Some interpreters (Dostaler 2007, 189) trace the multiplier to his May 24, 1924 article, "Does Unemployment Need a Drastic Remedy?" (CW 19, 219–223). There he suggests that "prosperity is cumulative" (CW 19, 220).

[26] See Dimand (1988, 158, 188) and Laidler (1999, 174, 336).

on May 28, 1929, Keynes gave a speech in London on "Support of the Liberal Party Candidate T.O. Jacobson."[27] As with *Can Lloyd George Do It?*, he discusses "indirect unemployment." But he takes another critical step: he introduces the central idea that indirect spending is generated in a geometric progression. PS/4/121 is reproduced here in Fig. 3.2, and it shows that Keynes did attempt a formal statement of the multiplier by May 28, 1929.

> A man who is unemployed spends perhaps 30 a week. When employed he spends 60.
>
> Some imports for food and raw materials. This may stimulate exports or a little diminish foreign investment
>
> Indirect employment. But of the 30 extra he spends a good deal goes to home industry. He buys boots and clothing. Suppose 25 goes in this way
>
> A man is taken off the dole and nearly half is found in this way
>
> A long series
>
> I have calculated that if 1/4 is imported
>
> $$\begin{aligned} &1/2 + 3/4(1/4 + 1/8 + \ldots) \\ &\quad + 3/16(1 + 1/2 + 1/4 + \ldots) \\ &\quad + 3/8 \\ &= 7/8 \end{aligned}$$

PS/4/121 proves that Keynes did attempt a formal statement of the multiplier in May 1929. Kahn presented an early draft of his classic paper by September 1930, and the paper was published in June 1931.[28] Hence, Keynes attempted a formal statement of the multiplier sixteen months before Kahn. While he deserves credit for emphasizing the document, Kent seems to have missed a connection between PS/4/121 and Keynes's key 1933 article on the multiplier, as will be shown below.

The evidence shows that Keynes incorporated the basic multiplier process underlying IS into his theory by early 1933. The key article is "The Means to Prosperity," published March 13–16 in *The Times*.[29] In this article, Keynes coins the term "the multiplier."

> Let us call the gross amount of expenditure, provided out of additional borrowing, the primary expenditure and the employment directly created by this expenditure the primary employment.... This primary expenditure will, in any of these cases, set up a series of repercussions leading to what it is convenient to call secondary employment. Our problem is to ascertain the total employment, primary and secondary together, created by a given amount of additional loan-expenditure, i.e. to ascertain the multiplier relating the total employment to the primary employment.[30]

---

[27] Keynes (Keynes Papers, PS/4/120–140). See Kent (2007).

[28] See Moggridge (1973, 74–75; 1976, 81; 1993, 89), Patkinin (1982, 197), and Kahn (1984, 95–96).

[29] Keynes (CW 9, 335–366). Also see Dimand (1988, 158) and Moggridge (1992, 563–564).

[30] Keynes (CW 9, 341).

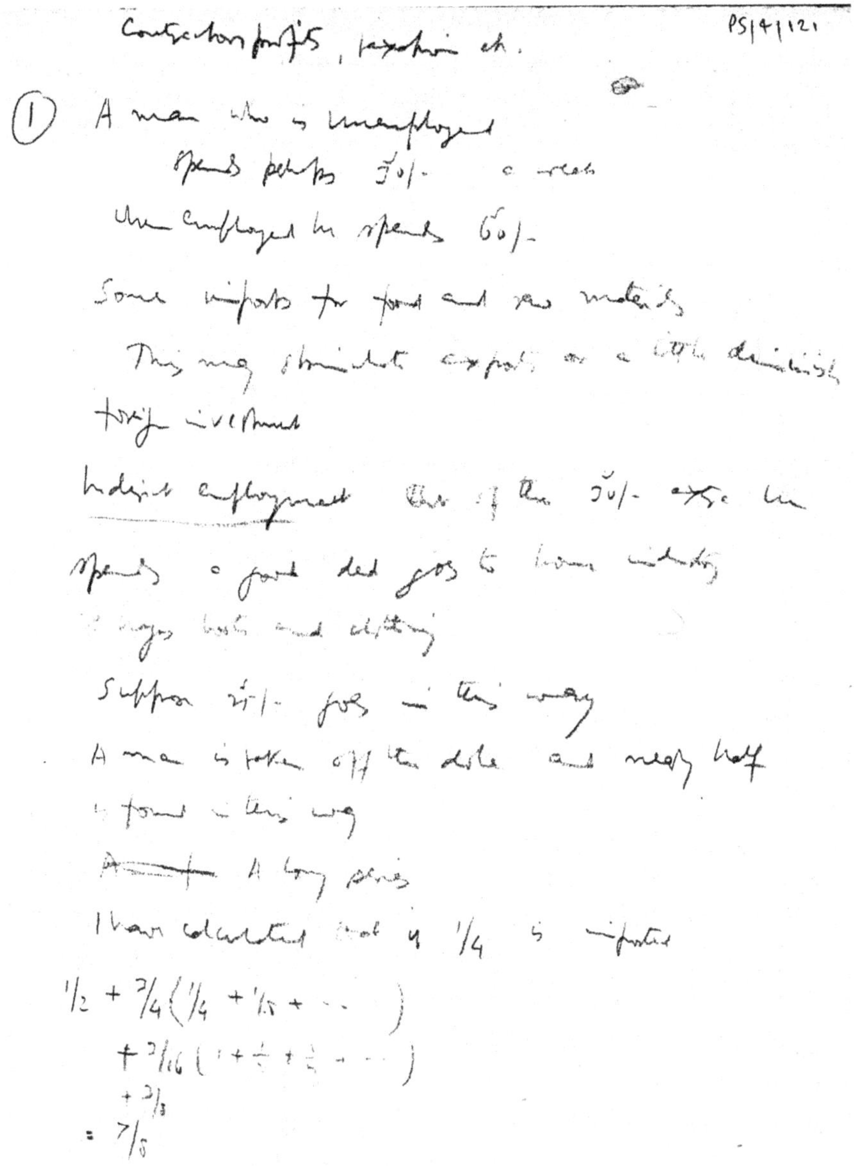
PS/4/121

A man who is unemployed
spends perhaps 50/- a week
when employed he spends 60/-
Some imports for food and raw materials
This may stimulate exports or a little diminish
foreign investment
Indirect employment of the 50/- extra he
spends a good deal goes to home industry
wages boots and clothing
Suppose 25/- goes in this way
A man is taken off the dole and nearly half
is found in this way
A long series
I have calculated that if 1/4 is imported

Fig. 3.2 Keynes Papers, PS/4/121

He argues that an increase in primary employment creates secondary employment in a "series of repercussions."[31] Initially, he suggests the multiplier is 2, meaning the amount of secondary employment generated is equal to the increase in

[31] Keynes (CW 9, 342).

primary employment. Although he does not use the term, he recognizes that primary employment generates secondary employment in a geometric progression.

> [T]he first repercussion will be 49 per cent (since 7x7 = 49) of the primary effect, or (say) one-half; the second repercussion will be one-half of the first repercussion, i.e. one-quarter of the primary effect, and so on. Thus the multiplier is 2, since, if I may take the reader back to his schooldays, he will remember that $1 + \frac{1}{2} + \frac{1}{4} + \text{etc.} = 2$. The amount of time which it takes for current income to be spent will separate each repercussion from the next one. But it will be seen that seven-eights of the total effects come from the primary expenditure and the first two repercussions, so that the time-lags involved are not unduly serious.[32]

The number "seven-eights" might be significant, for this is the same number he arrives at in PS/4/121. This suggests a connection between his May 1929 multiplier analysis and the March 1933 article "The Means to Prosperity." In the remainder of the article, he introduces additional considerations and reduces his estimate of the multiplier from 2 to $1\frac{1}{2}$ and, finally, to $1\frac{1}{3}$. While he does not use the term, his multiplier estimate of $1\frac{1}{3}$ implies the marginal propensity to consume is $\frac{1}{4}$.

On April 1, he published an article in *New Statesman and Nation* entitled "The Multiplier."[33] This article is a response to criticisms of "The Means of Prosperity." Critics argued his estimates of the multiplier in "The Means to Prosperity" are too high. In his reply to critics, he maintains that his estimates of the multiplier are too low: "The actual calculations of my first article were based, however, on a multiplier, not of 2, but of $1\frac{1}{2}$ or $1\frac{1}{3}$. In existing circumstances, therefore, I left myself a very wide margin for various contingencies."[34] Although he does not use the term, he suggests the marginal propensity to consume is probably $\frac{2}{3}$, meaning the multiplier is 3.[35] He concludes by insisting, "There is no magic here, no mystery; but a reliable scientific prediction."[36]

In summary, Keynes created the traditional wisdom that Kahn introduced the multiplier. Today, scholars recognize that figures like Meade, Hawtrey, Giblin, Warming, and others played a role.[37] Now it is common to attribute the multiplier to a group of economists. But this group does not typically include Keynes. PS/4/121 shows that he was one of the earliest formalizers of the multiplier. Thus, he was a key member of the group of economists who formalized the multiplier. And he was the significant popularizer. Keynes incorporated the basic multiplier process into his theory in 1933 and the IS-LM consumption function was born.

---

[32] Keynes (CW 9, 343; CW 21, 175). Kahn notes, "Keynes was not interested in the actual process of movement from one position to another" (1984, 124). On the issue of time in the multiplier process, see Dillard (1948, 88), Hansen (1953, 113), Presley (1979, 165–177), Fletcher (1987, 52–53, 56, 81; 2008, 189, 191), and Meltzer (1988, 142).

[33] Keynes (CW 21, 171–178). Keynes was chairman of *New Statesman and Nation* from early 1931 until his death in April 1946. See Moggridge (1992, 508).

[34] Keynes (CW 21, 175–176).

[35] Keynes (CW 21, 176).

[36] Keynes (CW 21, 177).

[37] See Dimand (1994) on Meade. See Davis (1980) and Dimand (1988, 107–111; 1997) on Hawtrey. See Dimand (1988, 115–118) and Laidler (1999, 172–177) on Warming. See Wright (1956) and Dimand (1988, 105) on Giblin.

3.4 The Marginal Efficiency of Capital

Keynes coined the term marginal efficiency of capital sometime in 1933.[38] But his use of the term emerged from his 1932 work on investment theory. The *Collected Writings* contain an undated draft chapter entitled "Quasi-Rent and the Marginal Efficiency of Capital."[39] There is no supporting draft table of contents, but the editors of the *Collected Writings* presume it dates to 1933–34.[40] On the contrary, the original manuscript almost certainly dates to late 1932. The original title was "Quasi-Rent and the Marginal Productivity of Capital," and he used the term "marginal productivity of capital" throughout the manuscript. Then, sometime in 1933, he amended the document, and all seventeen instances of "marginal productivity of capital" were changed to "marginal efficiency of capital."[41]

The main significance of this document is that it links the notion of the marginal efficiency of capital to Keynes's 1932 lectures. As noted, on November 14, 1932, Keynes adopts a present-value approach to his theory of investment.[42]

> p_r = the cost of production of capital assets at time *r*.
>
> k_r = marginal productivity of capital at time *r*
>
> q_r = profit at time *r*
>
> d_r = present value of £1 deferred *r* years.
>
> Present value of an asset $= \sum (p_r k_r + q_r) d_r$.

Keynes's analysis in the 1932 lectures is virtually identical in "Quasi-Rent and the Marginal Efficiency of Capital." In fact, he almost certainly lectured from this document in 1932. The only difference in 1933 is that he changes the "marginal productivity of capital" to "marginal efficiency of capital." Indeed, he maintains the notation k_r for the m.e.c, or marginal efficiency of capital.

> Thus, apart from allowance for risk, the money value of capital assets at any time, which we have analyzed above as depending on prospective quasi-rent in conjunction with the rate of interest, can be further analyzed as depending on four factors,—(1) prospective m.e.c, (2) prospective windfall profit and loss, (3) prospective value of money in terms of cost of production, and (4) the complex of current rates of interest.
>
> Let p_r be the cost of production at time *r*
>
> Let k_r be the m.e.c. at time *r*
>
> Let q_r be the profit at time *r*

---

38 As Moggridge puts it, by 1933, "Keynes had the glimmerings of the marginal efficiency of capital" (1976, 105; 1992, 561, 565).

39 Keynes (CW 29, 111–120).

40 Keynes (CW 29, 111).

41 Moggridge writes in his editorial comments in the *Collected Writings*: "Throughout the first two sections of the manuscript of this draft, except in paragraph four, Keynes crossed out the word 'productivity' and replaced it with the word 'efficiency' after he originally wrote out the chapter. Where these changes occurred the word 'efficiency' is underlined. The same occurs when m.e.c. replaced m.p.c. as a short form" (CW 29, 111n17).

42 Keynes (1932–35, D17, A37–38, I20–21).

Let d_r present value of *£1* deferred r years.

Then $\sum (p_r k_r + q_r) d_r$ is the present value of an equity assuming all the relevant quantities are known. In the case of a gilt-edged debt, expressed in terms of money $k_r = \frac{1}{p_r}$ and $q_r = 0$, so that its value is $\sum d_r$.[43]

Clearly, Keynes's conception of the marginal efficiency of capital in 1932–33 is not identical to its final conception in the *General Theory*. His 1932–33 presentation is confused.[44] He initially aligns the marginal efficiency with quasi-rent, meaning it is a sum of money: "quasi-rent [is], so to speak, the short-period version of m.e.c."[45] No doubt, the m.e.c. (k_r) must be a sum of money to be included in his present value expression $\sum (p_r k_r + q_r) d_r$. But then he says the marginal efficiency of capital is a ratio, or percentage.

> I said above that quasi-rent is so to speak the short-period version of the marginal efficiency of capital, because there are also two other respects in which it differs.... [Q]uasi-rent is an absolute sum, whereas m.e.c. is a ratio, namely the ratio of the net yield of an asset to its cost of production. To this extent m.e.c. is a concept more nearly analogous to the rate of interest.[46]

All this indicates that, in 1932–33, Keynes was using the term marginal efficiency of capital inconsistently, as both a sum of money and as a rate of return. In the *General Theory*, the marginal efficiency of capital is defined as the discount rate that makes the present value equal to the supply price.[47] Thus, it is a percentage rate, not a sum of money. Keynes did not achieve his final definition of the marginal efficiency of capital in 1933. Still, the broad notion is there: he had the name and he related it to the present value.[48]

3.5 Keynes's 1933 Lectures

Keynes was on the verge of the IS-LM model by mid-1933. Indeed, as shown above, it is possible to piece together the IS-LM model from various documents he produced just before mid-1933. By summer 1933, he acknowledged his theory was at an advanced stage of development. It was so well developed, in fact, he thought his

---

[43] Keynes (CW 29, 114).

[44] This is not a moot point, for the marginal efficiency of capital is "absolutely vital" to Keynes (CW 13, 549). Kahn describes the marginal efficiency of capital as "the most important [subject] in the *General Theory*" (1984, 145). As Moggridge notes, "Keynes also made mistakes, let his intuition rush beyond the limits of his current technical ability and his formal argument" (1992, 558).

[45] Keynes (CW 29, 113).

[46] Keynes (CW 29, 114).

[47] Keynes (CW 7, 135).

[48] In this manuscript, Keynes includes an extended note on the origins of the term 'marginal efficiency.' There, he traces the term to Alfred Marshall's *Principles*: "The phrase which Marshall himself uses is 'marginal efficiency' of a factor of production" (CW 29, 113n). Keynes then cites the relevant passage from Marshall.

book could be published in mid-1934. He wrote to his publisher, Daniel Macmillan, on August 17, 1933:

> I have been working at my next contribution to monetary theory, which will probably appear, I hope, some time in the first half of next year. In view of this I have not been wanting to spend time revising my *Treatise on Money*, even in minor particulars, and am anxious to put off doing so until after my next book has appeared.[49]

Keynes's lectures in the fall of 1933 represent a great watershed in this history of macroeconomic thought, and IS-LM in particular. Six sets of student notes from the 1933 lectures have taken on a central role in the study of the Keynesian Revolution. The six student note takers are Robert Bryce, Alec Cairncross, Marvin Fallgatter, Walter Salant, Lorie Tarshis, and Bryn Thring. Robert W. Dimand describes the notes taken by these six students as "comparable in importance and fascination to the rediscovered lectures of Adam Smith."[50] Robert Skidelsky writes,

> Six sets of students' notes have survived of the lectures Keynes gave in the Michaelmas (autumn) term of 1933. They show that the lectures were much sharper than those of the year before, the theory in much better focus. Had they been published as delivered, the world would have got a pretty clear idea of what it later received as the *General Theory of Employment, Interest, and Money*.... The world would also have got a more vivid idea, because in lecturing Keynes was less restrained in his expression. In the *General Theory* the iconoclasm was largely covered up by technical drapery. Here it can be grasped more directly.[51]

Keynes delivered his first lecture on October 16. He starts by acknowledging that his *Treatise on Money* lacks a theory of output. Salant records, "Since *Treatise*, Keynes has changed emphasis of his thought from prices to output and employment."[52] According to Bryce,

> He has lectured in this general course for six-seven years. They have always been different, but form and substance only—underlying ideas still very much the same. Started on Quantity Theory, i.e., early lectures trying to get a new quantity theory. But later abandoned as in Fundamental Equations in the *Treatise*. In the *Treatise* he was assuming monetary positions and was not so much interested in the occurrence of movement but thought he had the clue. Lectures since then were aimed at making good their monetary analysis and making it more general. General trend of the course has been toward what determines output and its change and the rate of change of output and hence employment.[53]

---

[49] Keynes (CW 20, 420).

[50] Dimand (2019, 181). Also see King (2002, 149).

[51] Skidelsky (1992, 496). We agree with this statement. But Skidelsky's endorsement of the 1933 lectures seems inconsistent with his repeated rejections of the IS-LM interpretation of Keynes's theory.

[52] Keynes (1932–35, M1).

[53] Keynes (1932–25, B1). As Patinkin observed, this and other statements show that "Keynes is succumbing to the natural temptation of an author to present himself as having been consistent over time, and that he accordingly attempts to minimise the difference between the *Treatise* and the *General Theory*" (1993, 648).

Keynes devotes the first lecture to the classical theory of wages. According to Keynes, the classical economists argued that involuntary unemployment is impossible. The classical argument is based on the two classical wage postulates.[54] Tarshis records:

> Two fundamental postulates—
>
> (1) The wage is equal to the marginal product….
>
> (2) In equilibrium the utility of wage when a given volume of labor employed is equal to the marginal disutility of that amount of employment….
>
> The first postulate of classical theory gives us the demand function for employment. The second gives us the supply schedule…. Hence the volume of employment is, for the classical theory, determined…. Note that if postulate 2 of classical theory holds good there can be no person unemployed in the above (involuntary) sense. So if classical theory is correct involuntary unemployment in strict sense is impossible[55]

Keynes accepts the first classical wage postulate: "Keynes continues to maintain the first postulate."[56] In sharp contrast, however, he rejects the second postulate: "postulate No. 2 wrong," and "We must drop the second postulate of Classical doctrine—But not the first postulate."[57] And since the second postulate is incorrect, Keynes holds that involuntary unemployment is possible.[58] Thring records his definition of unemployment as follows:

> Keynes definition of unemployment: Men are involuntarily unemployed if the supply of labor willing to work for a money wage worth less, in terms of product, than the existing money wage is greater than the existing volume of employment.[59]

For Keynes, the classical theory is problematic, because it does not properly distinguish between the real wage and money wage. Salant reports,

---

[54] Keynes first wrote about these postulates in his second 1933 manuscript (CW 29, 70–72). See Hansen (1953, 20–25) for a general overview of Keynes's analysis, and Dimand (1988, 160–161) for the analysis in the 1933 lectures.

[55] Keynes (1932–35, J2, B1, M1, N2).

[56] Keynes (1932–35, B7).

[57] Keynes (1932–35, M2, J4, N3).

[58] Keynes writes in the *General Theory*, "We need to throw over the second postulate of the classical doctrine and to work out the behavior of a system in which involuntary unemployment in the strict sense is possible" (CW 7, 16–17). However, he admits in his famous 1937 article, "this part of my book is particularly open to criticism" (CW 14, 110). Dennis Robertson wrote to Harrod in October 1936: "the generally recognized traditional … doctrines with which the *General Theory* is contrasted often seem to me a kind of bogey man, created out of straw" (in Young 1989, 59). Harrod agreed, "[Keynes] himself was in some confusion about what the classical position really was" (1951, 453). Kahn mostly ignores Keynes's analysis of the classical wage postulates and describes the analysis as "unnecessarily complex" (1984, 120). Also see Moggridge (1976, 106), Coddington (1983, 65, 92), Darity and Young (1997), Laidler (1999, 278–279; 2006, 39–40), and Leeson and Schiffman (2013).

[59] Keynes (1932–35, N2, B5, J2–3, M2). It appears Keynes wrote this definition on the chalkboard, for it is virtually identical in all student notes (Rymes 1989, 22). He gives a similar definition in the *General Theory* (CW 7, 15).

> Also classical treatment always assumes real wages will be reduced as a result of reduction in money wages. According to this, unemployment could be completely wiped out by sufficient reduction of wages. In real world, actual wages are money wages. Refusal to accept lower real wages and to accept lower money wages is not the same thing. If reduction of money wages wouldn't reduce volume of labor offering itself, there is involuntary unemployment. Reduction of money wages, Keynes believes will not reduce unemployment.... Keynes accepts correlation between real wage and unemployment but not that between real wages and money wages.[60]

He agrees that a reduction in the real wage will reduce unemployment: "Keynes wouldn't deny that a change in real wages then would have a real influence on employment" and "increase in employment can only come about by decrease in real wage."[61] But a reduction in the money wage will not always eliminate unemployment. In fact, a reduction in the money wage can lead to even more unemployment: "There is no reason to expect higher employment by reduction in money wages—rather opposite is more possible."[62]

It is not necessary to review the second and third lectures in great detail. These lectures are largely devoted to definitions, and much of this material did not survive into the *General Theory*. Tarshis recalled, "An awful lot of the lectures were filled with his fiddling over definitions."[63] Indeed, Keynes acknowledged that his long deliberations on definitions were a "great drag" on the presentation of his theory: "The chapters dealing with income, user cost and the rest of the definitions ... were a great drag on getting to the real business."[64] Still, there a few points in these lectures worth noting.

On October 23, Keynes addresses the classical theory and Say's Law. He proclaims, "Ricardo foisted on economics the idea that supply creates its own demand.... Celebrated optimism of classical theory is traceable to this—also its devotion to laissez-faire."[65] Opposed to the Commodity–Money–Commodity (*C–M–C'*) approach of classical economics, he endorses Karl Marx's Money–Commodity–Money (*M–C–M'*) approach.[66] He says, "situation is not *C–M–C'* but *M–C–M'*."[67] We read in Fallgatter's notes,

[60] Keynes (1932–35, M2, B5–B6, J3–4, N3).

[61] Keynes (1932–35, B2, N3).

[62] Keynes (1932–35, B6, J4, N3).

[63] Tarshis (1996, 55). Rymes observes, "The notes of the second lecture are replete with references to ... a classification scheme which Keynes largely abandoned in the *General Theory*" (1989, 22–23; 12n37). Dimand (1988, 157–163, 181–184) mostly ignores this material in his treatment of the 1933 lectures.

[64] Keynes (CW 13, 537, 469–470; CW 14, 206). Moggridge notices Keynes's "constant fretting—understandable after his experience with the *Treatise*—over matters of definitions" (1992, 557).

[65] Keynes (1932–35, B12, E3, G2, J8, M4, N4). Keynes alludes to this in the third 1933 manuscript (CW 29, 80). Also see his comments on Say's Law in the *General Theory* (CW 7, 18).

[66] Keynes (1932–25, B13, N4). Keynes compares the classical *C–M–C'* approach to the Marxian *M–C–M'* approach in some draft fragments from 1933 (CW 29, 81). On Keynes and Marx's *M–C–M'* approach, see Moggridge (1976, 104), Fitzgibbons (1988, 78–80), Skidelsky (1992, 497–498), and Dostaler (2007, 172).

[67] Keynes (1932–35, E3).

> Marx pointed out that the purpose of an economic system should be to increase the supply of consumers goods, and that money's function is to serve as an intermediary to that process. Money is accepted in return for goods in order that the money may be so used as to produce more goods than before, through the employment of labor on them. This may be symbolized
>
> *C–M–C'*
>
> But under capitalism, he pointed out, production is carried out rather so that money invested in labor and goods will produce more:
>
> *M–C–M'*
>
> ... Marx's view is right[68]

Keynes offers additional criticisms of the classical theory on October 30. Most importantly, he distinguishes the entrepreneur economy from the neutral economy.[69] He declares "In an entrepreneur economy the postulates of classical economy never fulfilled."[70] He alerts his audience that he will "construct a model of an entrepreneur economy."[71] In other words, entrepreneurs' uncertain expectations play a central role in Keynes's 1933 model.[72]

Keynes's delivered his fourth lecture on November 6. This lecture is significant because he presents the IS-LM consumption function for the first time in public. He came extremely close to the form of the IS-LM investment function in his 1933 draft *The Monetary Theory of Employment*. Although analytically equivalent, that function is not immediately recognizable as the IS-LM investment function, for consumption is a function of aggregate disbursements (D) rather than income (Y).[73] On November 6, he explicitly makes consumption a function of income.[74]

$$C = f(Y, A) \tag{3.14}$$

where C is consumption, Y is income, and A is windfall appreciation. There are two points worth noting. First, the consumption function only appears in the Tarshis notes. This suggests that Keynes did not heavily emphasize the function in the lecture. Second, he includes windfall profits (A). This is the only difference between the November 6 consumption function and the standard IS-LM consumption function. The inclusion of A is notable, however, for it ties his consumption function back to

68 Keynes (1932–35, G3).

69 It appears Keynes lectured from "The Characteristics of an Entrepreneur Economy" (CW 29, 87–101).

70 Keynes (1932–35, J9).

71 Keynes (1932–35, B16, E5).

72 As Moggridge writes, "uncertainty dominated the *General Theory*" (1976, 92). Meltzer notes the "dominant role of expectations in the *General Theory*" (1981, 62; 1988, 201). According to Kahn, "Expectations play a dominating part" (1984, 142, 159).

73 On November 13, Keynes explicitly states "Aggregate Disbursements equals Y [income]" (Keynes 1932–35, J19, B39). Thus, in form, the early 1933 consumption function is essentially the IS-LM investment function.

74 Keynes (1932–35, J17).

his *Treatise on Money*. Although he is developing a theory of output, he is eager to present his new theory as an extension of the *Treatise*.[75]

Also, on November 6, Keynes hints at his theory of uncertain expectations. Specifically, he differentiates between long-term and short-term expectations.[76] We read in Fallgatter's notes,

> 1. Long Period Expectations determine decisions as to fixed capital, organization, etc. ....
> 2. Short Period Expectations lead the firms to decide how intensively (if at all) to use its equipment in current production and employment[77]

Keynes emphasizes that the cash flows from an investment depend on the investor's expectations: "Quasi-rent [i.e. cash flow], note, is determined by expected and not the actual values."[78] Finally, the November 6 lecture contains some interesting remarks on method. As many scholars have noted, Keynes's intuition ran ahead of his formal analysis.[79] He declares, "the precision of thought comes usually toward the end of the argument."[80]

> Even in mathematics, when it is a matter of original work, you do not think always in precise terms. The precise use of language comes at a late stage in the development of one's thoughts. You can think accurately and effectively long before you can so to speak photograph your thought.[81]

Keynes is suggesting his new theory is an extension of the *Treatise*. He confesses that he was not yet thinking in totally "precise terms" during the development of the *Treatise*. Still, he was thinking "accurately and effectively." By late 1933, however, he had arrived at point where he could finally "photograph" his thought.[82]

---

[75] Patinkin observes, "Keynes was so interested in presenting the *General Theory* as a further development of the *Treatise*" (1976, 78).

[76] Keynes writes in the *General Theory*, "it will often be safe to omit express reference to short-term expectation.... [L]ong-term expectations [are] liable to sudden revision. Thus the factor of current long-term expectations cannot be even approximately eliminated or replaced by realised results" (CW 7, 50). For more on the short-term and long-term expectations in Keynes's theory, see O'Donnell (1989, 239–241) and Meltzer (1996, 41).

[77] Keynes (1932–35, G8).

[78] Keynes (1932–35, B31).

[79] Moggridge writes, "Keynes had intuitively grasped many of the essentials of his system as early as 1932. However, if there was no doubt about the truth, there was considerable trouble over the proof, and it took another three years of re-drafting and discussion to clothe that intuition in what he regarded as a technically adequate form for the purposes at hand. For with Keynes intuition represented an early, but essential, stage in the act of creation. Very hard, systematic work then went into developing the scheme of thought for the consumption and persuasion of the world at large" (1976, 32–33; 1992, 552).

[80] Keynes (1932–35, B25).

[81] Keynes (1932–35, G7).

[82] Keynes wrote to O.T. Falk, "The extent to which one sees one's destination before one discovers the route is the most obscure problem of all in the psychology of original work. In a sense, it is the destination on sees first" (in Moggridge 1992, 551).

Keynes's lecture on November 13 is dedicated to defining income.[83] For the first time, Keynes presents the standard IS-LM income equation: $Y = C + I$. In other words, he presents the condition for equilibrium in the goods market. He starts the lecture with the equations.[84]

$$Y = E + Q = C + I \tag{3.15}$$

$$S = Y - C \tag{3.16}$$

He spends most of the lecture relating his new definitions to his definitions from the *Treatise*. Finally, he gives the following equations at the end of the lecture.[85]

$$Y = E + Q = C + I = D \tag{3.17}$$

$$I = Y - C \tag{3.18}$$

$$I = S \tag{3.19}$$

Moreover, Keynes advocated the simultaneous equations approach to his theory on November 13. Fallgatter records, "Of course, these things operate backwards and forwards, and you really have, so to speak, a set of simultaneous equations."[86] Just like his *Treatise* model and *Parameters* model, Keynes's 1933 model is a general equilibrium, simultaneous equations model.[87]

Keynes's lecture on November 20 outlines his theories of consumption and investment. He starts with the income equation.[88]

$$Y = C + I = E + Q \tag{3.20}$$

Keynes expressed the positive investment--income relation in 1932. However, he only sensed intuitively that his theory required this relation; he did not have the

---

[83] It appears Keynes lectured from "Certain Fundamental Equations" (CW 29, 68–73; Keynes Papers, GTE/5/99–106).

[84] Keynes (1932–35, B33, G10, J18, M11, N8).

[85] Keynes (1932–35, G15, J22).

[86] Keynes (1932–35, G14).

[87] This passage contradicts Skidelsky when he insists, "what did not come naturally to [Keynes] was simultaneous equilibrium analysis. His mind did not work that way" (1992, 560). He claims, "the simultaneous equations … approach … was not true to Keynes's own spirit" (2005, 96). These statements are curious. It seems Skidelsky must be aware that Keynes consistently endorsed the simultaneous equations approach in his lectures, for he provides a somewhat detailed analysis of the 1932 lectures and 1933 lectures (Skidelsky 1992, 460–466, 496–502).

[88] Keynes (1932–35, B41, G16, J23, M13, N11).

underlying output-adjustment mechanism. On November 20, he outlines his output-adjustment mechanism publically for the first time. He begins with the consumption function. Significantly, the November 20 consumption function is identical to the standard IS-LM consumption function in theory and form.[89]

$$C = f(Y) \tag{3.21}$$

Next, Keynes introduces the Fundamental Psychological Law. As Bryce reports, "This 'psychological law' is that increment of consumption is less than the increment of income. When total income of community increases not the whole of the increase is spent on consumption."[90] Armed with his Fundamental Psychological Law, Keynes defines the propensity to spend as "the money value of consumption which would follow on an expectancy of income."[91] He stresses that there are only two ways to increase income: "Any increase in income can follow from either of two alternatives: 1. you may alter, as by propaganda, the Propensity to Spend. 2. Or, you may alter the Investment. These are the only two ways of bringing about a change in Income."[92] For Keynes, "This is 'a law' of the most tremendous importance."[93]

Then Keynes turns to his theory of investment. He notes, the "great omission so far is what determines investment."[94] He only attempts a "rough answer" on November 20.[95] However, as in the *Treatise*, he holds that the volume of investment depends on expected future cash flows (prospective yield) and the interest rate:

> What determines volume of investment? Present value of capital asset depends on expected consumption of goods which it will deliver or help deliver at some date in future (earnings) and rate at which future is discounted. The change in investment cannot be positive unless something has changed expectation of future consumption or caused a fall in the rate of interest.[96]

As this passage indicates, Keynes's theory of investment is based on the present value. Thus, "we can't get an increase in investment unless either future expectations of returns increase or the rate of interest falls."[97]

His sketch of his investment theory leads him into a short digression on the paradox of thrift. An increase in saving means a decrease in consumption. But when consumption drops, investors reduce their expectations of future consumption: "Saving does

---

[89] Keynes (1932–35, G17).

[90] Keynes (1932–35, B41–42, E9, G17, J23, M13, N11).

[91] Keynes (1932–35, G18). According to Tarshis and Thring, Keynes uses the terms propensity to save and propensity to spend (Keynes 1932–35, J24, N11–12). Bryce, Fallgatter, and Salant only use propensity to spend (Keynes 1932–35, B42–43, G18, M13). Cairncross only uses propensity to save (Keynes 1932–35, E9).

[92] Keynes (1932–35, G18).

[93] Keynes (1932–35, B43).

[94] Keynes (1932–35, B44).

[95] Keynes (1932–35, N12).

[96] Keynes (1932–35, M13–14).

[97] Keynes (1932–35, B44, G19, J25, N12).

not improve expectations of future demand. Instead you cause a total diminution of expectancy of consumption."[98] Thus, an increase in saving reduces investors' cash flow expectations and, in turn, investment. Given the investment-income relation, the reduction in investment causes income to fall. In short, an increase in saving reduces income: "effective demand is therefore curtailed by savings".[99]

Keynes closes his lecture with some comments on uncertain expectations and investment. As he had stressed earlier in the lecture, "Income of community must be governed by volume of investment."[100] But since investment depends on investors' expectations, "you can only change income by changing the entrepreneurs' expectations."[101] National income is normally suboptimal under capitalism because entrepreneurs' expectations about investment are extremely precarious.[102] The solution to the economic problem requires designing and implementing the proper controls on investment.

> The system of investment is actually less clear-cut than here portrayed, because of the enormous practical difficulty of making the requisite estimates with any good probability of accuracy. Investments occur only because investors have a high power of kidding themselves as to their powers of prediction.... Once we have grasped the nature of the social machine, there is no reason it should be recalcitrant. Without this knowledge of controls you will get all kinds of random dislocations and maladjustments in our economy. With an understanding of the essential nature of the beast, and the concomitant knowledge of it controls, it is entirely possible to raise output in the neighborhood of the optimum.[103]

On November 27, Keynes expands on his theories of consumption and investment. He starts by introducing the marginal propensity to consume for the first time. Then he derives the multiplier from the marginal propensity to consume.

---

[98] Keynes (1932–35, G20).

[99] Keynes (1932–35, G20, J23). He repeats on December 4: "the bad effect saving must be recognised" and "As soon as one saves, entrepreneurs make losses and capital will not be replaced—stock of capital becomes less" (Keynes 1932–35, G37, B60, J38). On the paradox of thrift, see Robinson (1937, 12–14), Klein (1947, 178), Hansen (1953, 154), Fletcher (1987, 75–77), and Meltzer (1988, 70–72).

[100] Keynes (1932–35, E9, B42, G18, J24, N11–12). As he wrote in his famous 1937 article, "the level of output and employment as a whole depends on the amount of investment" (CW 14, 121).

[101] Keynes (1932–35, J27, B47).

[102] Keynes wrote in 1932, "For a modern community one may say that it is a normal thing ... for output to be below the optimum level" (CW 13, 407). The *General Theory* is concerned with "a chronic condition of sub-normal activity ... [F]ull, or even approximately full, employment is of rare and short-lived occurrence" (CW 7, 249–250). As Meltzer writes, for Keynes, "uncertainty is the major reason the rate of investment [and thus income] is suboptimal" (1988, 120). O'Donnell agrees, "Keynes expressly based his account of long-term unemployment equilibrium on entrepreneurial [investor] expectations" (1989, 242).

[103] Keynes (1932–35, G21–22). According to Patinkin, "the fundamental policy conclusion of the *General Theory* [is] the advocacy of direct government investment" (1976, 136). As Meltzer writes, "Keynes favored state direction of investment from the mid-1920s" and "Keynes's main recommendation is for social management of investment" (1988, 5, 115). O'Donnell writes, "Keynes constantly viewed the volume of investment as a variable with which society, and hence the state, had a direct concern" (1992, 795).

Suppose a man's income commands quantity N of employment, and he actually consumes N_1—then the ratio of N_1 to N is the propensity to consume. Then $\Delta N_1/\Delta N$ is called his marginal propensity to consume ... In a given state of expectations let his N_1/N be measured by $\left(1 - \frac{1}{K}\right)$. Hence,

$$K(\Delta N - \Delta N_1) = \Delta N$$
$$\Delta N_2 = \Delta N - N_1$$
$$K \Delta N_2 = \Delta N$$

This ΔN_2 represents the increment of labour directed to output not consumed[104]

Keynes continues, "K here is the multiplier—giving relation between change in total employment corresponding to the primary employment resulting from the increment in investment."[105] He gives an example: "if people are in the habit of spending, say 90% of their increased incomes, then $K = 10$."[106] He suggests that the marginal propensity to consume must be less than one, otherwise the multiplier would be infinite.[107] He goes on to estimate the multiplier: "in US multiplier is perhaps quite large. In Great Britain perhaps 2, 3, or even 4—the US multiplier probably much larger".[108]

After deriving the multiplier, Keynes proceeds to his theory of investment. He stresses that investment determines income and employment: "We've discussed the relationship between consumption and income. But we cannot tell what absolute value of consumption and income will be—Thus, we need information as to what determines the rate of investment."[109] Again, his theory of investment is based on the present value:

d_r is present value of £1 deferred for r years. Asset will be worth

$$\sum Q_1 d_1 + Q_2 d_2 + Q_3 d_3 \; etc.$$

---

[104] Keynes (1932–35, B48–49, G22, N14). Also see Keynes (CW 7, 115). The references here are to Bryce, Fallgatter, and Thring, because they all use the same notation. Tarshis is excluded because there are errors in his recording. Salant and Caircross are excluded because of idiosyncrasies in their notation. See Rymes (1989, 117n52).

[105] Keynes (1932–35, J28).

[106] Keynes (1932–35, G23). Also see the *General Theory* (CW 7, 116).

[107] Keynes (1932–35, E11, G23). In the *General Theory*, Keynes explicitly states that the marginal propensity to consume is "positive and less than unity" (CW 7, 96). He writes, "If, on the other hand, they seek to consume the whole of any increment of income, there will be no point of stability and prices will rise without limit" (CW 7, 117). Also see Dillard (1948, 91, 96) and Hansen (1953, 95).

[108] Keynes (1932–35, J29, G24). Of course, Keynes had no real basis for these estimates. He admitted he was prone to making "bold guesses" when he lacked statistical data (CW 21, 409). Patinkin notes Keynes was "a person who was not too meticulous in his handling of data, and who sometimes succumbed to the temptation to bend the data to fit his preconceptions" (1982, 238). Moreover, Austin Robinson observed that he "would instinctively reject a figure which he felt could not be right" (1947, 44). Dennis Proctor worked with Keynes in the British Treasury, and he bluntly states that Keynes "handled statistics like India rubber" (in Annan 1999, 24). Also see Klein (1951, 446) and Moggridge (1992, 553).

[109] Keynes (1932–35, J30).

> Compare with cost of production. If surplus, produce. Improvement in price of capital assets will vary with Q and d, i.e., state of expectation and on rate of interest. Rate of investment varies with prospective quasi-rents and rate of interest.[110]

Accordingly, there are only two ways to increases investment and, by extension, income and employment: "there are only two things than can increase investment. 1. Higher expected Q's. 2. Fall in the rate of interest."[111]

As noted, from a strictly mechanical view, the present value framework underlying Keynes's investment theory is not original. However, his theory of cash flow forecasting differentiates his theory of investment from many of his contemporaries.[112] For Keynes, investor's erratic cash flows expectations are the key to economic problem.[113]

> [P]rospective quasi-rent is a very fluctuating thing. In case of a durable good—any estimates must be very precarious—the Q's are very much influenced by early factors—though because of compound interest the later Q's have little influence anyways. So in fact valuations are tremendously influenced by the early Q's of the series. Value of assets hence fluctuate widely and of course it pays to not estimate the Q's but to estimate the public's estimates of Q.[114]

Keynes starts his lecture on December 4, 1933, with the liquidity-preference theory of the interest rate. He says, "Liquidity preference really 'the demand for money'—the way of summing up the eagerness of people to hold their wealth in the form of money rather than other forms."[115] He argues there are four motives to hold money:

> 1. The Income motive. This corresponds with the similar item in the *Treatise on Money*. Individuals hold money for the purpose of smoothing out irregularities or intervals in the receipt of income as compared to the routine uses for it. (It is the thing which I would term the flywheel effect.)

---

110 Keynes (1932–35, E12, B51, G25, J31, M16, N15).

111 Keynes (1932–35, B51). Moggridge notes, "his theory of investment was taking on the recognisable form which he would later call the marginal efficiency of capital" (1992, 565).

112 Kahn observes, "Keynes' insistence on the overwhelming importance of expectations, highly subject to risk and uncertainty, was one of his biggest contributions" (1984, 159, 142). However, as O'Donnell says, "Keynes was far from original in focusing on uncertainty and expectations" (1989, 245). Uncertain expectations played a key role in Alfred Marshall's theory of economic depressions: "the chief cause of the evil is a want of confidence" (Marshall and Marshall 1879, 154). See Eshag (1963, 101–102), Moggridge (1976, 50), Presley (1979, 69–70), and Laidler (1999, 83–86) for an overview of how Keynes's predecessors—The Cambridge Cycle Theorists like Lavington and Pigou—highlighted uncertain expectations in the years before the *General Theory*.

113 Keynes writes in the *General Theory*, "expectations of the future should play a dominant part in determining the scale on which new investment is deemed advisable. But, as we have seen, the basis for such expectations is very precarious. Being based on shifting and unreliable evidence, they are subject to sudden and violent changes" (CW 7, 315). For Keynes, "economic decisions are unavoidably based on highly uncertain expectations as to future developments. By definition, this is particularly true for decisions with respect to investment" (Patinkin 1976, 98, 141). Kahn writes, "The determination of the rate of investment is the subject to which, for obvious reasons, the bulk of the *General Theory* is devoted.... Expectations play a dominating part" (1984, 142).

114 Keynes (1932–35, J31, N15). Kahn writes, "the symbol Q was clearly intended by Keynes to serve as a proxy for the state of mind of entrepreneurs" (1984, 149).

115 Keynes (1932–35, B54, E14).

2. The Business motive. This is the similar motive in the case of the business man. It is the working capital held for the purpose of tiding over intervals between the receipt of income from sales and operations.
3. The Precautionary motive. One keeps money to provide for contingencies of an unforseen kind; and, one mustn't forget, to take advantage of unforseen opportunities for advantageous purchases; and in order to meet a future fixed obligation.

   The strength of each of these three motives depends not only upon the state of trade, but also upon the ease and cheapness of credit; and the rate of deposit interest, and all such matters, in a way which is quite evident.
4. The Speculative motive. This depends upon the state of expectation with regard to the trends of trade, and also upon the expectation as to the trend of the price level. If it is anticipated that prices will fall, one has a motive for holding money, while if it is expected that prices will rise, one will rather tend to hold equities.[116]

In this passage, Keynes traces the income motive back to the *Treatise*. Beyond that, he also traces the speculative motive back to the *Treatise*. Bryce records, the speculative motive "depends on what Keynes called 'State of Bearishness'" in the *Treatise*.[117] Thus, in both the 1932 and 1933 lectures, Keynes explicitly acknowledges that his liquidity-preference theory has its origins in the *Treatise*.

As noted, Keynes gave a formal liquidity-preference function by late 1932 in *Parameters of a Monetary Economy*. Furthermore, GTE/5/423 contains a formal liquidity-preference function. Keynes refines the liquidity-preference function in the 1933 lectures.[118]

$$M = A(w, \rho) \tag{3.22}$$

where M is the quantity of money, A is liquidity preference, w is state of the news, and ρ is the interest rate. He observes, "It is the rate of interest which brings the quantity of money into alignment with the state of liquidity preference having regard for the state of the news. We now have the essential determinants of the rate of interest: M, w and A."[119] Finally he aligns state of the news with "expectations" and "confidence," meaning his 1933 liquidity-preference function explicitly includes expectations.[120]

---

[116] Keynes (1932–35, G30, B54–55, E14, J34, M18).

[117] Keynes (1932–35, B55, E14, J34).

[118] Keynes (1932–35, B57, E15, G33, J36, M19, N16). Fallgatter uses slightly different notation.

[119] Keynes (1932–35, B57, J36).

[120] Keynes (1932–35, G32, B59, J37, N17). Keynes writes, "The rate of interest is, on my theory, essentially an uncertainty phenomenon" (CW 29, 221). According to Meltzer, "Uncertainty increases the demand for money and raises the interest rate" (1988, 147, 151, 172). O'Donnell agrees, "if confidence weakens, as a result of greater uncertainty and doubt attaching to future forecasts, the demand for money and interest rates will rise" (1989, 269).

After presenting his liquidity-preference theory, Keynes criticizes the classical theory of interest. He argues the classical theory of interest is circular:

> This [liquidity-preference theory] is the alternative to the two classical views already discussed and seen to be abortive.
>
> 1. The rate of interest is given by the intersection of two curves, the supply of Savings, and the Demand for Capital.
> 2. The other attempted to get it out of the Marginal Efficiency of Capital, i.e, the *Q*'s. In Marshall's half-hearted attempt, he saw that he was becoming circular. But there are plenty of others who have adopted this view without seeing that it is circular. In the present view [liquidity-preference theory], we avoid this circularity.[121]

There are two points worth noting in this passage. First, Keynes argues the classical (and loanable funds) theory of the interest rate is indeterminate.[122] Liquidity preference is necessary for a determinate theory of interest.[123] Second, this passage shows that Keynes used the term "marginal efficiency of capital" by the end of 1933. Although he does not carefully define the marginal efficiency of capital, there is no doubt that he used the term by December 1933 at the latest.[124]

Keynes winds down his 1933 lecture series by summarizing his theory with a four-equation IS-LM model. As outlined above, he introduced the four elements of

---

[121] Keynes (1932–35, G33, B58, J36, N16).

[122] Keynes wrote, "the rate of interest is not determined by saving and investment in the same way in which price is determined by supply and demand" (CW 14, 212). He says, "In truth there are no such things as these [saving and investment] schedules. They are completely bogus" (CW 13, 551). As Hansen explains, "we cannot know what the rate of interest will be unless we already know the income level. And we cannot know the income level without already knowing the rate of interest, since a lower interest rate will mean a larger volume of investment and so, via the multiplier, a higher level of real income. The classical analysis, therefore, offers no solution" (1953, 140). Also see Dillard (1948, 190, 198), Patinkin (1976, 63, 99), Milgate (1982, 111–124), Fletcher (1987, 120), Carabelli (1988, 207), Fitzgibbons (1988, 113–123), Meltzer (1988, 153, 173), Laidler (1999, 256), and King (2002, 15).

[123] Keynes stressed "the essential independence of the rate of interest" by late 1932 (CW 29, 113). He wrote in August 1935, "any method, such as the classical one, which endeavors to arrive at the rate of interest without bringing in liquidity preference is bound to be circular in the worst possible sense of the word" (CW 13, 551). Hansen writes, "Keynes did, however, supply the missing link (liquidity preference) needed for a determinate theory" (1953, 148).

[124] Keynes (1932–35, G33, G35, M19, N16). Moggridge is correct when he states, "He appears to have coined the term [marginal efficiency of capital] by the end of the calendar year [1933]" (1992, 565). But it is not quite correct to say, "the phrase does not appear in the students' notes" (1992, 565). It is true that Bryce records "marginal productivity of capital" rather than "marginal efficiency of capital" (Keynes 1932–35, B60, J38). Both Bryce and Tarshis had attended Keynes's 1932 lectures, in which he used the term "marginal productivity of capital" (Keynes 1932, A37–38, I20–121). As noted above, in the 1932 lectures, Keynes lectured from a draft chapter called "Quasi-Rent and the Marginal Productivity of Capital." However, he changed the title to "Quasi-Rent and the Marginal Productivity of Capital" (CW 29, 114; Keynes Papers, GTE/5/189). It seems Bryce recalled Keynes's use of the term "productivity" in 1932 and substituted that term for "efficiency" in 1933. This substitution was repeated in the Tarshis notes, as he copied Bryce's notes. Still, Fallgatter, Salant, and Thring independently confirm that Keynes did indeed use the term "marginal efficiency of capital" in late 1933.

the Keynesian IS-LM model throughout the lecture series. Finally, on December 4, he brought all the elements together to summarize his general theory. In doing so, Keynes presented the very first four-equation IS-LM model.[125]

$$M = A(w, \rho) \tag{3.23}$$

$$Y = C + I \tag{3.24}$$

$$C = \phi_1(w, Y) \tag{3.25}$$

$$I = \phi_2(w, \rho) \tag{3.26}$$

After his IS-LM equations, he gives a verbal summary of his theory. Specifically, "the quantity of employment is a function of four things: 1. The State of Confidence, 2. Previous Consumption, 3. The Liquidity Propensity, 4. The Quantity of Money. This may be called the General Law of Employment."[126] This informal summary of his theory represents a verbal statement of Keynes's IS-LM approach. However, as we shall see in Chap. 4, there is much more to the story of the December 4, 1933 lecture, its impact on students who attended and took notes, and the actual basis for the lecture itself, the implications of which change the history of IS-LM as it has been presented by many, including one of the authors of the present volume.[127]

As in the *General Theory*, Keynes closes his 1933 lecture series with some comments on the sociopolitical implications of his theory. He alludes to the euthanasia of the rentier: "one can imagine a society so well equipped with capital that marginal productivity of capital is zero or negative.... Keynes wants to see this gradual reduction of the minimum profitable rate of interest—hence get rid of the troubles of capitalist system."[128] We read, "the evils of capitalism could be gradually and effectively eliminated by this process of the evaporation of the rate of interest."[129] With the proper understanding and application of Keynes's theory, humanity can achieve optimal material prosperity in a matter of decades.

> All past teaching has (if my view here given is correct) been either irrelevant, or else positively injurious. We have not only failed to understand the economic order under which we live, but we have misunderstood it to the extent of adopting practices which operate most harshly

[125] Keynes (1932–35, B57–59, E15, G33–34, J36–37, M19, N17). Patinkin was the first to report some of these equations (1976, 79n; 1977, 16; 1982, 29). Young wrote in 1987: "the equational representation presented by Keynes in his 1933 lectures does go some way towards the IS-LM approach" (1987, 13). Also see Dimand (1988, 181; 2007, 86–86; 2019, 184) and Rymes (1989, 125). Later, Solow (1991, 971–972) aligns Keynes's lectures with IS-LM, although he does not report the equations.

[126] Keynes (1932–35, G35, B59, J37, N17).

[127] See Young (1987).

[128] Keynes (1932–35, J38–39).

[129] Keynes (1932–35, G36).

to our detriment, so that we are tempted to cure the ills arising out of our misunderstanding, by resort to further destruction in the form of revolutions.

This instead of the sensible procedure of understanding the remarkably efficient machine which we have built up, whose smooth workings will yield in the course of a relatively few years an optimum of material prosperity; understanding it to keep it in running order and letting it serve our purposes instead of defeating them. At the rate we were going before the last dislocation, 30 years would have sufficed to build up our capital to the optimum level.[130]

References

Annan, N. (1999). Keynes and the Bloomsbury group. *Biography, 22*(1), 16–31.

Bagehot, W. (1873). *Lombard Street: A description of the money market*. Henry S. King & Co.

Blaug, M. (1990). *John Maynard Keynes: Life, ideas, legacy*. St. Martin's Press.

Brunner, K. (1996). *Economic analysis and political ideology*. Edward Elgar.

Carabelli, A. M. (1988). *On Keynes's method*. Macmillan.

Chick, V. (1992). The nature of the Keynesian revolution: A reassessment. In P. Arestis, D. Meghnad, & S. Dow (Eds.), *On money, method and Keynes: Selected essays* (pp. 55–79). Palgrave Macmillan.

Coddington, A. (1983). *Keynesian economics: The search for first principles*. George All & Unwin.

Darity, W. J., & Young, W. (1997). On rewriting chapter 2 of the general theory. In G. C. Harcourt & R. A. Riach (Eds.), *A 'second edition' of the general theory* (Vol. 1, pp. 2–27). Routledge.

Davis, E. G. (1980). The correspondence between R.G. Hawtrey and J.M. Keynes on the treatise: The genesis of output adjustment models. *The Canadian Journal of Economics, 13*(4), 716–724.

Dillard, D. (1948). *Economics of John Maynard Keynes*. Prentice-Hall.

Dimand, R. W. (1988). *The origins of the Keynesian revolution*. Stanford University Press.

Dimand, R. W. (1994). Mr Meade's relation, Kahn's multiplier, and the chronology of the general theory. *The Economic Journal, 104*(426), 1138–1142.

Dimand, R. W. (1997). Hawtrey on the multiplier. *History of Political Economy, 29*(3), 549–556.

Dimand, R. W. (2007). Keynes, IS-LM, and the Marshallian tradition. *History of Political Economy, 39*(1), 81–95.

Dimand, R. W. (2019). Lectures on the monetary theory of production and the general theory of employment. In R. W. Dimand & H. Hagemann (Eds.), *The Elgar companion to John Maynard Keynes* (pp. 181–185). Edward Elgar.

Dostaler, G. (2007). *Keynes and his battles*. Edward Elgar.

Eshag, E. (1963). *From Marshall to Keynes: An essay on the monetary theory of the Cambridge school*. Basil Blackwell.

[130] Keynes (1932–35, G37–38). Keynes described himself as "among the last of the utopians" (CW 10, 447; CW 9, xviii, 321–32; CW 21, 37–38). Hansen admits that Keynes "could daydream and speculate about utopia" (1953, 215). As Meltzer notes, "Throughout his life, his main goals included satiation of the capital stock" (1981, 43, 53, 56; 1988, 135, 169, 185; 1996, 44). O'Donnell writes, "Conventional portraits present Keynes as the intentional saviour of capitalism ... The conventional picture, however, is badly incomplete and misleading.... Keynes was very much concerned with the long term abolition of capitalism as he conceived it. His ultimate goal was a non-capitalist, ethically rational utopia, whose characteristics resembled more closely those of communist or left-wing utopias" (1991, 15–16; 1992, 787–788; 1999, 166). On Keynes's utopianism, see Minsky (1975, 152, 154), Moggridge (1976, 96, 128, 162; 1992, 454–455, 466), Fitzgibbons (1988, 68, 191), Mini (1991, 190), Skidelsky (1992, 234–238; 2000, 478; 2009, 135, 164), Brunner (1996, 208), Dostaler (2007, 99), and Fletcher (2008, 175).

Fitzgibbons, A. (1988). *Keynes's vision: A new political economy*. Clarendon Press.
Fletcher, G. A. (1987). *The Keynesian revolution and its critics*. Macmillan.
Fletcher, G. A. (2008). *Dennis Robertson*. Palgrave Macmillan.
Hansen, A. H. (1947). The general theory. In S. E. Harris (Ed.), *The new economics: Keynes' influence on theory and public policy* (pp. 133–144). Alfred A. Knopf.
Hansen, A. H. (1953). *A guide to Keynes*. McGraw-Hill.
Harrod, R. F. (1951). *The life of John Maynard Keynes*. Macmillan.
Johannsen, N. A. J. (1908). *A neglected point in connection with crises*. Bankers Publishing Co.
Kahn, R. F. (1931). The relation of home investment to unemployment. *The Economic Journal, 41*(162), 173–198.
Kahn, R. F. (1984). *The making of Keynes' general theory*. Cambridge University Press.
Kent, R. J. (2007). A 1929 application of multiplier analysis by Keynes. *History of Political Economy, 39*(3), 529–543.
Keynes, J. M. (CW). *The collected writings of John Maynard Keynes* (Vols. 1–30). Macmillan and Cambridge University Press for the Royal Economic Society
Keynes, J. M. (1932–35). Keynes's lectures, 1932–35: notes of students. In T. K. Rymes (Ed.), unpublished typescript. Carleton University, Ottawa, 1988.
King, J. E. (2002). *A history of post Keynesian economics since 1936*. Edward Elgar.
Klein, L. R. (1947). *The Keynesian revolution*. Macmillan.
Klein, L. R. (1951). The life of John Maynard Keynes. *Journal of Political Economy, 59*(5), 443–451.
Laidler, D. E. (1999). *Fabricating the Keynesian revolution*. Cambridge University Press.
Laidler, D. E. (2006). Keynes and the birth of modern macroeconomics. In R. E. Backhouse & B. W. Bateman (Eds.), *The Cambridge companion to Keynes* (pp. 39–57). Cambridge University Press.
Leeson, R., & Schiffman, D. (2013). The triumph of rhetoric: Pigou as Keynesian whipping boy and its unintended consequences. In R. Leeson (Ed.), *Hayek: A collaborative biography* (pp. 79–126). Palgrave Macmillan.
Marshall, A., & Marshall, M. P. (1879). *The economics of industry*. Macmillan and Co.
Meltzer, A. H. (1981). Keynes's general theory: A different perspective. *Journal of Economic Literature, 19*(1), 34–64.
Meltzer, A. H. (1988). *Keynes's monetary theory: A different interpretation*. Cambridge University Press.
Meltzer, A. H. (1996). The general theory after sixty years. *Journal of Post Keynesian Economics, 19*(1), 35–45.
Milgate, M. (1982). *Capital and employment*. Academic Press.
Mini, P. V. (1991). *Keynes, Bloomsbury, and the general theory*. St. Martin's Press.
Minsky, H. P. (1975). *John Maynard Keynes*. Columbia University Press.
Moggridge, D. E. (1973). From the treatise to the general theory: An exercise in chronology. *History of Political Economy, 5*(1), 72–88.
Moggridge, D. E. (1976). *Keynes*. Macmillan.
Moggridge, D. E. (1992). *Maynard Keynes: An economist's biography*. Routledge.
Moggridge, D. E. (1993). *Keynes*. University of Toronto Press.
O'Donnell, R. M. (1989). *Keynes: Philosophy, economics, and politics*. St. Martin's Press.
O'Donnell, R. M. (1991). Keynes's political philosophy. In W. J. Barber (Ed.), *Perspectives on the history of economic thought* (Vol. 5, pp. 3–28). Edward Elgar.
O'Donnell, R. M. (1992). The unwritten books and papers of J.M. Keynes. *History of Political Economy, 24*(4), 767–817.
O'Donnell, R. M. (1999). Keynes's socialism: Conception, strategy, and espousal. In P. Kriesler & C. Sardoni (Eds.), *Keynes, post-Keynesianism and political economy: Essays in honour of Geoff Harcourt* (Vol. 3, pp. 149–175). Routledge.
Patinkin, D. (1976). *Keynes' monetary thought: A study of its development*. Duke University Press.
Patinkin, D. (1977). The process of writing the general theory: A critical survey. In D. Patinkin & J. C. Leith (Eds.), *Keynes, Cambridge and the general theory* (pp. 3–26). Macmillan.

Patinkin, D. (1982). *Anticipations of the general theory?* University of Chicago Press.
Patinkin, D. (1993). On the chronology of the general theory. *The Economic Journal, 103*(418), 647–663.
Presley, J. R. (1979). *Robertsonian economics: An examination of the work of Sir D.H. Robertson on industrial fluctuation.* Holmes and Meier.
Robinson, E. A. G. (1947). John Maynard Keynes 1883–1946. *The Economic Journal, 57*(225), 1–68.
Robinson, J. V. (1937). *Introduction to the theory of employment.* Macmillan.
Rymes, T. K. (1989). *Keynes's lectures, 1932–35: Notes of a representative student.* Macmillan.
Skidelsky, R. (1992). *John Maynard Keynes: The economist as savior, 1920–1937.* Viking.
Skidelsky, R. (2000). *John Maynard Keynes: Fighting for freedom, 1937–1946.* Viking.
Skidelsky, R. (2005). Interview with Robert Skidelsky. In B. Snowdon & H. R. Vane (Eds.), *Modern macroeconomics: Its origins, development and current state* (pp. 91–100). Edward Elgar.
Skidelsky, R. (2009). *Keynes: The return of the master.* PublicAffairs.
Solow, R. M. (1991). Keynes's lectures. *The Economic Journal, 101*(407), 971–972.
Straight, M. W. (1983). *After long silence.* W.W. Norton & Co.
Tarshis, L. (1996). Interview with Lorie Tarshis. In D. C. Colander & H. Landreth (Eds.), *The coming of Keynesianism to America.* Edward Elgar
Wright, A. L. (1956). The genesis of the multiplier theory. *Oxford Economic Papers, 8*(2), 181–193.
Young, W. (1987). *Interpreting Mr. Keynes: the IS-LM enigma.* Polity Press.
Young, W. (1989). *Harrod and his trade cycle group.* Palgrave Macmillan.

Chapter 4
"The Missing Link": Keynes's Own Lecture Notes, December 4, 1933, Impact and Implications

Six sets of student notes from Keynes's 1933 lectures suggest Keynes himself was the first to represent his *General Theory* with a four-equation IS-LM model. However, student notes do not represent primary evidence. Donald Moggridge endorses the student notes and highlights that they were produced by "good students, most of whom later became professional economists."[1] Still, he acknowledges the natural concerns scholars might have with student notes:

> Scholars might not normally put much weight on such notes, because if they were to compare their own students' notes with what they said or intended to say in class they might find large discrepancies. They are in the hands of the reporters on such occasions and may have to decide, if they are fortunate, among several reporters' versions when the lecturer's own notes do not survive.[2]

Furthermore, the nature of Keynes's lectures might create special challenges for note takers, especially undergraduates. A.F.W. Plumptre reported,

> [Keynes] put forward his new ideas in a series of eight lectures—one a week for one term. Obviously the lectures had to be highly condensed and, despite the pleasantness and clearness with which they were delivered, I doubt that many undergraduates got very much out of them. However, they were not primarily intended for undergraduates; Keynes was trying out his lectures on anyone who cared to listen, and there was always a group of his fellow dons at his lectures, as well as some graduate students who were still rather rare in Cambridge in those days. Keynes was teaching intensively, not extensively.... [H]is few lectures were, I think, primarily intended to help himself, rather than his audience, to give him practice in formulating his new ideas and to invite criticism of them.[3]

[1] Moggridge (1992, 556). Austin Robinson (1977, 33) notes the "astonishing vintage" of students.

[2] Moggridge (1992, 556). Paul Davidson seems to challenge the student notes, and Bryce's notes in particular: "those who have taught large lecture sessions at universities know that often what appears in a student's lecture notes can differ significantly from what we professed" (2005, 106).

[3] Plumptre (1947, 366).

W. Young and E. W. Fuller, *Reinterpreting Mr. Keynes*,
Springer Studies in the History of Economic Thought,
https://doi.org/10.1007/978-3-030-91342-7_4

4.1 Keynes's Handwritten IS-LM Model: GTE/5/419

The missing link in the history of IS-LM has been a formal IS-LM model written in Keynes's own hand. Document GTE/5/419 found in the *Keynes Papers* is the missing link. This critical document is reproduced here in Fig. 4.1. GTE/5/419 shows, in his

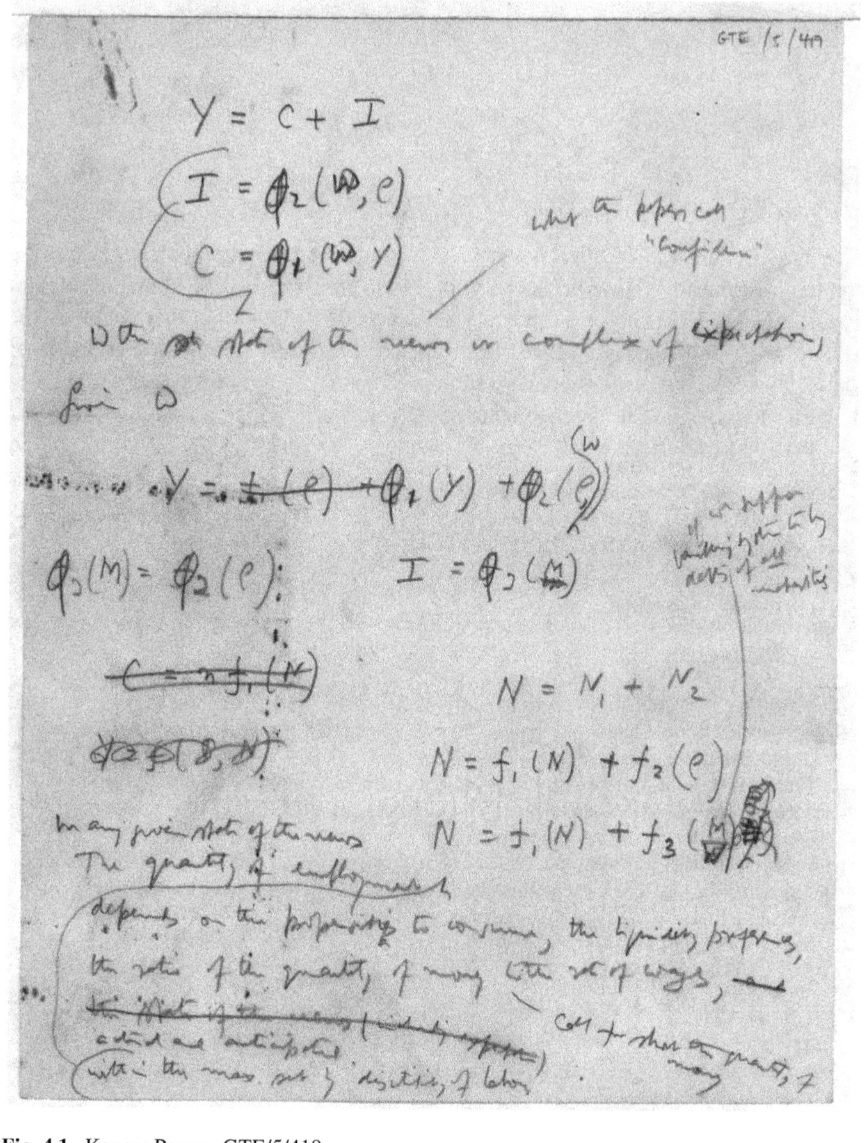

Fig. 4.1 Keynes Papers, GTE/5/419

own handwriting, that Keynes actually formalized a four-equation IS-LM model. The following is a transcription of GTE/5/419:

$$Y = C + I$$
$$I = \phi_2(w, \rho)$$
$$C = \phi_1(w, Y)$$

w the state of the news (what the papers call "confidence") is complex of expectations

Given w

$$Y = \phi_1(Y) + \phi_2(\rho)$$

$$\phi_3(M) = \phi_2(\rho) \qquad I = \phi_3(M)$$

$$N = N_1 + N_2$$
$$N = f_1(N) + f_2(\rho)$$
$$N = f_1(N) + f_3(M/W)$$

In any given state of the news, the quantity of employment depends on the propensity to consume, the liquidity preference, the ratio of the quantity of money to the rate of wages actual (call for short the quantity of money; if we suppose banking system to buy debts of all maturities) and anticipated with the maximum set by the disutility of labour.

GTE/5/419 proves beyond any doubt that Keynes did represent his *General Theory* with a formal, four-equation IS-LM model. His 1933 IS-LM model can be summarized as follows[4]:

$$Y = C + I \quad \text{[Income]} \tag{4.1}$$

$$C = \phi_1(w, Y) \quad \text{[Consumption Function]} \tag{4.2}$$

$$I = \phi_2(w, \rho) \quad \text{[Investment Function]} \tag{4.3}$$

$$\phi_3(M) = \phi_2(\rho) \quad \text{[Liquidity Preference]} \tag{4.4}$$

[4] There can be no doubt that Keynes's 1933 IS-LM model was a summary of his theory. Thring explicitly records "Summary" just before the IS-LM equations (Keynes 1932–35, N17). Fallgatter writes, "Now with all the materials at hand, let us pursue the analysis" (Keynes 1932–35, G34).

where Y is income, C is consumption, I is investment, w is state of the news (expectations or confidence), ρ is the interest rate, and M is the quantity of money.[5] Significantly, GTE/5/419 includes an additional relationship that is not present in the student notes. Keynes relates the volume of investment (I) to the quantity of money (M), which is the equilibrium condition for the economy, or IS = LM.[6]

$$I = \phi_3(M) \quad [\text{IS} = \text{LM}] \tag{4.5}$$

GTE/5/419 contains a formalized IS-LM model with an income equation, consumption function, investment function, and liquidity-preference function. Thus, there can be no doubt that, as early as December 1933, Keynes constructed a simultaneous equations IS-LM model to represent the *General Theory*. Finally, he provides an informal, verbal statement of his IS-LM approach at the end of GTE/5/419. As will be shown, this verbal IS-LM formulation is of the utmost significance, for it is consistently repeated in his subsequent works up to and including the *General Theory* and his seminal 1937 *QJE* paper.

4.2 GTE/5/419 Employment Equations

In addition to Keynes's 1933 IS-LM model, GTE/5/419 contains three employment equations. Although his 1933 IS-LM model is complete without them, these employment equations offer additional insights into the state of Keynes's theory in late 1933. The following are Keynes's 1933 employment equations.

$$N = N_1 + N_2 \tag{4.6}$$

$$N = f_1(N) + f_2(\rho) \tag{4.7}$$

$$N = f_1(N) + f_3(M/W) \tag{4.8}$$

[5] Keynes refers to "a change in the news" several times in the *General Theory* (CW 7, 153, 155, 198–199). Fallgatter associates "state of the news" with "state of expectation" (Keynes 1932–35, G33). Thring uses "state of news" and "state of expectation" interchangeably (Keynes 1932–35, N17). Bryce writes, "The state of news is something like the state of confidence" (Keynes 1932–35, B59, J37). For Cairncross, "state of news or of confidence" (Keynes 1932–35, E15).

[6] As Patinkin writes, "the spirit of IS-LM [is] the determination of the equilibrium level of income by the interaction between the markets for commodities and money" (1990, 224).

The first two employment equations are straightforward. Equation 4.6 is Eq. 4.1 in employment form rather than income form. Equation 4.7 corresponds to the extended income equation in GTE/5/419. Keynes explicitly includes state of the news (w) in the consumption function and investment function (Eqs. 4.2 and 4.3, respectively). He also provides an extended income equation in which the state of the news is given ("Given w"). Equation 4.9 below is Keynes's extended income equation from GTE/5/419.

$$Y = \phi_1(Y) + \phi_2(\rho) \tag{4.9}$$

In contrast to the first two employment equations, Keynes's third employment Eq. (4.8) has no clear connection to the other equations in GTE/5/419. The term $f_3(M/W)$ is introduced without any explanation. As will be seen below, the unannounced introduction of the money wage, W, confused the student note takers and scholars who analyzed the student notes later. Why did Keynes include $f_3(M/W)$ in the third employment equation?

The term $f_3(M/W)$ relates to his discussion of the two classical-wage postulates in his first lecture of 1933. In that lecture, he carefully distinguishes between the real wage and the money wage: "In actual world—wages are money wages. On Keynes theory real wages do not primarily depend on money wages.... What Keynes denies is that the level of real wages depends on the money level of wages."[7] He agrees that a reduction in the real wage will increase employment. By contrast, he claims a reduction in the money wage will not necessarily increase employment: "No reason to expect favorable repercussions on employment by reduction of money wages."[8]

In his first lecture of 1933, Keynes merely asserts that a reduction in money wages may not increase employment. He offers no theoretical explanation for this claim. Why not? Keynes felt he had to present his entire theory before he could discuss how changes in money wages affect employment. He explains in the *General Theory*:

> It would have been an advantage if the effects of a change in money-wages could have been discussed in an earlier chapter.... It was not possible, however, to discuss this matter fully until our own theory had been developed. For the consequences of a change in money-wages are complicated.... [I]t could not be set forth clearly until the reader was acquainted with my own method.[9]

Keynes's remarks on money wages in Chapter 2 of the *General Theory* are just a preview to his analysis in Chapter 19, "Changes in Money Wages." Similarly, Keynes's remarks on money wages in his first 1933 lecture are just a preview to the third employment equation in his last 1933 lecture.

---

[7] Keynes (1932–35, J3–4).

[8] Keynes (1932–35, J4, B6).

[9] Keynes (CW 7, 257).

In GTE/5/419, Keynes introduces *M* to show how the quantity of money influences the amount of income and employment. The liquidity-preference theory holds that an increase in the quantity of money reduces the interest rate. According to his investment theory, the amount of investment is negatively related to the interest rate. Thus, an increase in the quantity of money increases the amount of investment. Given Keynes's positive investment–income relation, an increase in the amount of investment necessarily raises income and employment. In short, other things equal, an increase in the quantity of money increases income and employment.[10]

Many interpreters claim that wages are fixed in Keynes's theory.[11] However, his theory does not depend on the assumption of wage rigidity.[12] In Chapter 2, he states that he will assume money wages are fixed. But he explicitly indicates that he will relax this assumption later in the book: "this simplification, which we shall dispense later, is introduced solely to facilitate the exposition."[13] Keynes's fixed-wage assumption is in force for most of the first eighteen chapters of the *General Theory*. Importantly, however, Keynes drops the fixed-wage assumption in Chapter 19 and analyzes how changes in money wages effect employment.[14]

In Keynes's theory, a decline in money wages increases employment by increasing the real quantity of money. To use modern terminology, he uses the money wage rate (rather than the price level) as a deflator for the nominal quantity of money. A money

---

[10] Meltzer writes, "Keynes does not deny—but strongly affirms—that, in the short term, changes in money increase employment" (1988, 5, 128). But he stresses, "Expansive monetary (or wage) policy is not a solution. These actions can increase output temporarily, but the level around which output fluctuates and the amplitude of fluctuations remain unchanged" (1988, 198).

[11] The orthodox view that wages are fixed in Keynes's theory is commonly associated with Modigliani (1944). However, Herald Hagemann (2017, 9658; 2019, 239) shows that Modigliani discusses money wage cuts in Section 25 of his PhD dissertation. See Meltzer (1988, 255–266) for a review of orthodox interpretations of Keynes's theory in which money wages are fixed.

[12] Patinkin writes, "the analysis of the *General Theory* as a whole does not depend on the assumption of absolutely rigid wages" (1976, 108; 1982, 138; 1990, 215). According to Meltzer, "the main propositions of the *General Theory* do not depend on wage rigidity" (1981, 44, 52, 60; 1988, 250, 265–266). As O'Donnell observes, the *General Theory* would not be truly general if he assumed wage rates were always fixed: "The *GT* is intended to apply to all circumstances, irrespective of social, political or institutional variation, under which capitalist production could take place. Its relevance is claimed to be independent, for instance, of whether the state is democratic or totalitarian, or of whether prices and wages are rigid, sticky or perfectly flexible ... The textbook view of Keynesian economics as dependent upon some form of inflexibility is, as the *GT* also indicates, exactly contrary to Keynes's own conception" (1989, 176). Also see Klein (1947, 89), Dillard (1948, 25), Moggridge (1976, 193), Kahn (1984, 128), and Tobin (1997, 19).

[13] Keynes (CW 7, 27). Patinkin notes, "Keynes first presents (in Book I of the *General Theory*) a 'brief summary' of his theory on the simplifying assumption ... that money wages are constant" (1976, 101–102, 90). Meltzer agrees, "at the start of the *General Theory*, wages are fixed ... [P]rices and wages [are] fixed through most of his discussion in the first eighteen chapters" (1988, 164).

[14] Meltzer writes, "the assumption that wages are rigid is advanced as a working hypothesis not a firm conclusion" (1981, 51). As Patinkin explains, "in 'Book V: Money-Wages and Prices', Keynes drops the assumption of a constant money-wage rate and applies the theory of effective demand that he had developed in Books I–IV to an analysis (in the first chapter of this Book, 'Chapter 19: Changes in Money Wages') of the effects of a decline in this rate" (1987, 27). Also see Dillard (1948, 207) and Hagemann (2019, 234).

wage reduction increases the quantity of real-money balances.[15] In turn, the interest rate falls, and the amount of investment rises. Given the positive investment–income relation, an increase in the amount of investment must increase employment. In the same way that an increase in the quantity of money increases employment, a decline in the money wage increases employment. For Keynes, then, "a flexible wage policy and a flexible money policy come, analytically, to the same thing."[16]

No doubt, $f_3(M/W)$ caused much confusion for the student note takers. Bryce and Tarshis recalled that Keynes lectured at a quick pace, and Tarshis was afraid he copied imprecisely.[17] The student notes suggest Keynes only briefly mentioned his employment equations and $f_3(M/W)$. Fallgatter records Keynes saying directly after $f_3(M/W)$, "for a reason I cannot go into now, tho I give it to you to think over."[18] Bryce wrote directly after $f_3(M/W)$, "which he [Keynes] can't elaborate."[19] In the originals, Thring records a "?" next to the term $f_3(M/W)$. Although Tarshis missed the lecture and copied his notes from Bryce, $f_3(M/W)$ led him to scribble, "why in hell? See Bob!".[20]

Admittedly, Keynes's approach to introducing the quantity of money and the money wage rate into his employment equations is clumsy. Rather than introducing the new term $f_3(M/W)$, he could have expressed his theory by expanding $f_2(\rho)$. Recall Keynes's liquidity-preference function and investment function from the December 4 lecture.

$$M = A(w, \rho) \tag{4.10}$$

$$I = \phi_2(w, \rho) \tag{4.11}$$

Keynes could have expanded his investment function in the following way:

$$I = \phi_2(w, A, M/W) \tag{4.12}$$

[15] According to Klein, "The most direct effect of wage cuts is to increase the stock of real balances ... [R]eal cash balances are the ratio of money balances and the wage rate" (1947, 88). Patinkin writes that, for Keynes, "the primary way in which a decline in wages and prices can possibly stimulate the aggregate level of employment is by the increase that it generates in the real quantity of money" (1976, 102; 1982, 12, 141). As Meltzer puts it, in Keynes's theory, "A change in W also affects M/W, however. Money wage reductions increase the stock of real balances, shift LM to the right, and lower the rate of interest" (1988, 259). Also see Kahn (1984, 126).

[16] Keynes (CW 7, 267). As Hansen writes, "a fall in wages and prices has monetary consequences similar to an outright increase in the quantity of money" (1953, 173). Also see Dillard (1948, 215), Fletcher (1987, 273), Dimand (1988, 174–175), and Laidler (1999, 332).

[17] Rymes (1989, 21–22). Tarshis reported, "He talked quickly and clearly, with no bombast, and very much down to business" and "He kept you in rapt attention for the 50 min of the lectures. He covered an enormous amount of ground in that time" (1977, 50, 72).

[18] Keynes (1932–35, G35).

[19] Keynes (1932–35, B59).

[20] Keynes (1932–35, J37).

Next, he could have augmented his second employment equation (4.7) with his expanded investment function (Eq. 4.12). This would yield the following employment equation.

$$N = f_1(N) + f_2(w, A, M/W) \tag{4.13}$$

With this, his analysis can be expressed as follows: A decrease in the money wage increases the real quantity of money (in terms of wage units). This reduces the interest rate and thereby increases the amount of investment. Since investment and employment always move in the same direction, the amount of employment rises. In short, other things equal, a decrease in the money wage increases employment: "A reduction in money-wages is quite capable in certain circumstances of affording a stimulus to output, as the classic theory supposes."[21]

It seems Keynes's employment equations contradict his claims in the first lecture. His employment equations show that a decline in money wages (W) will increase employment. But he claimed in his first lecture, "There is no reason to expect higher employment by reduction in money wages—rather opposite is more possible."[22] Given his employment equations, how can he argue a decline in the money wage will likely reduce employment?

The state of the news, w, is the key to Keynes's argument. All else equal, a decline in the money wage increases employment in Keynes's theory. But all else will not remain equal. A decline in money wages will have a negative effect on the state of the news—that is, expectations. Lower money wages impair workers' ability to consume. And if workers reduce consumption due to a drop in money wages, investors will reduce their cash flow expectations from investment projects. This leads investment to fall. In the end, the negative effect from the change in the state of the news (w) offsets the positive effect from lower money wages (W). As Keynes writes in the *General Theory*,

> We can, therefore, theoretically at least, produce precisely the same effects on the rate of interest by reducing wages, whilst leaving the quantity of money unchanged, that we can produce by increasing the quantity of money whilst leaving the level of wages unchanged. It follows that wage reductions, as a method of securing full employment, are also subject to the same limitations as the method of increasing the quantity of money. The same reasons as those mentioned above, which limit the efficacy of increases in the quantity of money as a means of increasing investment to the optimum figure, apply *mutatis mutandis* to wage reductions. Just as a moderate increase in the quantity of money may exert an inadequate influence over the long-term rate of interest, whilst an immoderate increase may offset its other advantages by its disturbing effect on confidence; so a moderate reduction in money-wages may prove inadequate, whilst an immoderate reduction might shatter confidence even if it were practicable.[23]

[21] Keynes (CW 7, 257).

[22] Keynes (1932–35, B6).

[23] Keynes (CW 7, 266–267). Joan Robinson writes, "Keynes' argument was not the one which has been foisted on him by the bastard Keynesians—that money-wage rates are rigid for institutional reasons. It was that if wages could be cut, in a slump, it would make the situation worse, because it would lead to falling prices and expectations of further falls, so that investment was discouraged"

What is the significance of the Keynes's 1933 employment equations? They contain the first glimmerings of his analysis of money wages in Chapter 19 of the *General Theory*. Chapter 19 has been described as "the apex of the *General Theory*."[24] Keynes's 1933 employment equations are somewhat maladroit. Still, they show his analysis of changes in money wages was in place by late 1933. This is significant, for one of Keynes's major objectives in the *General Theory* is to show that lower money wages will not eliminate unemployment.[25]

4.3 The Rashomon Effect

Student notes suggest Keynes provided an IS-LM type representation of his *General Theory* in December 1933. GTE/5/419 confirms this. While substantiating Keynes's own IS-LM approach, GTE/5/419 also reveals some problems with the student notes. First, the number of equations recorded varies across the notes, meaning some note takers missed writing down equations. Second, the equations are not always recorded the same way, meaning some note takers made mistakes when recording equations. Finally, there are instances where the students' notes contradict each other.

The Rashomon Effect is a phenomenon in which the same event is described in contradictory ways by different witnesses. A Rashomon is an inconsistency in the reports of witnesses. Although student notes from Keynes's lectures are an invaluable resource, they contain Rashomons. Unfortunately, scholars have been unable to make conclusive statements about the Rashomons in Keynes's December 4, 1933 lecture. Between 1976 and 1989, Patinkin, Dimand, and Rymes published equations from this crucial lecture. But without Keynes's own notes, it was impossible to conclude which students actually reported the equations correctly. GTE/5/419 makes this possible. As will be shown below, Patinkin and Rymes inadvertently perpetuated some of the errors in the student notes.

Figures 4.2, 4.3, 4.4, and 4.5 show Keynes's December 4, 1933, equations in the original handwriting of four note takers: Bryce, Salant, Tarshis, and Thring.[26] The appendix at the back of this volume contains full transcriptions of all six sets

(1937, 51; 1971, 90). According to Patinkin, "in Chapter 19 Keynes also stresses the adverse expectations that might be generated by a wage reduction. Thus one can conceive of circumstances in which such expectations might be sufficiently strong to prevent the reduction the money-wage rate from having any net effect on aggregate demand, hence on equilibrium output, and hence on employment" (1982, 141; 1990, 210). Meltzer writes, "money wage changes are no more reliable than changes in money for restoring full employment.... [T]he effect on expectations, and therefore on investment, is destabilizing" (1981, 50; 1988, 262).

24 Patinkin (1976, 106). As Patinkin notes, Chapter 19 is where Keynes "tie[s] together all the analytical elements of the preceding chapters" (1990, 210).

25 Patinkin (1976, 106).

26 Although available, the faded notes of Cairncross are not suitable for reproduction. Fallgatter only kept the typed versions of his notes, meaning there is little to be gained by reproduction of his typed notes. See the appendix at the back of this volume for transcriptions of their notes from this lecture.

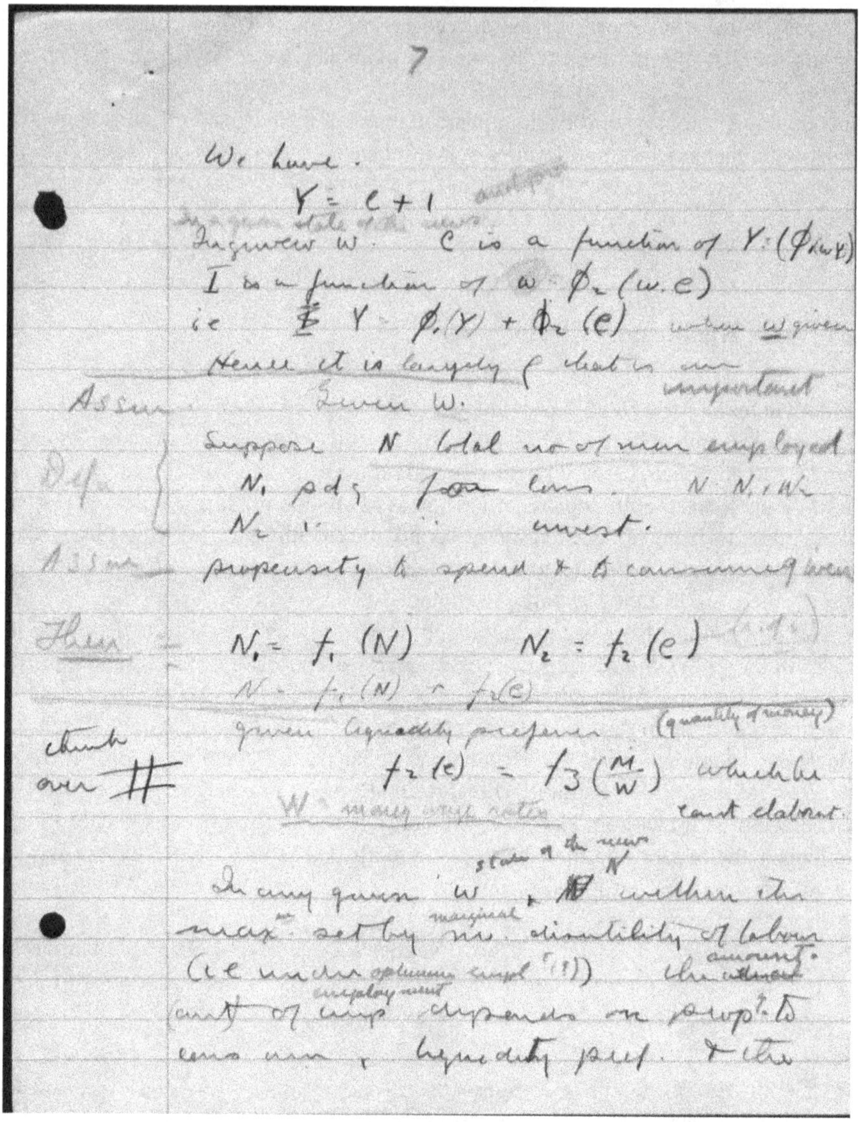

7

We have.

Y = C + I

In given W. C is a function of Y: (φ1 w Y)

I is a function of W: φ2 (w. e)

ie Y = φ1(Y) + φ2(e) when W given

Hence it is largely e that is an important

Assum Given W.

Suppose N total no of men employed

Def N1 ... for cons. N = N1 + N2

N2 ... invest.

Assum propensity to spend & to consume given

Then N1 = f1(N) N2 = f2(e)

N = f1(N) + f2(e)

given liquidity preference (quantity of money)

think over # f2(e) = f3(M/W) which he cant elaborate.

W = money wage rates

In any given state of the news W & N within the max^m set by marginal disutility of labour (i.e under optimum empl^t (?)) the amount of employment depends on prop^y to cons ... liquidity pref. & the

Fig. 4.2 Bryce notes, December 4, 1933

of student notes for this critical lecture. The first point worth noting is the number of equations in the relevant section of each set of notes (excluding Eq. 4.10 above). GTE/5/419 contains nine equations. The Bryce and Tarshis notes contain eight equations; Thring's notes contain seven equations; the Cairncross, Fallgatter, and Salant notes contain five equations.

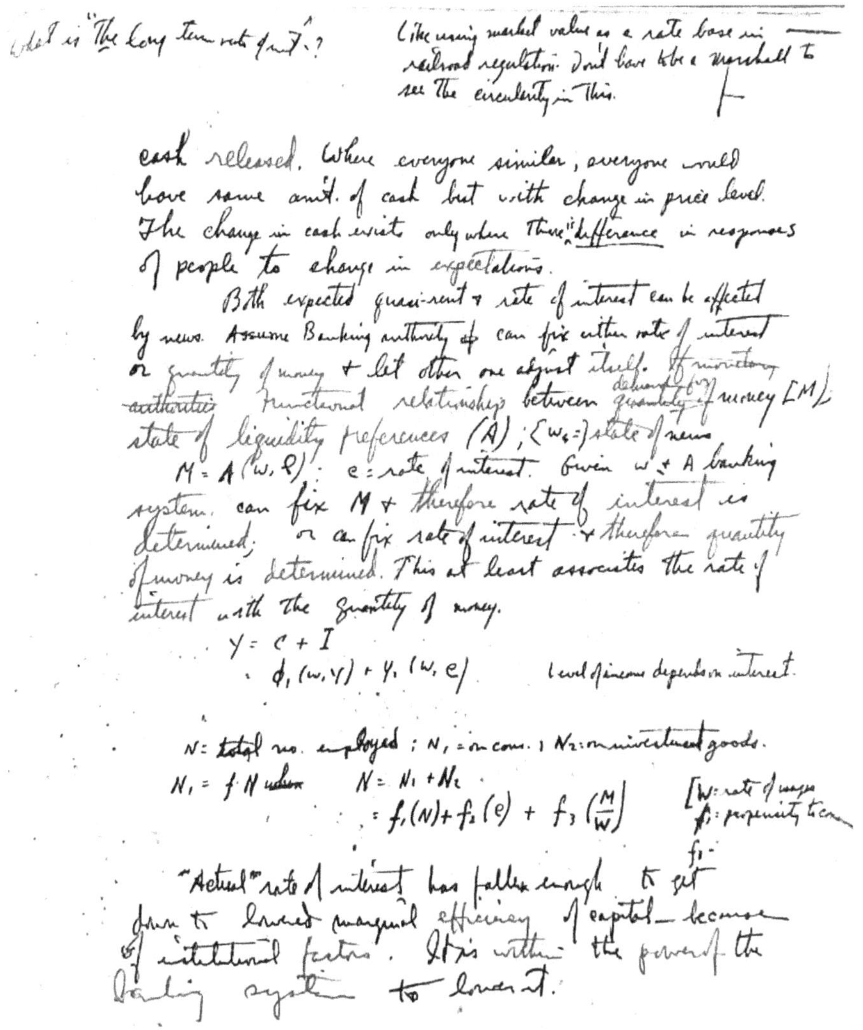
What is "the long term rate of int."?

Like using market value as a rate base in railroad regulation. Don't have to be a Marshall to see the circularity in this.

cash released. Where everyone similar, everyone would have same amt. of cash but with change in price level. The change in cash exists only where there's "difference" in responses of people to change in expectations.

Both expected quasi-rent & rate of interest can be affected by news. Assume Banking authority can fix either rate of interest or quantity of money & let other one adjust itself. ~~If monetary authorities~~ functional relationship between demand for quantity of money [M], state of liquidity preferences (A); [W =] state of news

$M = A(W, \rho)$: ρ = rate of interest. Given W & A banking system can fix M & therefore rate of interest is determined; or can fix rate of interest & therefore quantity of money is determined. This at least associates the rate of interest with the quantity of money.

$Y = C + I$

$= \phi_1(W, Y) + \psi_1(W, \rho)$ level of income depends on interest.

N = total no. employed; N_1 = on cons.; N_2 = on investment goods.

$N_1 = f\,N$ where $N = N_1 + N_2$

$= f_1(N) + f_2(\rho) + f_3\left(\frac{M}{W}\right)$ [W = rate of wages; f_1 = propensity to con.; f_2 –]

"Actual" rate of interest has fallen enough to get down to lowered marginal efficiency of capital — because of institutional factors. It is within the power of the banking system to lower it.

Fig. 4.3 Salant notes, December 4, 1933

All of the note takers recorded Keynes's IS-LM equations correctly. The only slight deviation is in Fallgatter. His record of the IS equations matches GTE/5/419 and the other students, but he uses the notation *f* rather than *A* in the liquidity-preference function. This is a minor notational Rashamon, as he explicitly writes "*f* the liquidity propensity functional relation."[27] The deviation in notation is perplexing, but it has no real analytical significance. In summary, as Table 4.1 illustrates, all the student notes are remarkably consistent with respect to Keynes's 1933 IS-LM equations.

[27] Keynes (1932–35, G33).

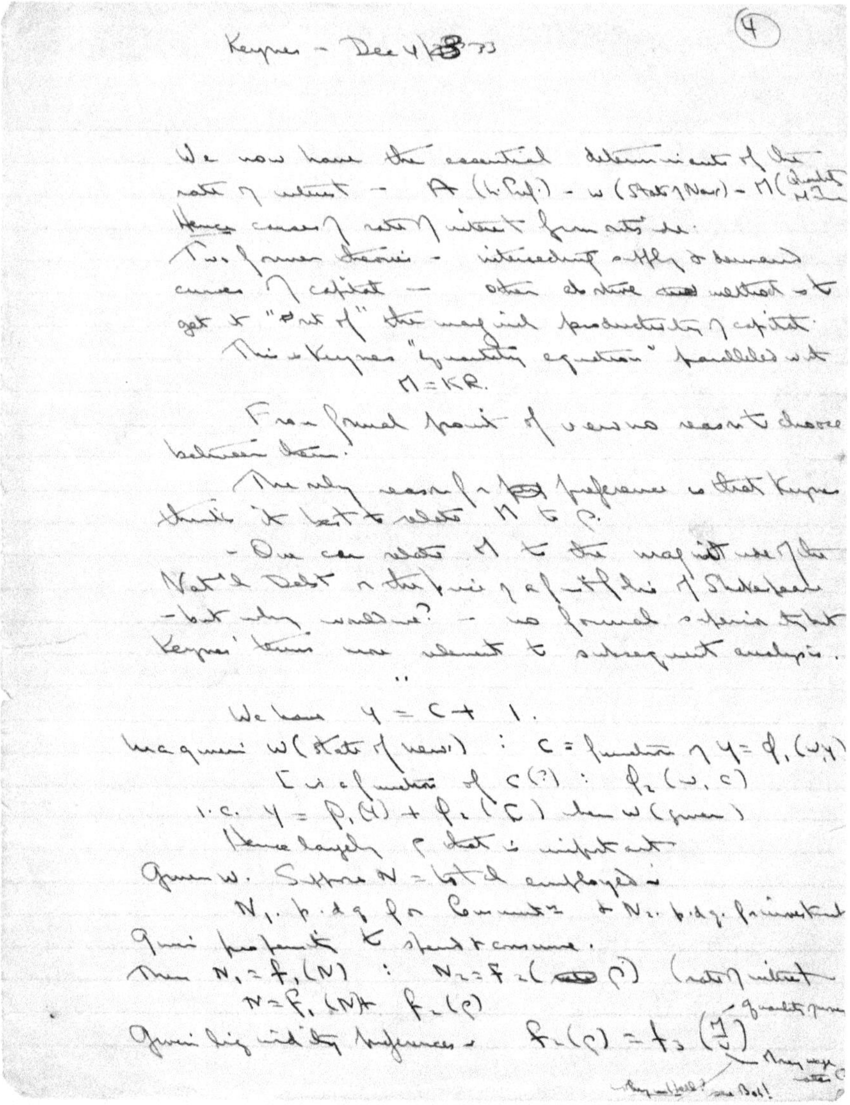

Fig. 4.4 Tarshis notes, December 4, 1933

However, all the student notes are missing the same equation from GTE/5/419. As mentioned above, in GTE/5/419, Keynes provides the equilibrium condition for the economy (Eq. 4.5). This enabled Keynes to link the real and nominal sides of his IS-LM approach and thereby deal with the problem of the Classical Dichotomy accordingly. Given the confines of the lecture, it seems Keynes realized that he could not adequately present his resolution of the issue of the Classical Dichotomy. Rather

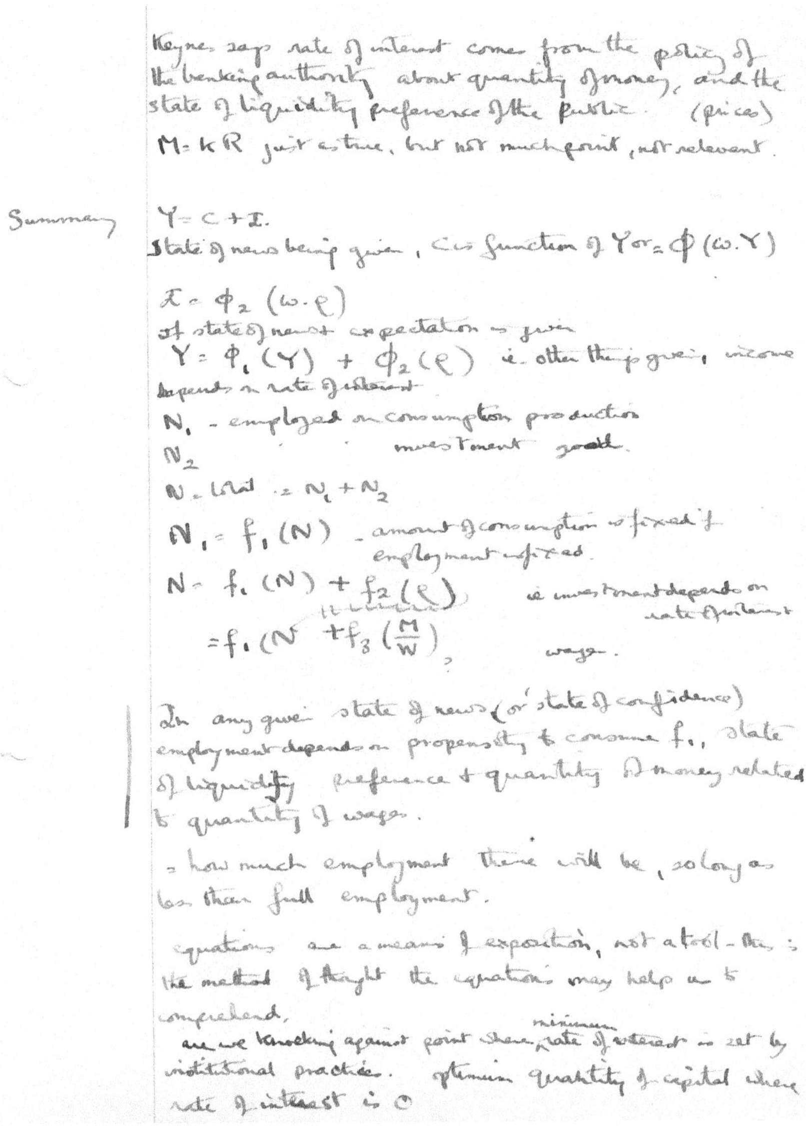

Keynes says rate of interest comes from the policy of the banking authority about quantity of money, and the state of liquidity preference of the public. (prices)
M = kR just as true, but not much point, not relevant.

Summary Y = C + I.
State of news being given, C is function of Y or = φ (ω.Y)
I = φ2 (ω.ρ)
if state of news & expectation is given
Y = φ1 (Y) + φ2 (ρ) i.e. other things given, income depends on rate of interest
N1 - employed on consumption production
N2 investment goods.
N = total = N1 + N2
N1 = f1 (N) - amount of consumption is fixed if employment is fixed.
N = f1 (N) + f2 (ρ) i.e. investment depends on rate of interest
= f1 (N) + f3 (M/W) wages.

In any given state of news (or state of confidence) employment depends on propensity to consume f1, state of liquidity preference + quantity of money related to quantity of wages.
= how much employment there will be, so long as less than full employment.
equations are a means of exposition, not a tool of thought; the method of thought the equations may help us to comprehend.
are we knocking against point where minimum rate of interest is set by institutional practice. optimum quantity of capital where rate of interest is 0

Fig. 4.5 Thring notes, December 4, 1933

than further complicating the lecture, he skipped over his equilibrium condition functional relationships (Eq. 4.5).

In contrast to the IS-LM type equations, there are significant Rashomons surrounding Keynes's 1933 employment equations. The most important problems stem from Robert Bryce's notes. Unfortunately, Lorie Tarshis did not attend Keynes's

Table 4.1 Keynes's IS-LM equations and the Rashomon effect

Source	Goods Market Equilibrium	Consumption Function	Investment Function	Equil. Cond./Liq. Pref. Func
Keynes	$Y = C + I$	$C = \phi_1(w, Y)$	$I = \phi_2(w, \rho)$	$\phi_3(M) = \phi_2(\rho); I = \phi_3(M)$
Bryce, Tarshis	$Y = C + I$	$C = \phi_1(w, Y)$	$I = \phi_2(w, \rho)$	$M = A(w, \rho)$
Cairncross	$Y = C + I$	$C = \phi_1(w, Y)$	$I = \phi_2(w, \rho)$	$M = A(w, \rho)$
Fallgatter	$Y = C + I$	$C = \phi_1(w, Y)$	$I = \phi_2(w, \rho)$	$M = f(w, \rho)$
Salant	$Y = C + I$	$C = \phi_1(w, Y)$	$I = \phi_2(w, \rho)$	$M = A(w, \rho)$
Thring	$Y = C + I$	$C = \phi_1(w, Y)$	$I = \phi_2(w, \rho)$	$M = A(w, \rho)$
Patinkin (1976)	$Y = C + I$	$C = \phi_1(w, Y)$	$I = \phi_2(w, \rho)$	N/A
Dimand (1988)	$Y = C + I$	$C = \phi_1(w, Y)$	$I = \phi_2(w, \rho)$	$M = A(w, \rho)$
Rymes (1989)	$Y = C + I$	$C = \phi_1(w, Y)$	$I = \phi_2(w, \rho)$	$M = A(w, \rho)$

Note 1 Y = income, C = consumption, I = investment, w = state of the news (expectations, confidence), ρ = interest rate, M = quantity of money, A = liquidity preference. This notation is based on Keynes and not Rymes, as Rymes did not use consistent notation in his transcriptions
Source Patinkin (1976, 79n22), Dimand (1988, 181), and Rymes (1989, 125–126)

lecture of December 4, 1933, and he copied Bryce's notes after the lecture. In turn, the Tarshis notes were the basis for Rymes's 1989 volume *Keynes's Lectures, 1932–35: Notes of a Representative Student.*[28] Thus, the problems in Bryce's notes from December 4 tend to be repeated in the literature. Bryce records the following employment equations:

$$N_1 = f_1(N) \tag{4.14}$$

$$N_2 = f_2(\rho) \tag{4.15}$$

$$N = f_1(N) + f_2(\rho) \tag{4.16}$$

$$f_2(\rho) = f_3(M/W) \tag{4.17}$$

Only Eq. 4.16 appears in GTE/5/419; Eqs. 4.14, 4.15, and 4.17 are not from Keynes's own notes. Cairncross records Eq. 4.17, but Eqs. 4.14 and 4.15 are not in his notes. Although Salant and Thring contain verbal expressions of Eqs. 4.14 and 4.15, Eq. 4.17 is absent in both. Fallgatter does not record any of these equations. The significant Rashomon surrounds Eq. 4.17, or what might be called the Bryce–Cairncross composite equation.

While the Bryce–Cairncross composite equation is not in Keynes's own notes, it does seem to have some basis in GTE/5/419. Recall that Keynes provides the

[28] Rymes reports, "The main thread of the synthesis is supplied by those notes taken by Lorie Tarshis" (1989, 10).

following equations in his own notes:

$$\phi_3(M) = \phi_2(\rho) \tag{4.18}$$

$$N = f_1(N) + f_3(M/W) \tag{4.19}$$

This equation is not found in any of the student notes. It would seem the Bryce–Cairncross composite Eq. (4.17) and Keynes's Eq. (4.18) are related. Still, there are two notable differences. First, Keynes's equation is in income form (ϕ), while Bryce–Cairncross equation is in employment form (f). Second, Keynes's equation does not include the wage rate (W). Thus, it appears Bryce and Cairncross pieced together Eq. 4.17 from Eqs. 4.18 and 4.19.

Keynes's analysis of changes in money wages does not follow directly from the Bryce–Cairncross composite equation. However, with some manipulation, it is possible to derive Keynes's third employment equation from the notes of Bryce and Cairncross. More specifically, combining Eqs. 4.16 and 4.17 leads to Keynes's Eq. 4.19, albeit in a more roundabout way than Keynes's own direct approach.

The employment equations in the Fallgatter and Salant notes are more problematic than those in the Bryce and Cairncross notes. Fallgatter and Salant record the following employment equation:

$$N = f_1(N) + f_2(\rho) + f_3(M/W) \tag{4.20}$$

The Fallgatter–Salant equation is more conducive to Keynes's analysis of money wages than the Bryce–Cairncross equation. It reflects that, all else equal, a fall in the money wages increases employment in Keynes's theory. But the Fallgatter–Salant equation is analytically flawed. Specifically, the equation contains redundant terms, because f_2 and f_3 are equal. Fallgatter and Salant overlooked this equality and thus included both terms in the employment equation.

As Table 4.2 shows, Thring was the only note taker to record Keynes's employment equations correctly. Unfortunately, the erroneous employment equations are the ones found in the literature. Fragments from December 4, 1933, lecture were first published by Don Patinkin in his 1976 classic, *Keynes' Monetary Thought*.[29] Patinkin only referred to Bryce's notes, and he omitted the problematic Bryce–Cairncross composite Eq. (4.17 above). Thomas K. Rymes's 1989 volume *Keynes's Lectures, 1932–35: Notes of a Representative Student* (1989) is the standard source on Keynes's lectures. In the body of the text, Rymes reports the incorrect equations from Bryce, Cairncross, Fallgatter, and Salant. Unfortunately, Thring's correct equation is only mentioned in the footnotes. In summary, Keynes's employment equations are widely misreported in the literature, and consequently, it is commonly overlooked

[29] Patinkin (1976, 79n22). The equations are repeated in Patinkin (1977, 16) and Patinkin (1982, 23).

Table 4.2 Keynes's employment equations and the Rashomon effect

Source	Employment equations
Keynes	$N = f_1(N) + f_2(\rho)$ $N = f_1(N) + f_3(M/W)$
Bryce, Cairncross, Tarshis	$N = f_1(N) + f_2(\rho)$ $f_2(\rho) = f_3(M/W)$
Fallgatter, Salant	$N = f_1(N) + f_2(\rho) + f_3(M/W)$
Thring	$N = f_1(N) + f_2(\rho)$ $N = f_1(N) + f_3(M/W)$
Patinkin (1976)	$N = f_1(N) + f_2(\rho)$
Rymes (1989)	$N = f_1(N) + f_2(\rho)$ $f_2(\rho) = f_3(M/W)$

Note 1 N = employment, ρ = interest rate, M = quantity of money, W = money wage rates. This notation is based on Keynes and not Rymes, as Rymes did not use consistent notation in his transcriptions
Note 2 Tarshis writes after $f_3(M/W)$: "why in Hell? See Bob!"
Note 3 Thring's original notes lack a parenthesis in the final employment equation: $N = f_1(N + f_3(M/W)$. Furthermore, there is a question mark (?) after the term $f_3(M/W)$
Source Patinkin (1976, 79n22) and Rymes (1989, 125–126)

that Keynes has already reached the "climax" of the *General Theory* by late 1933.[30] He writes in the *General Theory*,

> There is, therefore, no ground for the belief that a flexible wage policy is capable of maintaining a state of continuous full employment;any more than for the belief that an open-market monetary policy is capable, unaided, of achieving this result. The economic system cannot be made self-adjusting along these lines.[31]

References

Davidson, P. (2005). Galbraith and the post Keynesians. *Journal of Post Keynesian Economics, 28*(1), 103–113.

Dillard, D. (1948). *Economics of John Maynard Keynes*. Prentice-Hall.

Dimand, R. W. (1988). *The origins of the Keynesian revolution*. Stanford University Press.

Fletcher, G. A. (1987). *The Keynesian revolution and its critics*. Macmillan.

Hagemann, H. (2017). Franco Modigliani as American Keynesian: How the university in Exile economists influenced economics. *Social Research, 4*(40), 955–985.

Hagemann, H. (2019). Wages and employment. In R. W. Dimand & H. Hagemann (Eds.), *The Elgar companion to John Maynard Keynes* (pp. 233–241). Edward Elgar.

[30] Patinkin writes, "chapter 19 is the climax of the *General Theory*" (1987, 28). He repeats, "I have accordingly always regarded [Chapter 19] as the apex of the *General Theory*" (1990, 210).

[31] Keynes (CW 7, 267). Patinkin describes this statement as the "*quaesitum* of his *General Theory*" (1976, 106; 1990, 210).

Hansen, A. H. (1953). *A guide to Keynes*. McGraw-Hill.

Kahn, R. F. (1984). *The making of Keynes' general theory*. Cambridge University Press.

Keynes, J. M. (CW). The collected writings of John Maynard Keynes (Vols. 1–30). Macmillan and Cambridge University Press for the Royal Economic Society.

Keynes, J. M. (1932–35). Keynes's lectures, 1932–35: Notes of students. In T. K. Rymes (Ed.), unpublished typescript. Carleton University, Ottawa, 1988.

Klein, L. R. (1947). *The Keynesian revolution*. Macmillan.

Laidler, D. E. (1999). *Fabricating the Keynesian revolution*. Cambridge University Press.

Meltzer, A. H. (1981). Keynes's general theory: A different perspective. *Journal of Economic Literature, 19*(1), 34–64.

Meltzer, A. H. (1988). *Keynes's monetary theory: A different interpretation*. Cambridge University Press.

Modigliani, F. (1944). Liquidity preference and the theory of interest and money. *Econometrica, 12*(1), 45–88.

Moggridge, D. E. (1976). *Keynes*. Macmillan.

Moggridge, D. E. (1992). *Maynard Keynes: An economist's biography*. Routledge.

O'Donnell, R. M. (1989). *Keynes: Philosophy, economics, and politics*. St. Martin's Press.

Patinkin, D. (1976). *Keynes' monetary thought: A study of its development*. Duke University Press.

Patinkin, D. (1977). The process of writing the general theory: A critical survey. In D. Patinkin & J. C. Leith (Eds.), *Keynes, Cambridge and the general theory* (pp. 3–26). Macmillan.

Patinkin, D. (1982). *Anticipations of the general theory?* University of Chicago Press.

Patinkin, D. (1987). Keynes, John Maynard (1883–1946). In J. Eatwell, M. Milgate, & P. Newman (Eds.), *The new Palgrave dictionary of economics* (Vol. 3, pp. 19–41). Palgrave Macmillan.

Patinkin, D. (1990). On different interpretations of the general theory. *Journal of Monetary Economics, 26*, 205–243.

Plumptre, A. F. W. (1947). Keynes in Cambridge. *The Canadian Journal of Economics and Political Science, 13*(3), 366–371.

Robinson, E. A. G. (1977). Keynes and his Cambridge colleagues. In D. Patinkin & J. C. Leith (Eds.), *Keynes, Cambridge and the general theory* (pp. 25–38). Macmillan.

Robinson, J. V. (1937). *Introduction to the theory of employment*. Macmillan.

Robinson, J. V. (1971). *Economic heresies: Some old-fashioned questions in economic theory*. Basic Books.

Rymes, T. K. (1989). *Keynes's lectures, 1932–35: Notes of a representative student*. Macmillan.

Tarshis, L. (1977). Keynes as seen by his students in the 1930s. In D. Patinkin & J. C. Leith (Eds.), *Keynes, Cambridge and the general theory* (pp. 48–89). Macmillan.

Tobin, J. (1997). An overview of the general theory. In G. C. Harcourt & R. A. Riach (Eds.), *A 'second edition' of the general theory* (Vol. 2, pp. 3–27). Routledge.

Chapter 5
Reconstructing Keynes's IS-LM Approach, 1931 to 1937

Some influential observers reject the IS-LM interpretation of Keynes's *General Theory*. It is viewed by them as a perversion of his theory, developed by people other than Keynes after the *General Theory* was published. Some even call IS-LM Keynesianism "Bastard Keynesianism."[1] GTE/5/419 poses a serious challenge to interpreters who reject the IS-LM interpretation of Keynes's approach. Based on this document, in Keynes's own hand, we maintain that he was the originator of the IS-LM approach to the *General Theory*. Still, opponents of the IS-LM interpretation might contend that he abandoned the IS-LM approach after 1933. Thus, it is necessary to investigate whether there is continuity in Keynes's IS-LM approach.

5.1 1931 to 1933: A Review

There are three key elements of the IS-LM model: (1) the consumption (or saving) function, (2) the investment function, and (3) the liquidity-preference function. Keynes was the first economist to formalize the three component functions of the IS-LM model. Table 5.1 summarizes the development of Keynes's consumption (or saving) function from September 1931 to December 1933. He formalized a saving function for the first time in summer 1931. He worked with a saving function until late 1932, when he switched to a consumption function. Although he reverted back to a saving function in early 1933, he finally settled on using a consumption function rather than a saving function in the first half of 1933.

The development of the IS-LM consumption function began in September 1931. But it must be emphasized that it was not achieved until March 1933. Prior to this

[1] For examples, see Robinson (1962, 691; 1971, 90; 1974, 9, 11), Pasinetti (1974, 36–40; 2007, 33), Weintraub (1976, 618; 1977, 45), Kahn (1978, 548–549, 555; 1984, 160), Davidson (1978, 2–3, 175; 1990, 474), and Skidelsky (1992, 621).

W. Young and E. W. Fuller, *Reinterpreting Mr. Keynes*,
Springer Studies in the History of Economic Thought,
https://doi.org/10.1007/978-3-030-91342-7_5

Table 5.1 Keynes's saving and consumption functions, 1931–1933

Date	Function	Source
September 24, 1931	$S/E = f(O)$	GTE/1/21; CW 13, 374
Mid-1932	$S = \phi(E, Q, P_1, P_2)$	GTE/1/25
Late 1932	$R = H(P_1); P_1 = G(I, H) \therefore R = H(G, I)$	CW 13, 403
Early 1933	$S = f_2(\rho, B)$	GTE/5/423
Early 1933	$C = f_3(D)$	GTE/5/93; CW 29, 65
November 6, 1933	$C = f(Y, A)$	Tarshis, J17
November 20, 1933	$C = f(Y)$	Fallgatter, G17
December 4, 1933	$C = \phi_1(w, Y)$	GTE/5/419

Note 1 S = saving, E = income, O = physical output, ϕ = propensity to save, Q = profit, P_1 = price of consumer goods, P_2 = price of investment goods, ρ = interest rate, R = consumption, H = supply schedule of consumables, G = state of time preferences, I = investment, B = state of time preferences, C = consumption, D = aggregate disbursements, Y = income, A = windfall appreciation, w = state of the news

Note 2 References to Tarshis and Fallgatter are in Thomas Rymes's 1988 collection *Keynes's Lectures, 1932–35: Notes of Students*

period, Keynes did not underpin his saving or consumption functions with the multiplier. It is through the multiplier that changes in income equalize investment (I) and saving (S). Linking the consumption function to the multiplier was the critical step in the development of the *General Theory* and IS-LM, and this critical step was taken in the first half of 1933.

Table 5.2 summarizes the development of Keynes's investment function from mid-1932 to December 1933. He made several attempts at a formal investment function in 1932. In doing so, he linked the goods side of the economy to the money side. But his formalization of the investment function was somewhat convoluted in 1932. He achieved the basic form of the IS-LM investment function by early 1933 at the latest. Still, the IS-LM investment function is the least innovative element of the IS-LM model. As will be seen later, this is significant, for he omitted a formalized investment function from the *General Theory*.

Table 5.3 summarizes the development of Keynes's liquidity-preference function. He started with a hoarding function in mid-1932. But he coined the term liquidity preference by late 1932 and had a formalized liquidity-preference function by that time.

In summary, Keynes was the first to formalize all of the component functions of the IS-LM model. Beyond that, GTE/5/419 shows that Keynes was the first to bring the component functions of the IS-LM model together to summarize his theory. In

Table 5.2 Keynes's investment functions, 1932–1933

Date	Function	Source
Mid-1932	$P_2 = \psi'(M); I' = C(P_2) \therefore I' = C(\psi', M)$	GTE/1/26; GTE/1/32; GTE/1/34
Late 1932	$P_2 = B(\rho); I' = C(P_2) \therefore I' = C(B, \rho)$	GTE/5/61; CW 13, 398–99
Early 1933	$I = f_3(\rho, E)$	GTE/5/423
December 4, 1933	$I = \phi_2(w, \rho)$	GTE/5/419

Note 1 P_2 = price of investment goods, ψ' = propensity to hoard, M = quantity of money, I' = investment, C = the supply schedule of investment goods, B = quasi-rent, ρ = interest rate, I = investment, E = state of technique, w = state of the news
Note 2 Keynes writes in the *General Theory*: "The concept of hoarding may be regarded as a first approximation to the concept of liquidity-preference" (CW 7, 174)
Note 3 In GTE/1/34, Keynes uses the notation $I' = C.P_2$
Note 4 In GTE/5/423, Keynes uses C for state of technique rather than E. Here, C has been changed to E to avoid confusion with the supply schedule of investment goods

Table 5.3 Keynes's money-demand and liquidity-preference functions, 1932–1933

Date	Function	Source
Mid-1932	$M = \psi(H, P_2)$	GTE/1/25
Late 1932	$\rho = A(M)$	GTE/5/58–59; CW 13, 398
Early 1933	$\rho = f_1(M, A)$	GTE/5/423
December 4, 1933	$M = A(w, \rho)$	Bryce, B57; Cairncross, E15; Salant, M19; Thring, N16
December 4, 1933	$\phi_3(M) = \phi_2(\rho)$	GTE/5/419

Note 1 M = quantity of money, ψ = propensity to hoard, H = hoarding, P_2 = price of investment goods, ρ = interest rate, A = liquidity preference, w = state of the news
Note 2 Keynes writes in the *General Theory*: "The concept of hoarding may be regarded as a first approximation to the concept of liquidity-preference" (CW 7, 174)
Note 3 References to Bryce, Cairncross, Salant, and Thring are in Thomas Rymes's 1988 collection *Keynes's Lectures, 1932–35: Notes of Students*. Fallgatter (G33) uses slightly different notation and records $M = f(w, \rho)$. Tarshis (J36) copied the equation from Bryce

short, there can be no doubt that Keynes was the originator of IS-LM type models commonly used to represent his theory.

5.2 The Mid-1934 Drafts

The mid-1934 drafts of the *General Theory* have played a key role in studies on the origins of the IS-LM model. Don Patinkin was a staunch defender of the IS-LM interpretation of the *General Theory*, and he built his case around the mid-1934 drafts.[2] There are two drafts from mid-1934: one from spring and another from summer. The key chapter in the spring-1934 draft is Chapter 9, "The Functions Relating to Employment, Consumption and Investment."[3]

$$C_w = f_1(N, r, E) \tag{5.1}$$

$$I_w = f_2(N, r, E) \tag{5.2}$$

where C_w is consumption (in wage units), N is employment (or real income), r is the interest rate, E is the state of long-term expectations, and I_w is investment (in wage units). Next, he argues that consumption depends on employment, while investment depends on the interest rate and long-term expectations: "consumption will depend mainly on N and investment mainly on r and E. Thus the simplified expressions."[4]

$$C_w = f_1(N) \tag{5.3}$$

$$I_w = f_2(r, E) \tag{5.4}$$

Finally, Keynes provides the following equations, where D is effective demand (in wage units).[5]

$$D_w = C_w + I_w \tag{5.5}$$

$$F(N) = f_1(N, r, E) + f_2(N, r, E) \tag{5.6}$$

Keynes provides a similar set of equations in his summer-1934 draft. The title of Chapter 9 is changed to "The Functions Relating Employment to the Independent Variables of the System."[6] He provides the following equations.[7]

---

[2] Patinkin (1976, 74–75). Young (1987, 13, 24, 30, 179), Meltzer (1988, 143), and Dimand (2007, 82, 88, 91) note the connection between the mid-1934 drafts and the IS-LM model.

[3] Keynes (CW 13, 441; Keynes Papers, GTE/5/232). Also see Patinkin (1976, 74) and Meltzer (1988, 143).

[4] Keynes (CW 13, 441; Keynes Papers, GTE/5/233). Also see Patinkin (1976, 75).

[5] Keynes (CW 13, 442; Keynes Papers, GTE/5/233). Also see Patinkin (1976, 75).

[6] Keynes (CW 13, 480; Keynes Papers, NIS/1/250). The summer-1934 draft is misfiled in the *Keynes Papers*.

[7] Keynes (CW 13, 483; Keynes Papers, NIS/1/255).

$$C_w = Q_1(N, r, e) \tag{5.7}$$

$$I_w = Q_2(N, r, e) \tag{5.8}$$

$$N = N_1 + N_2 \tag{5.9}$$

$$N = f_1(N, r, e) + f_2(N, r, e) \tag{5.10}$$

where C_w is effective demand for consumption goods, N is aggregate employment, r is the interest rate, e is the marginal efficiency of capital, and I_w is effective demand for investment goods. Again, consumption depends mainly on employment, while investment depends mainly on the interest rate and the marginal efficiency of capital: "Both r and e are comparatively unimportant to C_w … N has not much bearing on I_w."[8]

$$N = f_1(N) + f_2(r, e) \tag{5.11}$$

Unfortunately, the mid-1934 draft chapters on liquidity preference did not survive.[9] Thus, the complete IS-LM model cannot be derived from the mid-1934 drafts. It is possible to derive the IS side of the model from the mid-1934 drafts; but not the LM side. This forced Patinkin to adopt a synthetic approach to reconstruct the IS-LM model from different drafts of the *General Theory*. In other words, Patinkin sought to defend the IS-LM interpretation by piecing together the IS-LM model from scattered fragments of Keynes's writings. In his synthetic approach, he took the IS side of the model from the mid-1934 drafts and the LM side from the late-1932 *Parameters of a Monetary Economy*.[10]

$$\rho = A(M) \tag{5.12}$$

It might be surprising that Patinkin did not use the liquidity-preference function from Keynes's lecture of December 4, 1933.[11]

$$M = A(w, \rho) \tag{5.13}$$

[8] Keynes (CW 13, 483–484; Keynes Papers, GTE/5/256).

[9] See Keynes (CW 13, 423) for the table of contents. Patinkin writes, "Unfortunately, those parts of the earlier drafts of the *General Theory* which deal with the theory of liquidity preference and might have provided a test for this conjecture have not survived" (1976, 112).

[10] Patinkin (1976, 72). Also see Eqs. 2.15 and 2.23.

[11] Keynes (1932–35, B57, E15, G33, J36).

Table 5.4 Keynes's synthetic IS-LM model—Patinkin (1976)

Component	Equation	Source
Consumption function	$C_w = f_1(N, r, E)$	CW 13, 441
Investment function	$I_w = f_2(N, r, E)$	CW 13, 441
Liquidity preference	$r = L(M)$	GTE/6/1/129
Effective demand	$F(N) = f_1(N, r, E) + f_2(N, r, E)$	CW 13, 442

Note 1 C_w = consumption, N = employment (income), r = interest rate, E = expectations, I_w = investment, L = liquidity preference, M = quantity of money
Note 2 On Keynes's 1934 liquidity-preference equation, also see Keynes (1932–35, C47, F15, H34, O27)

Patinkin was certainly familiar with this more refined function. He reports fragments of Bryce's notes and observes: "the lectures which Keynes gave in October–November 1933 were very similar to his presentation in the mid-1934 draft."[12] It seems Patinkin selected the liquidity-preference function from *Parameters* over the student notes for two reasons. First, *Parameters* came earlier in time. Patinkin was interested in presenting the liquidity-preference theory as an earlier contribution from the *Treatise on Money*. Using an earlier liquidity-preference function was conducive to his case against the novelty of the liquidity-preference theory.[13] Second, the *Parameters* materials are primary evidence from Keynes's own papers. By contrast, the student notes are secondary evidence and are hence less reliable.

Table 5.4 summarizes Patinkin's approach. It shows that Keynes did formalize all the elements of the IS-LM model by mid-1934. However, there is a potential drawback to the synthetic approach: It does not directly show that Keynes himself brought the components together. In sharp contrast, GTE/5/419 shows that Keynes did bring the formal elements of IS-LM together. In summary, although compelling, Patinkin's synthetic approach to defending the IS-LM interpretation is superseded by GTE/5/419.

5.3 The Marginal Efficiency of Capital

Of all the elements of Keynes's theory, the history of the marginal efficiency of capital is perhaps the longest and most complicated. The issues surrounding the emergence of this concept are critical, however. For as Keynes recognizes, "the marginal efficiency of capital is of fundamental importance."[14] In fact, Richard Kahn,

---

[12] Patinkin (1976, 79).

[13] Patinkin writes, "the essence of the theory of liquidity preference appears in the *Treatise*" (1976, 81).

[14] Keynes (CW 7, 145).

his protégé, describes the subject as the "the most important one in the *General Theory*."[15]

Since it is a present-value concept, the origins of the marginal efficiency of capital reach far back into recorded history. The ancient Sumerians were calculating compound interest by 2400 BC, and such calculations were common in Ancient Greece and Rome.[16] Discounting is the reverse of compounding. Just as it is possible to calculate the future value from the present value (compounding), it is possible to calculate the present value from the future value (discounting). Naturally, the study of compounding led to knowledge of its reverse—discounting. Present-value calculations have been common in major European trading centers since the Renaissance.[17] Of course, the marginal efficiency of capital is a present-value concept that involves discounting cash flows. In this sense, then, the marginal efficiency of capital has a long history.

In another sense, however, the marginal efficiency of capital was an original contribution of Keynes. He gave discounting a new twist. Prior to the *General Theory*, it was common to discount future cash flows at the interest rate. Time complicates the process of comparing the cash flows from investments. The interest rate is an "external rate" investors use to standardize cash flows and thus make them comparable across time. By contrast, Keynes suggested discounting cash flows at an "internal rate" unique to each investment. His procedure was to find the internal discount rate that makes the present value of an investment equal to the supply price. For this reason, his approach is commonly called the "internal rate of return." Today, the marginal efficiency of capital is better known as the internal rate of return in corporate finance, and it was popularized by Keynes.[18]

As emphasized, Keynes always based his investment theory on the present value. But he had the conventional external rate approach from 1909 up to the 1933 lectures. He introduced the name marginal efficiency of capital around mid-1933, although he still retained the external rate approach to the present value. Then, in spring 1934, he developed the central notion of the internal rate. He wrote in the spring-1934 draft of the *General Theory*:

> We have seen that a new investment has a prospective yield in the sense of a series of annuities or quasi-rents *Q1, Q2* ..., which it is hoped to gain from it on the successive occasions of using it over the course of its life. Given this series of annuities (and assuming, so as to avoid unnecessary complications, that the prospective yield will accrue at an even rate over the life of the investment) there is some rate of interest on the basis of which the present value

[15] Kahn (1984, 145). Moggridge describes Kahn as "Keynes's intellectual confessor on economic-theoretical issues" (1992, 532).

[16] See Muroi (1990, 2015) for examples of compound interest calculations in the ancient world.

[17] For notable early examples, see Fibonacci (1202, 384) and Stevin (1582, 107, 111). See Parker (1968), Poitras (2000), Goetzmann (2004, 2016), and Lewin (2019) on the history of compounding and discounting.

[18] Richard Kahn writes, "This [the marginal efficiency of capital] to-day is the familiar concept of the internal rate of return" (1984, 146). As Dimand says, "Keynes defined the marginal efficiencies of capital as the internal rates of return" (1988, 185). See Parker (1968) on Keynes's popularization of the internal rate of return.

> of the series of annuities will be equal to the supply price of the investment. The rate thus arrived at we may call the marginal yield (or efficiency) of capital.[19]

This is identical to the definition found in the *General Theory*: "I define the marginal efficiency of capital as being equal to that rate of discount which would make the present value of the series of annuities given by the returns expected from the capital-asset during its life just equal to its supply price."[20]

Unfortunately, Keynes's own remarks greatly complicate the history of the marginal efficiency of capital. In the *General Theory*, he erroneously attributes the marginal efficiency of capital to Irving Fisher:

> Although he does not call it the 'marginal efficiency of capital,' Professor Irving Fisher has given in his *Theory of Interest* (1930) a definition of what he calls 'the rate of return over cost' which is identical with my definition.... Professor Fisher uses his 'rate of return over cost' in the same sense and for precisely the same purpose as I employ 'the marginal efficiency of capital.'[21]

He repeated this claim in 1937:

> The meaning of 'marginal efficiency of capital' of which I make use—and which is, in my opinion, the only definition of the term which makes good sense—was first introduced into economic theory by Irving Fisher in his *Theory of Interest* (1930), under the designation 'rate of return over cost.' This conception of his is, I think, the most important and fruitful of his recent original suggestions.[22]

This is incorrect. Given his authority, however, Keynes's error has been widely repeated in the literature. It is common to find the marginal efficiency of capital aligned with Fisher.[23]

There are two approaches to showing that Keynes did not get the marginal efficiency of capital from Fisher: the mathematical approach and the archival approach. The mathematical approach is conclusive, although it is largely neglected in the literature on Keynes. As highlighted, he claims the marginal efficiency of capital is "identical" and used for "precisely the same purpose" as Fisher's rate of return over cost.[24] Mathematically, this is incorrect. Keynes's marginal efficiency of capital involves discounting the cash flows from only a single investment project. By contrast, Fisher's rate of return over cost involves discounting the cash flows from two different investment projects.[25] Thus, from a strictly mathematical perspective, it is illegitimate to associate the marginal efficiency of capital with Fisher.

[19] Keynes (CW 13, 453).

[20] Keynes (CW 7, 135).

[21] Keynes (CW 7, 140–141).

[22] Keynes (CW 14, 101n2).

[23] On the extent of the problem, see Hansen (1953, 118), Champernowne (1964, 182), Patinkin (1976, 80; 1982, 9, 78), Weintraub (1983, 618), Kahn (1984, 146), Fletcher (1987, 138), Carabelli (1988, 208), Fitzgibbons (1988, 120), Tobin (1990, 167), Skidelsky (1992, 555), O'Donnell (1997, 102), Laidler (1999, 254), Lawlor (2006, 150), and Backhouse and Bateman (2011, 24).

[24] Keynes (CW 7, 140–141).

[25] Fisher (1930, 155). Armen Alchian wrote in his seminal 1955 paper: "Fisher's rate of return over cost always involved a comparison of two options, not a discounting of merely one option" (1955,

The archival approach confirms that Keynes did not get the marginal efficiency of capital from Fisher. First, Keynes is incorrect when he claims Fisher introduced the rate of return over cost in 1930. Fisher originally introduced it in his classic work *The Rate of Interest* (1907), although he called it the "rate of return on sacrifice."[26] Keynes's error is perplexing, for he was certainly familiar with this book. He gave a series of lectures in 1909 called *Appreciation and Interest*. These lectures were "chiefly based" on Chapter 5 of Fisher's *The Rate of Interest*, titled "Appreciation and Interest."[27]

Comments by Joseph Schumpeter initiated the archival investigation into Fisher's place in the history of the marginal efficiency of capital. Schumpeter reported that Keynes "arrived at his concept quite independently ... [H]e inserted the acknowledgment in question upon his attention's [sic] having been drawn to Fisher's formulation."[28] Schumpeter did not indicate who had brought Fisher's formulation to Keynes's attention. Later, through the efforts of Paul Samuelson and Don Patinkin, it was confirmed that Redvers Opie was the source of Keynes's false attribution.[29]

> Samuelson has discussed this question with Redvers Opie himself, who in reply provided him with a copy of a handwritten note (dated August 5, 1935) which R. F. Kahn sent to Opie at Oxford, and which in its entirety reads:
>
> > "Guillebaud tells me that you maintain that Fisher, in his *Theory of Interest* (1930), has a definition identical with Keynes' definition of the 'marginal efficiency of capital.' I wonder if you could let me have the reference."
>
> A scribble at the bottom of this note indicates that Opie then referred Kahn to 'Fisher 155, 168.'[30]

Richard J. Kent discovered the August 1935 letter from Opie to Kahn in the *Keynes Papers* and published a transcription of the letter in 2014.[31] Kent's transcription might be misleading, for it contains the complete definition of the rate of return over cost from Fisher's *Theory of Interest*. In actuality, the definition in Opie's original letter is incomplete. The letter reads, "rate of return over cost is that rate which, employed in computing the present worth of all the costs and ---- all the returns, will make

939). Alchian's paper is a classic in the corporate finance literature. Unfortunately, it is almost totally neglected in the Keynes literature. For supplements to Alchian, see Weston (1962, 131), Hirshleifer (1970, 77), Fama and Miller (1972, 140), and Bodie and Merton (2000, 180).

26 Fisher (1907, 152–156). Patinkin (1976, 80n24) recognizes that the rate over return over cost is identical to the rate of return on sacrifice. But he does not indicate that the marginal efficiency of capital is not identical to the rate of return over cost.

27 Fisher (1907, 77) and Keynes (Keynes Papers, UA/6/1/5/2). Here, Keynes refers to Fisher's "monograph published some years ago," also titled *Appreciation and Interest* (1896). See Dimand (1995, 252).

28 Schumpeter (1954, 1178n15). Patinkin agreed as early as 1976, "to all appearances, Keynes arrived at the concept independently of Fisher" (1976, 80).

29 Patinkin (1976, 80n25).

30 Patinkin and Leith (1977, 89n6).

31 Kent (2014, 188).

these two equal. (168.)" Kent does not mention that Opie included "----" to indicate certain words are omitted from Fisher's definition.

Furthermore, Kent does not mention that there is some handwriting above the omitted words "----." The handwriting belongs to Keynes, and it reads: "the present worth of." This proves Kahn gave the letter to Keynes. Then, Keynes checked the passage in Fisher's original work and added Fisher's missing text to Opie's letter. The text Keynes added brought the definition in Opie's letter into perfect conformity with Fisher's definition. The handwriting on the letter proves that Opie, through Kahn, guided Keynes to Fisher's definition of the rate of return over cost approximately sixteen months after the development of the marginal efficiency of capital.

The archival approach confirms the mathematical approach: Keynes, not Fisher, was the originator of the marginal efficiency of capital. Keynes developed the concept around spring 1934, and he did not initially attribute it to Fisher. In fact, he stated in a lecture at Cambridge on November 26, 1934: "No clear definition of marginal efficiency in any economists' writing."[32] Later, in summer 1935, Opie told Kahn that the marginal efficiency of capital came from Fisher, and Kahn passed the letter to Keynes. Keynes and Kahn did not realize Fisher's concept differed. Regrettably, the false attribution found its way into the *General Theory* and has been perpetuated in the literature ever since.

5.4 Keynes's 1934 Lectures

Keynes did not submit *The General Theory* manuscript all at once. Rather, he submitted the manuscript chapters in batches over approximately sixteen months. This means he was drafting the later chapters as he was rewriting and revising the earlier chapters. Given this disjointed approach, the *General Theory* never reached its final form until about three weeks before publication. On September 13, 1934, he submitted the first three chapters of his manuscript for printing. He explicitly instructed the printer to return the proofs by the start of his 1934 lectures series on October 15.[33] He tended to lecture from proof pages of his books when they were available, meaning his 1934 lectures provide important insights into the progress of the book.

Opponents of the IS-LM interpretation might note that there is nothing corresponding to GTE/5/419 in the 1934 lectures. However, the 1934 lectures contain less of his theory than the 1933 lectures for at least two reasons. First, there were only seven lectures in 1934 compared to eight in 1933.[34] Even eight lectures at fifty minutes apiece were hardly enough time to cover the entire theory. As shown in

[32] Keynes (1932–35, O22, C38). Interestingly, Keynes explicitly mentioned Fisher in this lecture (Keynes 1932–35, C39, K18, O22).

[33] Keynes (CW 13, 484).

[34] King George V visited Cambridge on October 22, 1934 for the opening of the new University Library. Queen Mary described the tower of the library as a "magnificent erection." All lectures were suspended for the King's visit, meaning Keynes could not lecture. Keynes was in Cambridge

Chap. 3, he only presented the equations from GTE/5/419 in his eighth lecture, and he did not have enough time to fully explain his employment equations. Time was always an issue for Keynes when lecturing, but the problem was amplified in 1934.[35]

Second, the material covered in the 1934 lectures reflects the irregular organization of the early proofs of the *General Theory*. The chapters in the early proofs do not coincide with the chapters in the published version. The editors of the *Collected Writings* note, "In his [1934] lectures during the Michaelmas term, Keynes basically took his students through chapters 2–14 of the first proof version of the *General Theory*."[36] While the multiplier is treated in Chapter 10 of the published version, he treated the multiplier in Chapter 22 of the early proofs.[37] Consequently, the multiplier is missing from the 1934 lectures. As will be shown, an IS-LM type model can be extracted from the 1934 lectures. Still, the 1934 lectures are relatively lacking because of the time constraint and the irregular organization of the proofs.

Keynes opened the lecture series on October 15 with an analysis of the postulates of classical economics as he understood them. There is no need to review this material, as it mirrors his analysis in the 1933 lectures (see Chap. 3 above).[38] He did not lecture on October 22, meaning the second 1934 lecture was delivered on October 29.[39] Tarshis records an informal consumption function: "Current consumption depends (given data) on income."[40] This closely parallels his verbal approach from the mid-1934 drafts: "consumption will depend mainly on N."[41] Moreover, Champernowne records a formal consumption function.[42]

$$C = C(N) \tag{5.14}$$

where C is consumption, and N is employment (or income). The formal consumption function from the 1934 lectures is virtually identical to that of the spring-1934 draft of the *General Theory* (Eq. 5.3 above).

Next, Keynes provides a verbal statement of the investment function: "[Investment] will depend on marginal efficiency of capital and rate of interest."[43]

---

for the King's visit and wrote a letter to his wife Lydia Lopokova about the day's events (Keynes Papers, PP/45/190/6/171–172).

[35] On the time constraint, see Plumptre (1947, 366) and Rymes (1989, 21–22).

[36] In Keynes (CW 13, 485).

[37] Keynes (Keynes Papers, GTE/6/3/21). Similarly, the multiplier was treated in Chapter 21 of the mid-1934 drafts (CW 14, 423–424).

[38] Also see Dimand (1988, 160–161, 173).

[39] As Rymes (1989, 130n3) notes, there is some confusion in the literature over the dating of Keynes's 1934 lectures. The confusion stems from a dating error in the Tarshis notes, where he records that the first lecture was on October 22 (Keynes 1932–35, K1). Keynes's engagement diaries indicate that the lectures started on October 15, and there was no lecture on October 22.

[40] Keynes (1932–35, K4).

[41] Keynes (CW 13, 441; Keynes Papers, GTE/5/233).

[42] Keynes (1932–35, F5).

[43] Keynes (1932–35, K4, C9, O6, H10).

This is similar to what he writes in the spring-1934 draft: "investment [depends] mainly on r and E."[44] The only difference is that E is changed to e. But this change had already been made by summer 1934 (compare Eqs. 5.2 and 5.8 above). If formalized, the verbal investment function from the 1934 lectures takes the following form.

$$I = I(r, e) \tag{5.15}$$

where I is investment, r is the interest rate, and e is the marginal efficiency of capital. This formalized function is essentially identical to the formal investment function from the summer-1934 draft (Eq. 5.11). And Keynes's verbal investment functions from 1934 correspond closely to that of the *General Theory*: "the scale of investment depends on the relation between the rate of interest and the schedule of the marginal efficiency of capital."[45]

Keynes only gave an introduction to the consumption and investment functions on October 29, and there is no mention of liquidity preference. Still, he previews how the elements of his theory will fit together. Thring records the following: "The propensity to consume & the marginal efficiency of capital & and the rate of interest determine the level of employment."[46] Champernowne reports, "Everything depends on: propensity to consume, rate of interest, marginal efficiency of capital."[47] These statements are suggestive of Keynes's verbal IS-LM approach from GTE/5/419.

Finally, Keynes explicitly links his verbal IS-LM approach to his chronic stagnation thesis. Keynes's central thesis is that a capitalist economy has a chronic tendency to stagnate below its full productive potential.[48] He expresses his stagnation thesis in the context of his verbal IS-LM approach: "There is a level of investment which leads to full employment but no reason it should always exist. That is, marginal

---

[44] Keynes (CW 13, 441; Keynes Papers, GTE/5/233).

[45] Keynes (CW 7, 147, 137).

[46] Keynes (1932–35, O7).

[47] Keynes (1932–35, F6).

[48] Keynes wrote in 1932, "For a modern community one may say that it is a normal thing ... for output to be below the optimum level" (CW 13, 407). He writes in *The General Theory*, "It is an outstanding characteristic of the economic system in which we live that ... it seems capable of remaining in a chronic condition of sub-normal activity" (CW 7, 249). He states, "Full employment is of rare and short-lived occurrence" (CW 7, 250). As Meltzer says, "The central thesis of the *General Theory* is that a capitalist economy operating on the principles of laissez-faire fluctuates around a stable equilibrium at which there is less than full use of resources" (1988, 123, 172, 300; 1981, 43, 61). It must be emphasized that Keynes developed his chronic stagnation thesis long before the *General Theory*. Dennis Robertson worked closely with Keynes in the 1920s and could write in 1931: "Mr. Keynes's legend seems to be not so much one of cyclical depression as secular decay" (1931, 399n1). On Keynes's chronic stagnation thesis, see Klein (1947, 68), Dillard (1948, 99–100, 155, 269), Moggridge (1973, 75; 1976, 94), Minsky (1975, 64, 79, 85, 126, 128), Patinkin (1976, 113–114; 1982, xxiii; 1987, 29), Johnson and Johnson (1978, 27, 204), Kahn (1984, 142), Fletcher (1987, 165, 186, 209, 305), O'Donnell (1989, 242), Skidelsky (1992, 318, 462, 484, 545, 615; 2009, 97–99), Brunner (1996, 196), and Laidler (1999, 154, 265, 292).

efficiency of capital, the rate of interest, and the propensity to consume will give us all."[49] Hopkin reports,

> The level of effective demand which leads to full employment is a special case, and there is no automatic reason why that level should always exist. With $\phi(N)$ fixed there is a value of D which makes employment full. The propensity to consume, the marginal efficiency of capital, and the rate of interest determine the level of employment. This analysis explains the paradox of poverty and plenty. The richer the community the wider will be the gap between its actual and its potential output.[50]

The third and fourth lectures are devoted largely to definitions. Tarshis reported, "An awful lot of the lectures were filled with his fiddling over definitions."[51] According to Bryce, "[Keynes] told me that he too found it terribly tiresome—all this definition business."[52] There are indications that the student note takers grew weary during his long discourses on definitions.[53] Certainly, all the time he spent on definitional matters came at a cost. He only gave seven lectures in 1934, and the time he spent agonizing over definitions could have been dedicated to other material, like the multiplier, which is conspicuously missing from his 1934 lectures. The following paragraphs only contain the highlights of the third and fourth lectures.

Keynes treats expectations on November 7. As many commentators have noted, expectations play a central role in Keynes's theory, and the 1933 and 1934 lectures confirm this. First, he defines the amount of employment as the measure of economic activity: "The measure of economic activity is the number of men employed."[54] As he did in the 1933 lectures, he differentiates between short-term and long-term expectations.

> All production is to sell for consumption. A time elapses between the incurring of costs and the purchase; and the producer does not hold firm orders from the consumer. Hence his output is guided by his best expectations of future demand for his products. There are two groups of expectations:
>
> 1. Short term expectations, before the goods are finished. The forecast over the period between the beginning of production and completion. It relates mostly to the production of consumption goods. The producer of capital goods usually works to a firm order.

[49] Keynes (1932–35, K5).

[50] Keynes (1932–35, H11).

[51] Tarshis (1996, 55).

[52] Bryce (1977, 40). Also see Keynes (CW 13, 469–470; CW 14, 206) and Moggridge (1992, 557).

[53] See Rymes (1989, 12n37). For suspected examples in 1934, see Keynes (1932–35, K8, O8).

[54] Keynes (1932–35, H14, C14, O9). Elizabeth and Harry Johnson observe that, for Keynes, "'full employment' is an exclusive definition of social well-being, and as such is to be pursued at virtually any cost" (1978, 224). They note "the naiveté of the concept of full employment as a policy goal … That goal is very intimately related to Keynes's essentially aristocratic Victorian view of the economic requirements of a happy society. In that view, social happiness consisted of a job for everyone in his appointed place in life—Keynes was little concerned about providing more equal opportunities for advancement within the ordered hierarchy of employment" (1978, 217).

2. Long period expectations. The purchaser of capital goods has to form an expectation of the returns from the capital goods over a long period. It is on these expectations that the amount of employment depends[55]

After defining expectations, he stresses that the amount of economic activity ultimately depends on investors' long-term expectations: "Current employment depends on expectations," and "level of employment is determined by the expectation of entrepreneurs [investors]."[56] Finally, he hints that changes in investors' long-term expectations are the cause of the business cycle: "Thus a change in expectation may produce an oscillation similar to those of cyclical movements."[57] At this point, Hopkin and Thring include a crude drawing of the cycle. Still, this is just a brief preview, and Keynes describes his cycle theory in more detail on November 26.

While he begins with more definitions, Keynes finally gets back to the "real business" on November 19.[58] The discussion starts with an attack on forced saving—that is, the idea that banks can cause the amount of investment to exceed the amount of saving.[59] He declares, "Forced saving is sheer nonsense from beginning to end; nobody has explained what it means and no one can explain what it means, because it means nothing."[60] These comments might suggest that he recognized by late 1934 that the *General Theory* constitutes an attack on the doctrine of forced saving.[61]

Keynes's presentation of his theory of consumption is much briefer in 1934 than 1933. First, he expresses the Fundamental Psychological Law: "There is a general psychological law that, in a given state of habits (i.e., the propensity to spend), as people's real incomes increase they will increase their real consumption but not by the full amount of the increase in real income."[62] This law is of "fundamental importance."[63] For it means "income cannot increase without an increase in investment,

[55] Keynes (1932–35, H16, F7, K7, O11).

[56] Keynes (1932–35, F7, O13, C17).

[57] Keynes (1932–35, H17, O13).

[58] Keynes CW (13, 537).

[59] Keynes states in the 1935 lectures, "'Forced Saving' implies generally a difference between *S* and *I* when there is a change in the quantity of money" (1932–35, L15). He already rejected forced saving in the October 1931 preface to the German edition of the *Treatise* (CW 5, xxiv). He wrote to his wife on March 5, 1933: "Hayek has been here for the weekend.... We get on very well in private life! But what rubbish his theory is—I felt today that he was beginning to disbelieve it himself" (Keynes Papers, PP/45/190/6/26).

[60] Keynes (1932–35, H21, K14).

[61] Keynes (CW 7, 79–80) comments on forced savings in the *General Theory* and describes it as "one of the worst muddles of all" (CW 7, 183, 328). Presley writes, "The real Keynesian attack on forced saving came with the development of the multiplier analysis" (1979, 112, 168). As Fletcher explains, "The multiplier process generated just the right amount of voluntary saving to finance investment without any resort to the idea of forced saving" (2008, 189; 1987, 79).

[62] Keynes (1932–35, H25, C33, K14, O20). For the corresponding passage in the *General Theory*, see Keynes (CW 7, 96).

[63] Keynes (1932–35, C33).

i.e., more investment is a necessary condition of an increase in income."[64] The positive investment–income relation is at the core of IS-LM, and it is "the fundamental law of employment."[65]

Next, Keynes outlines the investment function. As mentioned, he gave a verbal investment function on October 29. He repeats it on November 19: "The propensity to invest depends on the relationship between the marginal efficiency of capital and the rate of interest."[66] Again, this is identical to Keynes's verbal investment function in the *General Theory*, and it is identical to Keynes's summer-1934 investment function when formalized (Eqs. 5.11 and 5.15).

The discussion at the end of the lecture returns to forced saving. The IS-LM consumption function underpinned by the multiplier makes forced saving impossible. An increase in the quantity of money by banks lowers the interest rate, and the lower interest rate increases the amount of investment. In turn, new investment generates new saving through the multiplier process. Whenever banks increase the quantity of money, just enough new saving is generated to finance the increase in the amount of investment. "Hence use of the term 'forced saving' is sheer nonsense" because "investment produces saving, not saving investment."[67]

> Lowering the rate of interest is certain to increase the amount of saving. Therefore, given habits and the distribution of wealth, the main influence on the volume of saving is the volume of real income. This depends on the amount of investment. Thus investment rules the roost & determines the volume of saving. Saving can look after itself. Except when employment is full, investment and consumption are not alternative but complementary.[68]

Lecture six on November 26 is the key lecture in 1934. He covers the marginal efficiency of capital, uncertain expectations, the business cycle, and his main policy proposal. He starts by defining the marginal efficiency of capital:

> 1. Prospective yield of an investment.
>
> $Q_1, Q_2, Q_3 \dots Q_n$.
>
> 2. Supply price of the asset is replacement cost.
>
> Marginal efficiency of the piece of capital considered is that rate of discount which will cause the present value of this series to be equal to the supply price.
>
> This has nothing to do with the rate of interest.

---

[64] Keynes (1932–35, C33, F12, H25, O20).

[65] Keynes (1932–35, H25).

[66] Keynes (1932–35, H25, C33, F12).

[67] Keynes (1932–35, C31, O21).

[68] Keynes (1932–35, H27, C35). Keynes attacked the forced saving doctrine in June 1937: "No amount of actual investment, however great, can exhaust and exceed the supply of savings, which will always exactly keep pace … [I]f the banking system chooses to make the finance available and the investment projected by the new issues actually takes place, the appropriate level of incomes will be generated out of which there will necessarily remain an amount of saving exactly sufficient to take care of the new investment" (CW 14, 210–211). He repeats in September 1939, "credit expansion provides not an alternative to increased saving, but a necessary preparation for it. It is the parent, not the twin, of increased saving" (CW 14, 281).

Rate of discount which will cause the present value of the series earned by one more unit of capital to equal the supply price of this one more unit.

3. Demand price is prospective yields discounted at the market rate of interest.

Investment will go on as long as there is any piece of equipment for which the marginal efficiency exceeds the market rate of interest.

Marginal efficiency falls, as investment increases, for prospective yield declines, and in the short period, the supply price rises.[69]

Uncertain expectations enter into all the elements of Keynes's theory. But the marginal efficiency of capital is the main outlet for uncertain expectations.[70] For Keynes, "Marginal efficiency of capital is very unstable."[71] Recall, the marginal efficiency of capital depends on the expected cash flows from the investment—the *Q*s. As Champernowne reports,[72]

Prospective Yields = $Q_1, Q_2, \ldots$

This means changes in expectations of the *Q*s cause the marginal efficiency of capital to change. For Keynes, the fundamental problem with private capital investment is that investors' expectations of *Q*s are highly uncertain and susceptible to rapid change: "We know very little about the future—it needs little to cause us to change our minds.... Of course our estimate of expected yields is very precarious. The basis of knowledge, for example, estimating yields of an asset ten year hence amounts to very little."[73]

According to Keynes, the business cycle is caused by fluctuations in the marginal efficiency of capital: "the trade cycle is nothing more than the fluctuations of the marginal efficiency of capital relative to the rate of interest. When the boom bursts sudden collapse of the marginal efficiency of capital and perhaps rise in the rate of interest."[74] Or more precisely, the business cycle is caused by fluctuations of the prospective yields (*Q*s) investors expect to receive from capital investment projects.

The marginal efficiency of capital is mainly dominated by the future. In durable goods it is the expected future returns [*Q*s] which mainly matter. Our expectations are very flimsily

[69] Keynes (1932–35, O21–22, C36, H27, K17).

[70] Keynes says in the 1935 lectures, "The marginal efficiency of capital is the way of bringing in the future (more than does the rate of interest)" (1932–35, L24).

[71] Keynes (1932–35, F13). Laidler writes, "It was Keynes's firmly held belief and frequently repeated view that the marginal efficiency of capital was extremely unstable in a market economy" (1999, 273–274).

[72] Keynes (1932–35, F13). For the corresponding statement in the *General Theory*, see Keynes (CW 7, 135).

[73] Keynes (1932–35, K19). For the corresponding statement in the *General Theory*, see Keynes (CW 7, 149–50). He claims, "the state of expectation is liable to constant change" (CW 7, 50). He writes of the "fickle and highly unstable marginal efficiency of capital" (CW 7, 204).

[74] Keynes (1932–35, C40). He writes in the *General Theory*, "The trade cycle is best regarded, I think, as being occasioned by a cyclical change in the marginal efficiency of capital" (CW 7, 313).

> based, and therefore very susceptible to changes in atmosphere; as a result the marginal efficiency is very subject to very rapid fluctuation. This is the fundamental explanation of the violent changes associated with the trade cycle, and of the general instability of the economic system.[75]

Keynes acknowledges that the *General Theory* is not about the business cycle.[76] The business cycle is just one aspect of a much greater problem: the institution of private capital investment. He explains, "most investment is not result of cold calculation but of taking a chance, desire for power.... Since conventional valuation of marginal efficiency of capital is the mass psychology of ignorant people, it is subject to great fluctuations."[77]

> There are waves of sentiment due to the mass psychology of a large number of ignorant individuals which influence the marginal efficiency of capital. The energies and skill of the professional investors and speculators are put not into making accurate long-term estimates of the value of an investment but into forecasting the behaviour of the market a short time hence, in order to 'beat the band.' ... The purchase by professionals of serious long-term investments on genuine long-term forecasts is uncommon, it is extremely difficult and risky.[78]

He is highly critical of the stock market: "The fetish of stock exchange providing liquidity of investment is very antisocial."[79] In an advanced economy with a privately organized stock market, "Capital development becomes a by product of a casino."[80] He compares the stock market to a "game of snap or musical chairs or old maid played by old men."[81]

Keynes's main policy recommendation is government control of investment. He contemplates reforms to improve the institution of private capital investment: "It is tempting to make the purchase of an investment, like marriage, only dissoluble at death or for very grave cause, so that investors would be forced to consider distant prospects."[82] Still, government control of investment is the only way to completely abolish the grave socioeconomic problems produced by private capital investment.

---

[75] Keynes (1932–35, H29). Bryce also reports the words "flimsily" and "violent" (Keynes 1932–35, C40). The *General Theory* reads, "expectations of the future should play a dominant part in determining the scale on which new investment is deemed advisable. But, as we have seen, the basis for such expectations is very precarious. Being based on shifting and unreliable evidence, they are subject to sudden and violent changes" (CW 7, 315).

[76] Keynes (CW 7, 313). Meltzer notes, "Business cycles are not a main concern of the *General Theory*" and "Keynes's applications to the business cycle are an afterthought" (1988, xi, 199). Also see Dillard (1948, 267), Minsky (1975, 60), and Laidler (1999, 248).

[77] Keynes (1932–35, O24).

[78] Keynes (1932–35, H31). Bryce's notes contain the phrase "mass psychology of a large number of ignorant outsiders" (Keynes 1932–35, C43). The *General Theory* contains the phrase "the mass psychology of a large number of ignorant individuals" (CW 7, 154).

[79] Keynes (1932–35, O25). Bryce's notes contain the phrase "socially dangerous fetish" (Keynes 1932–35, C43).

[80] Keynes (1932–35, H32).

[81] Keynes (1932–35, C43, K20, O25).

[82] Keynes (1932–35, H32).

He declares, "Perhaps the only solution is for long term investment to be controlled by the State—Private capital is an open scandal in this respect."[83]

Keynes saves the liquidity-preference theory for the final lecture of 1934, delivered on December 3. He starts his final lecture with a critique of the pre-Keynesian interest theories. He distinguishes "two older theories" and argues both are circular.[84]

1. The rate of interest is governed by the marginal efficiency of capital and depends on it. The expected rate of return as capital sets the pace, and the rate of interest on loans has to be in equilibrium with it. This will not do because the marginal efficiency of capital depends on the amount of investment and you cannot tell how much investment will be made until you know the rate of interest. The argument is circular.
2. The rate of interest is the balancing factor which brings the supply of and demand for capital into equilibrium. The demand is given (this is correct) by the marginal efficiency of capital, and the supply is given by saving. Two curves intersecting. This will not do if you accept the view that net investment and saving are necessarily always the same and equal. One might as well say that price is the factor which equates the value of goods sold and the value of goods bought.[85]

At this point, Thring draws a crude supply and demand diagram, representing saving (supply curve) and the marginal efficiency of capital (demand curve).[86] This might be suggestive of the Harrod–Keynes diagram in the *General Theory*.[87] However, it is not possible to determine whether Keynes drew the diagram himself, or whether Thring drew the diagram to summarize Keynes's verbal approach.

After criticizing the older theories, Keynes moves on to his own theory of interest ("My own answer").[88] He begins, "Psychological time preferences of an individual require two decisions."[89]

---

[83] Keynes (1932–35, O26, C45, H32, K20). Keynes writes in the *General Theory*, "A somewhat comprehensive socialisation of investment will prove the only means of securing an approximation of full employment" (CW 7, 378). As Meltzer notes, "Keynes first proposed either socialization of most investment or state direction in the mid-1920s and, to my knowledge, never abandoned the idea" (1998, 315; 1988, 5, 182, 189, 195, 198–199). O'Donnell observes, "[For Keynes] the state and not the private sector would be responsible for the aggregate level of investment," and "That the state should control the level of investment in the interests of macroeconomic efficiency was a key proposition of the *GT*, although public investment had been a key factor in Keynes's thought long before 1936" (1989, 323; 1999a, 171). On the socialization of investment, see Dillard (1948, 54, 156–159, 327–328), Minsky (1975, 12, 156–159), Patinkin (1976, 136), Fletcher (1987, 173, 178, 205), Skidelsky (1992, 558, 570), Brunner (1996, 199), Laidler (1999, 267, 292), Marcuzzo (2006, 132), and Dostaler (2007, 202, 259).

[84] Keynes (1932–35, K21).

[85] Keynes (1932–35, H33, C46, F15, K21, O26).

[86] Keynes (1932–35, O26). A similar construction appears in the 1935 lectures (Keynes 1932–45, L28). Austin Robinson reports that Keynes occasionally used diagrams in his lectures (in Tarshis 1977, 72).

[87] Keynes (CW 7, 180).

[88] Keynes (1932–35, H33).

[89] Keynes (1932–35, O26, C47, H33, K21).

Decisions:

1. Consumption or saving
2. How to hold savings

   Two Broad alternatives:

   (a) immediate liquid purchasing power (money)

   (b) non-liquid assets[90]

According to Keynes, "old theory tried to derive the interest rate from decision (1) not (2)."[91] He argues his predecessors ignored the second decision, between holding (a) liquid money, or (b) non-liquid assets. "The question is: what is the degree of his liquidity preference?"[92] He provides a formal liquidity-preference function.[93]

$$r = L(M) \tag{5.16}$$

where r is the interest rate, L is liquidity preference, and M is the quantity of money. He says just after his formal liquidity-preference function.

> The traditional theory of the rate of interest has forgotten the second of these two sets of decisions. The rate of interest cannot depend on the first decision, is not the reward of saving or waiting as such; it is not the reward of not spending but of not hoarding, the reward for parting with liquidity for a specified period, a measure of the unwillingness of those who possess money to part with their liquid control, the price which equilibrates the desire for control over cash with the available volume of cash. (This is the first point in the argument in which money appears.) The rate of interest must adjust the relative price of money and other assets so that the desire to hold money equals the amount of money to be held. If the rate of interest falls the sacrifice involved in keeping cash falls and therefore the amount of cash people will want to keep rises. Thus liquidity preference and the amount of money determine the rate of interest.[94]

The late-1934 liquidity-preference function is essentially identical to the late-1932 function emphasized by Patinkin (Eq. 5.12). The only difference is in notation. Whereas he had used A for liquidity preference in 1932 and 1933, he uses L by the end of 1934. Thus, by late 1934, Keynes introduced the standard LM notation common today. For the interest rate, he has settled on the notation r rather than ρ. Interestingly, Tarshis appears to have recognized the close link between the 1932 and 1934 functions, for he retains ρ for the interest rate in his notes for this lecture.[95]

---

90 Keynes (1932–35, F15, C47, H33, K21, O26). This scheme is a synthesis of Champernowne and Bryce. Champernowne's organization of the decision process is superior, while Bryce's terminology is more consistent with other note takers.

91 Keynes (1932–35, O27).

92 Keynes (1932–35, H34).

93 Keynes (1932–35, C47, F15, H34). Thring uses R rather than r (Keynes 1932–35, O27).

94 Keynes (1932–35, H34–35).

95 Keynes (1932–35, K21).

Keynes recommended a monetary policy of a permanently low and stable interest rate. He declared in his 1933 lectures, "it is of overwhelming importance that the optimum interest rate be determined by institutions and banking practice."[96] But he did not believe optimum income and employment can be attained with monetary policy alone.[97] All else equal, an increase in the money supply increases income and employment. Other things are not likely to remain equal, however. Changes in other factors are likely to offset any beneficial effects from monetary policy.

> An increase in the volume of money will tend to increase employment but may well fail to do so, especially if liquidity preference is for other reasons increasing; a fall in r [the interest rate] will tend to increase investment, but not if the marginal efficiency of capital is for other reasons falling more rapidly; an increase in investment will tend to increase output and employment, but not if the propensity to spend is falling.[98]

He closes the lecture with some brief comments on the "cause of liquidity preference."[99] But he warns, "This is an elusive subject and there is no final truth."[100]

Unfortunately, the 1934 series was cut short to seven lectures, meaning material from the 1933 lecture series is missing in 1934. Following Patinkin's approach for the spring-1934 drafts, however, it is possible to construct a synthetic IS-LM model from the late-1934 lectures.

$$C = C(N) \tag{5.17}$$

$$I = I(r, e) \tag{5.18}$$

$$r = L(M) \tag{5.19}$$

$$D = C + I \tag{5.20}$$

---

[96] Keynes (1932–35, G37).

[97] Keynes declared in his 1932 lectures, "There is no inherent tendency for economic system to react back to the optimum output regardless of the monetary policy followed—that is even when there is complete fluidity" (1932–35, I19). The *General Theory* reads, "It seems unlikely that the influence of banking policy on the rate of interest will be sufficient by itself to determine an optimum rate of investment" (CW 7, 378, 316). Patinkin writes, "the problem of unemployment could not be solved by monetary policy alone … [A] program of government investment was necessary" (1982, 212–213, 1976, 137). Also see Robinson (1937, 79, 121), Klein (1947, 66), Dillard (1948, 188, 328), Hansen (1953, 221), Moggridge (1976, 103), Fletcher (1987, 173), Meltzer (1988, 160, 188, 198, 294, 308; 1992, 155), and Laidler (1999, 9, 263).

[98] Keynes (1932–35, H35, O27, C48, F15, K22).

[99] Keynes (1932–35, F15).

[100] Keynes (1932–35, H36). Bryce uses the words "difficult subject" (Keynes 1932–35, C49). Thring records that this is "Puzzling as yet" (Keynes 1932–35, O28).

where D is effective demand.[101] Moreover, it is important to emphasize that Keynes was still using a simultaneous equations approach to his theory during the 1934 lectures. None of the note takers mention the words "simultaneous equations" in the 1934 lectures. However, Keynes received a set of proofs from his publisher on December 13, just days after the lecture series ended. This suggests he sent the proofs in the same period as the 1934 lectures. He explicitly advocates the simultaneous equations approach to his theory in the December 1934 proof: "Thus we are still left with one equation too few to enable use to solve our set of simultaneous equations, until we can obtain the value of the rate of interest from another source."[102]

5.5 1935: De-formalizing and Re-formalizing the *General Theory*

Advocates of the IS-LM approach to Keynes's theory must acknowledge that there is no unified IS-LM model in the *General Theory*. In other words, the *General Theory* does not contain all the formalized IS-LM equations neatly organized together on a single page. The lack of textbook style presentation of the IS-LM model might lead a superficial observer to believe the model is not there.

The IS-LM model is in the *General Theory*; but it must be extracted from different sections of the book.[103] Furthermore, the process of extraction is complicated by the investment function. The *General Theory* contains a formal consumption function and a formal liquidity-preference function. In sharp contrast, it does not contain a formal, equational investment function like GTE/5/419 or the mid-1934 drafts. An informal (or "literary") investment function is certainly there. Still, as Don Patinkin notes, "an explicit [mathematical] description of [the investment function] is curiously absent from the *General Theory*."[104] This led Patinkin to write,

> [T]he exposition of this mid-1934 draft is more systematic and mathematically elegant than the one which finally appeared in the *General Theory*.... Now it is true that all of these points are fully expounded in a literary fashion in the *General Theory* as published. Nevertheless, it is worth noting that—to judge from the subsequent rapid acceptance of the Hicks-Modigliani IS-LM model as the standard interpretation of the *General Theory*—the revealed preference

[101] On the effective demand equation, see Keynes (1932–35, C33, F5, F12, H4, K14). Keynes also uses this equation in the first proof (Keynes Papers, GTE/6/1/87).

[102] Keynes (Keynes Papers, GTE/6/1/142). This seems to contradict interpreters who claim Keynes rejects the simultaneous equations approach: "Those who actually read the *General Theory* recognised that Keynes had not presented a simultaneous equation system" (Nevile 2000, 141).

[103] Meltzer writes, "Since Keynes did not set out an explicit set of equations, later readers have to do this work for themselves" (1992, 155). Laidler writes, "A careful, not to say selective, reading will confirm that an informal version of the [IS-LM] model was there to be found" (1999, 4, 12). Harcourt and Turnell agree, "IS/LM is there" (2012, 35).

[104] Patinkin (1976, 75).

> of the profession is actually for the more formal style of presentation of analysis of his 1934 draft, as against his presentation in the final form the *General Theory*.[105]

This statement applies equally to Keynes's style of presentation of analysis in his 1933 lectures, as summarized in GTE/5/419. For, as Patinkin noticed, "the lectures which Keynes gave in October–November 1933 were very similar to his presentation in the mid-1934 draft."[106]

The *General Theory* underwent a drastic process of de-formalization between late 1934 and mid-1935. As illustrated, Keynes had a formal style of presentation from 1932 to 1934. Then, his style of presentation became much less formal after autumn 1934. This de-formalization of the *General Theory* might suggest that he abandoned his IS-LM approach to his theory. This would be incorrect, however, as will be demonstrated below.

The first proof of the *General Theory* shows that the de-formalization process was underway by winter 1934. Student notes suggest Keynes presented a formal consumption function on October 29, 1934 (Eq. 5.14). However, there is no formal consumption function in the first proof, dated December 7.[107] As noted, the 1934 lectures ended on December 3, meaning he likely drafted this material in the same period as the 1934 lectures. In short, Keynes decided to omit a formal consumption function from the first proof of *General Theory*.

Two points must be stressed. First, Keynes's presentation of his theory is even more informal in the first proof than the *General Theory* itself. The first proof does not contain a formal consumption function, but the *General Theory* does. As this indicates, there was a process of re-formalization in the second half of 1935. Second, de-formalization does not necessarily constitute abandonment. For example, the first proof contains an informal, verbal statement of the consumption function:

> The amount that the community spends on consumption obviously depends partly on the amount of its income, partly on the other objective attendant circumstances, and partly on the subjective needs and the psychological propensities and habits of the individuals composing it and the principles on which the income is divided between them.[108]

This exact passage appears in the proof dated April 26–27, 1935.[109] Additionally, it appears in the *General Theory* itself.[110] Thus, Keynes took the same verbal approach to the consumption function from December 1934 through April 1935 and into the *General Theory*.

Then, sometime after April 1935, Keynes re-formalized his theory. He inserted a formal consumption function into the text.

---

105 Patinkin (1976, 75–76).

106 Patinkin (1976, 79). Young (1987, 13, 24, 30, 179) and Dimand (2007, 82, 88, 91) also connect the 1933 lectures and mid-1934 drafts.

107 Keynes (Keynes Papers, GTE/6/1/87).

108 Keynes (Keynes Papers, GTE/6/1/87).

109 Keynes (Keynes Papers, GTE/6/3/17).

110 Keynes (CW 7, 90–91).

$$C_w = \chi(Y_w) \tag{5.21}$$

And where is the formal consumption function? Directly above his verbal consumption function from the December 1934 and April-1935 proofs.[111] Hence, he engaged in a process of re-formalization: He linked his formal consumption function back to his verbal consumption function. This indicates that Keynes's adoption of a purely verbal approach in December 1934 and April 1935 did not mean he abandoned his formal function. Rather, the informal and formal statements are complimentary and mutually reinforcing.

Keynes never brought his equational investment function back into the *General Theory* as he did with the consumption function. This might suggest the re-formalization of his theory remained incomplete. However, there is only one diagram in the *General Theory*, and it constitutes important evidence of re-formalization after mid-1935. Keynes sent proofs to Roy Harrod on June 5, 1935 for critical comments.[112] This means the proofs Harrod reviewed did not contain formal consumption or investment functions. The diagram emerged in September 1935 out of the correspondence between Keynes and Harrod.[113] As explained below, it is appropriate to call it the Harrod–Keynes diagram.

As with the multiplier and the marginal efficiency of capital, Keynes's own comments in the *General Theory* have complicated the history of the Harrod–Keynes diagram. He wrote in the accompanying footnote to the diagram, "This diagram was suggested to me by Mr. R. F. Harrod."[114] Harrod was the author of Keynes's official biography, *The Life of John Maynard Keynes* (1951), and he reported: "I supplied a diagram purporting to reconcile the classical theory with his theory, and he incorporated this in the volume—the only diagram in it!"[115] Given these comments, the Harrod–Keynes diagram is widely attributed solely to Harrod.

As Rod O'Donnell discovered, however, the genesis of the Harrod–Keynes diagram is more complicated than Keynes and Harrod suggest.[116] Their comments imply that Harrod conceived and drew the diagram, and that Keynes simply incorporated a finished diagram into the *General Theory*. On the contrary, there is no evidence that Harrod ever drew the diagram himself. Rather, Harrod provided Keynes with a verbal description of the diagram. He wrote to Keynes on August 30, 1935,

> Let y_1, y_2 etc. be rates of interest and Y_1, Y_2 etc. incomes corresponding to them (Y_1 being derived from y_1 via marginal efficiency of cap. and the multiplier). For each value of Y draw classical supply curves, of which *each* curve shows amount of saving corresponding to various values of y at a given level of Y. Then according to you it will be found that the

---

[111] Keynes (CW 7, 90).

[112] Keynes (CW 7, 526).

[113] Keynes (CW 7, 180). For the letters that led to the emergence of the diagram, see Keynes (CW 13, 543–559). For the diagram itself, see Keynes (CW 13, 557). It should be noted, however, that this diagram is flawed.

[114] Keynes (CW 7, 180n1).

[115] Harrod (1951, 453).

[116] See O'Donnell (1999b).

value of y at which the curve appropriate to income Y_r intersects the demand curve is in fact y_r, where y_r represents any given rate of interest whatever. The so-called supply curve in the passage from your letter which I have quoted is the locus of points on the classical supply curves for that value of y corresponding to the level of income on the assumption of which each was drawn.[117]

After receiving Harrod's informal description, Keynes actually drew the diagram. He sent the drawing to Harrod on September 14 and wrote: "I think the construction in the note, of which I attach a copy to remind you of it, is both correct and very useful as a help to exposition, and I shall like to appropriate it."[118] Harrod replied on September 20, "By all means use my construction of a family of classical supply curves if you feel so disposed."[119]

Contrary to the conventional wisdom, Keynes played an active role in formulating the only diagram in the *General Theory*. No doubt, Harrod initiated the process that led to the diagram. As O'Donnell suggests, there would probably be no diagrams in the *General Theory* without Harrod.[120] But Keynes actually formalized the diagram found in the *General Theory*.[121] In summary, it is appropriate to include both Harrod and Keynes in the name of the diagram, and the name "Harrod–Keynes diagram" is appropriate given the direction of causation from Harrod to Keynes.

The Harrod–Keynes diagram means there is a formal investment function in the *General Theory*. It is just presented in diagrammatic rather than equational form. The investment demand schedule (X_1X_1') in the diagram can be translated into equational form.

$$I = I(r, e) \tag{5.22}$$

where I is investment, r is the interest rate, and e is the marginal efficiency of capital. This is equivalent to the equational function in the summer-1934 drafts (Eq. 5.11). Beyond that, the Harrod–Keynes diagram constitutes evidence of a formal saving function in the *General Theory*. The saving function from the Harrod–Keynes diagram (Y_1) can be translated into equational form:

$$S = S(r, Y) \tag{5.23}$$

where S is saving, r is the interest rate, and Y is income. Together, these two functions can be used to derive the IS relation. The Harrod–Keynes diagram is logically equivalent to the IS curve, meaning Keynes was the first to draw a diagram of the

---

[117] Harrod in Keynes (CW 13, 556–557; Keynes Papers, GTE/1/335). Unfortunately, O'Donnell (1999b) does not include this highly significant passage.

[118] Keynes (CW 13, 557). This letter is incorrectly dated September 10 in the *Collected Writings*. The correct date is September 14 (O'Donnell 1999b, 29).

[119] Harrod in Keynes (CW 13, 560).

[120] O'Donnell (1999b, 36).

[121] O'Donnell writes, "while the idea of this diagram originated with Harrod, it was Keynes who seized on the idea and produced the drawings of both the initial and final diagrams" (1999b, 28).

IS relation.[122] Along with the A curve from his 1932 lectures, the Harrod–Keynes diagram shows that Keynes himself initiated the diagrammatical approach to his theory.[123]

Moreover, the investment demand schedule (X_1X_1') in the Harrod–Keynes diagram can be linked to his informal approach in the proofs. Two examples are provided here: the Chapter 11 verbal function and the Chapter 12 verbal function. The Chapter 11 verbal function from the first proof reads: "changes in the rate of investment depend partly on changes in the marginal efficiency of capital and partly on changes in the rate of interest."[124] This exact wording is retained in the April proof.[125] In the *General Theory*, however, the words "marginal efficiency of capital" are changed to "investment demand schedule." The final Chapter 11 verbal function reads: "the inducement to invest depends partly on the investment demand schedule and partly on the rate of interest."[126]

The Chapter 12 verbal function underwent less change. The function reads in the first proof: "the rate of investment depends on the relation between the marginal efficiency of capital and the rate of interest."[127] By the April proof it reads, "the rate of investment depends on the relation between the rate of interest and the schedule of the marginal efficiency of capital."[128] This is identical to the passage found in the *General Theory*, except "rate of investment" is changed to "scale of investment."[129]

As noted, the mid-1934 draft chapters on liquidity preference did not survive. Chapters 15 and 16 would almost certainly have contained a formal liquidity-preference function.[130] But these fragments are not available. As noted, Keynes presented a formal liquidity-preference function in his lecture on December 3. This same equation appears in the first proof, dated December 13, and the *General Theory* itself.[131]

$$r = L(M) \tag{5.24}$$

[122] See Young (1987, 95, 138, 191n80). Patinkin writes "the one diagram that we do find in the *General Theory* (p. 180) is logically equivalent to the IS curve" (1990, 224). He describes the diagram as a "general-equilibrium analysis" (1982, 12).

[123] Keynes's A curve and the Harrod–Keynes diagram contradict Joan Robinson's position: "An attempt to submit the *General Theory of Employment* to a diagrammatic treatment is subject to grave objections, since few of the concepts can be reduced to precise quantitative terms" (1947, 119).

[124] Keynes (Keynes Papers, GTE/6/1/102).

[125] Keynes (Keynes Papers, GTE/6/3/19).

[126] Keynes (CW 7, 137).

[127] Keynes (Keynes Papers, GTE/6/1/109).

[128] Keynes (Keynes Papers, GTE/6/3/21).

[129] Keynes (CW 7, 147).

[130] Keynes (CW 13, 423).

[131] Keynes (Keynes Papers, GTE/6/1/129) and Keynes (CW 7, 168).

As of December 1934, there is no indication that Keynes has introduced income (Y) into the liquidity-preference function. He takes an important step in this direction in the April proof.[132]

$$M = M_1 + M_2 = L_1(D) + L_2(r) \tag{5.25}$$

where M_1 is the amount of cash held to satisfy the transaction and precautionary motives, M_2 is the amount of cash held to satisfy the speculative motive, L_1 is liquidity preference corresponding to M_1, L_2 is liquidity preference corresponding to M_2, D is effective demand, and r is the interest rate. This is virtually identical to the final function in the *General Theory*. The only difference is that L_1 depends on effective demand (D) in the April proof, whereas it depends income (Y) in the *General Theory*.[133] Student notes from Keynes's 1935 lectures show that he finally introduced income (Y) into the liquidity-preference function by November 25, 1935.[134]

Finally, the de-formalization of the *General Theory* between December 1934 and April 1935 must not give the impression that Keynes abandoned his simultaneous equations approach. Keynes explicitly states in the proof dated May 7–17, 1935, "we are still left with one equation too few to enable use to solve our set of simultaneous equations, until we can obtain the value of the rate of interest from another source."[135] As mentioned, this statement also appears in the December 1934 proof.[136] Furthermore, he introduces a new endorsement of the simultaneous equations approach in the May-1935 proof: "if we have all the facts before us, we shall have enough simultaneous equations to give us a determinate result."[137] This passage survived into the final version of the book. As Table 5.5 shows, there can be no doubt that Keynes consistently endorsed the simultaneous equations approach from 1932 until the *General Theory* itself.[138]

5.6 *The General Theory*: Extracting the IS-LM Model

On January 9, 1936, Keynes announced to his publisher that he finished *The General Theory of Employment, Interest and Money*. He submitted the work on January 19, and it was finally published on February 4.[139]

---

132 Keynes (Keynes Papers, GTE/6/3/29).

133 Keynes (CW 7, 199).

134 Keynes (1932–35, L29).

135 Keynes (Keynes Papers, GTE/3/6/26) and Keynes (CW 14, 478).

136 Keynes (Keynes Papers, GTE/6/1/142).

137 Keynes (Keynes Papers, GTE/6/3/51).

138 Keynes (CW 7, 299).

139 Keynes (CW 13, 653) and Moggridge (1992, 570).

Table 5.5 Keynes and simultaneous equations

Source	Passage
"The Parameters of a Monetary Economy." Chapter 5 of Late-1932 Draft of *GT*	We should write in terms of simultaneous equations (just as we should strictly, since all the factors are in some measure interdependent, write the whole of this discussion in terms of multiple simultaneous equations). (CW 13, 403)
"The Parameters of a Monetary Economy." Chapter 5 of Late-1932 Draft of *GT*	These Parameters themselves are not entirely independent of one another, and the schedules expressing them should be stated, strictly, in the form of simultaneous equations. (CW 13, 405)
"A Summary of the Argument So Far." Chapter 6 of 1933 Draft of *GT*	The amount of employment will be determined by a set of simultaneous equations. (CW 29, 65)
"The Characteristics of an Entrepreneurial Economy." Chapter 3 of 1933 Draft of *GT*	The aggregate volume of employment is determined in a similar way … so that a set of simultaneous equations has to be satisfied. (CW 29, 98)
December 13, 1934 Proof of *GT*	Thus, we are still left with one equation too few to enable use to solve our set of simultaneous equations, until we can obtain the value of the rate of interest from another source. (Keynes Papers, GTE/6/1/142)
May 7–17, 1935 Proof of *GT*	As above (CW 14, 478)
The General Theory 1936	If we have all the facts before us, we shall have enough simultaneous equations to give us a determinate result (CW 7, 299)

As mentioned, the *General Theory* does not contain a unified IS-LM model in equational form. Rather, the model must be extracted from different sections of the book. The extraction process begins with the income equation from Chapter 6.[140]

$$Income = value\,of\,output = consumption + investment.$$
$$Saving = income - consumption.$$
$$Therefore\,saving = investment.$$

The consumption function comes shortly after the income equation. In Chapter 8, the *General Theory* contains a formal consumption function in equational form.[141]

$$C_w = \chi(Y_w) \tag{5.26}$$

Unlike the consumption function, the *General Theory* does not contain a mathematical description of the investment function in equational form. As outlined above,

[140] Keynes (CW 7, 63).

[141] Keynes (CW 7, 90).

the work contains informal statements of the investment function in verbal form, particularly in Chapter 11 and Chapter 12.[142] Moreover, an equational function can be derived from the Harrod–Keynes diagram.[143] Either way, the *General Theory* investment function takes the following form.

$$I = I(r, e) \tag{5.27}$$

Finally, the *General Theory* contains the liquidity-preference function in equational form. There is a preview of the function in Chapter 13.[144] But the liquidity-preference function in its final form is located in Chapter 15.[145]

$$M = M_1 + M_2 = L_1(Y) + L_2(r) \tag{5.28}$$

As this process shows, all the elements of the IS-LM model are in the *General Theory*.[146] Keynes did not bring all the elements together in the book as he had in earlier sources. Still, it is possible to do so. And the result is the IS-LM model.

$$Y = C + I \tag{5.29}$$

$$C = C(Y) \tag{5.30}$$

$$I = I(r, e) \tag{5.31}$$

$$M = L(Y, r) \tag{5.32}$$

5.7 Keynes's Verbal IS-LM Approach and *QJE* 1937

After the publication of the *General Theory*, Keynes's most important statement of his theory was his February 1937 article published in the *Quarterly Journal of Economics*, entitled "The General Theory of Employment."[147] The article has been interpreted as either a stand-alone reply to the November 1936 critiques of the

---

142 Keynes (CW 7, 137, 147).

143 Keynes (CW 7, 180).

144 Keynes (CW 13, 168).

145 Keynes (CW 7, 199).

146 Patinkin writes, "all of these points are fully expounded in a literary fashion in the *General Theory* as published" (1976, 75). Laidler observes, "its components were certainly to be found in the *General Theory*" (1999, 12, 275). Backhouse and Bateman agree, "the *General Theory* contains all the components of the IS-LM model" (2010, 21).

147 See Keynes (CW 14, 109–123).

General Theory, or as a reaction against mathematical models like IS-LM. On the contrary, the *QJE* article contains Keynes's final restatement of the central message of his December 1933 IS-LM verbal approach. Recall Keynes's verbal IS-LM approach from GTE/5/419:

> In any given state of the news, the quantity of employment depends on the propensity to consume, the liquidity preference, the ratio of the quantity of money to the rate of wages actual and anticipated (call for short the quantity of money; if we suppose banking system to buy debts of all maturities) with the maximum set by the disutility of labour.

Keynes called his IS-LM verbal approach "the General Law of Employment."[148] He provides a strikingly similar statement in his summer-1934 draft, just before his IS-LM type equations.

> Thus eventually our independent variables will prove to be (1) the state of long-term expectation, (2) the state of liquidity preference and (3) the quantity of money measured in terms of wage units. This means that, if we take as given the factors catalogued above including the subjective factors which determine the propensity to spend, the national income (or dividend) and the quantity of employment will depend on the values assumed by the above three variables. In some contexts, however, it may be advisable to include the propensity to spend amongst the variables of the system rather than amongst the factors taken as given.[149]

Importantly, just after this statement, Keynes writes: "We can express the above symbolically as follows."[150] Then he introduces his IS-LM type equations (Eqs. 5.7–5.11). Thus, originally, this passage was directly linked to Keynes's formal IS-LM approach.

As emphasized, Keynes started de-formalizing the *General Theory* in late 1934. He removed his IS-LM type equations in the de-formalization process. However, he retained his verbal IS-LM approach. He wrote in the proof dated May 7–17, 1935:

> Thus we can sometimes regard our ultimate independent variables as being (1) the prospective yield of capital, (2) the state of liquidity preference, (3) the quantity of money, and (4) the wage unit; so that, if we take as given the factors specified above, including the subjective factors which determine the propensity to consume, the national income (or dividend) and the quantity of employment will depend on the values assumed by these four variables.[151]

The link between this passage and the summer-1934 draft is unmistakable. He continues,

> The rate of investment depends on the relationship between the marginal efficiency of capital and the rate of interest. The propensity to consume determines a relationship between the rate of investment and aggregate income in terms of wage-units. The expectation of aggregate income constitutes the effective demand which sets the productive machine in motion. Thus the current productivity of the economic system as given, in other words the National Dividend, is determined by the interactions of the propensity to consume, the marginal efficiency of capital, the wage unit in terms of money, and the rate of interest.[152]

---

[148] Keynes (1932–35, G35).

[149] Keynes (CW 13, 482).

[150] Keynes (CW 13, 483).

[151] Keynes (Keynes Papers, GTE/6/3/39; CW 14, 503–504).

[152] Keynes (Keynes Papers, GTE/6/3/39; CW 14, 504).

Chapter 18 of the *General Theory* is titled "The General Theory of Employment Re-Stated." It is a summary of the work.[153] Keynes restates the central message of his December 1933 IS-LM verbal approach:

> Thus we can sometimes regard our ultimate independent variables as consisting of (1) the three fundamental psychological factors, namely, the psychological propensity to consume, the psychological attitude to liquidity and the psychological expectation of future yield from capital-assets, (2) the wage-unit as determined by the bargains reached between employers and employed, and (3) the quantity of money as determined by the action of the central bank; so that, if we take as given the factors specified above, these variables determine the national income (or dividend) and the quantity of employment.[154]

Clearly, this passage is a re-working of the passage from the summer-1934 draft. Consequently, there is a link between this passage in the *General Theory*, his mid-1934 IS-LM type equations, and GTE/5/419. Finally, his *QJE* article in February 1937 reads:

> More comprehensively, aggregate output depends on the propensity to hoard [liquidity preference], on the policy of the monetary authority as it affects the quantity of money, on the state of confidence concerning the prospective yield of capital assets; on the propensity to spend and on the social factors which influence the level of the money wage.[155]

In summary, GTE/5/419 contains the very first IS-LM model and a verbal statement of Keynes's IS-LM approach. He refined this verbal approach in mid-1934 and maintained his IS-LM type equations. He decided to remove the equations in late 1934 during his de-formalization process. But he retained his verbal IS-LM approach in the proofs and the published version of the *General Theory*. Finally, his 1937 *QJE* article contains his ultimate restatement of his verbal IS-LM approach developed in 1933. All this shows that Keynes consistently maintained the IS-LM approach to his theory from 1933 through the publication of the *General Theory* and into his seminal *QJE* article of 1937 (see Table 5.6).

5.8 De-formalization: Did Keynes "Do a Marshall?"

Opponents of the IS-LM interpretation might claim the de-formalization of the *General Theory* in early 1935 shows Keynes abandoned his IS-LM approach. As explained, this view must be rejected for at least two reasons. First, the re-formalization period of late 1935 indicates de-formalization did not mean abandonment for Keynes. Second, he consistently maintained his verbal IS-LM approach from 1933 through 1937. The question still remains: why did Keynes de-formalize the *General Theory* in early 1935?

---

[153] Patinkin agrees Chapter 18 "summarizes the argument of his book up to that point" (1976, 116). Meltzer describes Chapter 18 as "the summary of the *General Theory*" (1988, 125).

[154] Keynes (CW 7, 246–247). Patinkin associates this passage with "a general-equilibrium analysis" and "the IS-LM interpretation" (1982, 12).

[155] Keynes (CW 14, 121). For the early draft of the paper, see Keynes (Keynes Papers, GTE/2/3/).

Table 5.6 GTE/5/419 restatements and Keynes's IS-LM model of December 1933

Source	Passage
GTE/5/419 (Late 1933)	In any given state of the news, the quantity of employment depends on the propensity to consume, the liquidity preference, the ratio of the quantity of money to the rate of wages actual and anticipated (call for short the quantity of money; if we suppose banking system to buy debts of all maturities) with the maximum set by the disutility of labor
Summer-1934 draft	Thus, eventually, our independent variables will prove to be (1) the state of long-term expectation, (2) the state of liquidity preference, and (3) the quantity of money measured in terms of wage units. This means that, if we take as given the factors catalogued above including, the subjective factors which determine the propensity to spend, the national income (or dividend) and the quantity of employment will depend on the values assumed by the above three variables. (CW 13, 482)
May-1935 proofs	Thus, we can sometimes regard our ultimate independent variables as being (1) the prospective yield of capital, (2) the state of liquidity preference, (3) the quantity of money, and (4) the wage unit; so that, if we take as given the factors specified above, including the subjective factors which determine the propensity to consume, the national income (or dividend) and the quantity of employment will depend on the values assumed by these four variables. (CW 14, 503–4)
General Theory (February 1936)	Thus, we can sometimes regard our ultimate independent variables as consisting of (1) the three fundamental psychological factors, namely the psychological propensity to consume, the psychological attitude to liquidity and the psychological expectation of future yield from capital-assets, (2) the wage-unit as determined by the bargains reached between employers and employed, and (3) the quantity of money as determined by the action of the central bank; so that, if we take as given the factors specified above, these variables determine the national income (or dividend) and the quantity of employment. (CW 7, 246–47)
QJE Article (1937)	More comprehensively, aggregate output depends on the propensity to hoard, on the policy of the monetary authority as it affects the quantity of money, on the state of confidence concerning the prospective yield of capital assets, on the propensity to spend, and on the social factors which influence the level of the money wage. (CW 14, 121)

The conventional wisdom is that Keynes violently opposed mathematical economics. As O'Donnell notes, "According to the traditional account, Keynes was either totally or preponderantly hostile towards the use of mathematics and statistical inference in economics."[156] Of course, IS-LM is a mathematical model. If Keynes

[156] O'Donnell (1997, 133; 1990, 39).

rejected mathematical economics, then it seems he would oppose a mathematical model like IS-LM as a representation of the *General Theory*.

The view that Keynes totally opposed mathematical economics must be rejected. Even a cursory look at his lectures reveals that he used mathematics somewhat extensively. In addition to his lectures, the *Treatise on Money* and the *General Theory* are relatively mathematical. It is true that he was not highly mathematical by modern standards. And some of his contemporaries were more mathematical, like Irving Fisher for example. Still, Patinkin seems justified to suggest that "a comparison of the *General Theory* (and a fortiori the *Treatise*) with other works on economic theory that were written during that period would actually show Keynes' works to be among the more mathematical of them."[157]

Rather than totally rejecting mathematical economics, scholars increasingly maintain that Keynes embraced the approach of Alfred Marshall. For Robert W. Dimand, Keynes's adoption of Marshall's approach might explain the de-formalization of the *General Theory*: "Keynes, far from rejecting the IS-LM approach, was following Marshall's 1906 rules, using mathematics as an aid to thought but publishing only the translation in English."[158] Dimand notes the following passage from a letter Marshall wrote in 1906:

> Mathematics used in a Fellowship thesis by a man who is not a mathematician by nature—and I have come across a good deal of that—seems to me an unmixed evil. And I think that you should do all you can to prevent people from using Mathematics in cases in which the English language is as short as the Mathematical.[159]

Marshall continues,

> I went more and more on the rules—(1) Use mathematics as a shorthand language, rather than as an engine of inquiry. (2) Keep to them till you have done. (3) Translate into English. (4) Then illustrate by examples that are important in real life. (5) Burn the mathematics. (6) If you can't succeed in 4, burn 3. This last I did often.[160]

There is certainly good evidence to support Dimand's claim that Keynes agreed with Marshall's approach to mathematical economics. The young Keynes declared in his 1910 lectures:

> With regard to the use of mathematics:—
>
> The line taken by Marshall in his preface to be agreed with:—
>
> "The chief use of pure mathematics in economic questions seems to be in helping a person to write down quickly, shortly and exactly some of his thoughts for his own use ... but when a great many symbols have to be used, they become very laborious to anyone but the writer himself." See also Appendix D with regard to long trains of reasoning.
>
> A mathematical mind rather than a mathematical technique.
>
> Very easy qua mathematics, and very limited usefulness.

---

[157] Patinkin (1976, 22; 1982, 227).

[158] Dimand (2007, 92).

[159] Marshall in Dimand (2007, 90).

[160] Marshall in Dimand (2007, 90).

> Diagrams on the other hand rather useful.
>
> In these lectures I shall make some use of diagrams, but not—with one or two exceptions—of algebraical mathematics.[161]

Furthermore, there is evidence the mature Keynes maintained this attitude. He published a lengthy obituary for Marshall in September 1924, and he seems to uphold Marshall's approach to mathematical economics: "in 1890, in the preface to the *Principles*, he first emphasizes his preference for diagrams over algebra, then allows the former a limited usefulness and reduces the latter to the position of a convenience for private uses."[162] Keynes retained this passage in his March 1933 collection *Essays in Biography*, and this was published in the same period he was developing his IS-LM approach.[163]

Although Dimand's explanation for de-formalization is compelling, there is an apparent problem that needs explaining. Namely, the *General Theory* is less formal than the *Treatise*. As Patinkin recognized, "it is significant that in the *General Theory*—in contrast with the *Treatise*—Keynes did not attempt to provide a formal mathematical statement of the theory of employment that constitutes the major theme of the book."[164] If he was committed to Marshall's approach to mathematical economics, why are there different levels of mathematical formalization in the *Treatise* versus the *General Theory*?

Recall, Keynes developed and wrote the *Treatise* between 1924 and 1930. As shown above, he appealed to Marshall's approach to mathematical economics in September 1924. In that same work, however, he suggests Marshall's approach might be too severe: "In his reaction against excessive addiction to these [mathematical] methods, and also (a less satisfactory motive) from fear of frightening 'business men' away from reading his book, Marshall may have gone too far."[165] This passage might indicate that Keynes was more tolerant of mathematical economics than Marshall in the period of the *Treatise*.

So what moved Keynes to a less formal approach in the *General Theory*? Patinkin argues the failure of the *Treatise* had a profound effect on Keynes and his approach to writing the *General Theory*. First, the failure of the *Treatise* taught him to take a more collaborative approach. Patinkin highlights that he did not subject the *Treatise* to professional criticism before publication:

> [T]here is little if any evidence that the *Treatise* was subjected to much effective prepublication criticism.... Correspondingly, there are many serious deficiencis in the *Treatise* which were pointed out immediately after its publication and which (I conjecture) would have been avoided if only it had been subjected to such criticism. I would also conjecture that it was precisely this unfortunate experience with the *Treatise* that made Keynes so eager to seek out criticism at every stage of the writing of the *General Theory*.[166]

---

161 Keynes in O'Donnell (1997, 137).

162 Keynes (1924, 334).

163 Keynes (CW 10, 187–188).

164 Patinkin (1976, 22).

165 Keynes (1924, 334; CW 10, 188).

166 Patinkin (1976, 20–21).

After the failure of the *Treatise*, Keynes collaborated closely with a group of young Oxbridge economists called by one observer, the "General Theory Group."[167] The group consisted of Richard Kahn, Joan and Austin Robinson, Roy Harrod, and James Meade. These young economists served as Keynes's critique partners, and they helped purge the *General Theory* of errors.[168] This collaborative approach is significant, for it indicates a deep commitment to insulate the work from professional criticism.

Second, Patinkin suggests the failure of the *Treatise* moved Keynes to adopt a less formal style of presentation in the *General Theory*. He writes, "Indeed, it may have been Keynes's lack of success with such formal model building in the *Treatise* that led him to the more critical attitude expressed [in the] *General Theory*."[169] Put somewhat differently, Keynes came to the realization that "his strength did not lie in the use of [mathematical] methods."[170]

There is evidence that Keynes lost some confidence in his mathematical abilities as he grew older. While mathematically "competent," Harrod reports that "he had no specific genius for mathematics."[171] Keynes graduated from Cambridge in 1905 with a degree in mathematics. Moggridge notes, however, "His degree in mathematics, twelfth in first class honors, was respectable, especially given the relatively little work he had put into it, but it was not of a standard to suggest further research in the area."[172] Kahn describes Keynes in the late 1920s as "a poor mathematician" and noticed by 1933 that "Keynes had come to feel curiously insecure in doing even simple arithmetic calculations."[173]

Why did Keynes de-formalize the *General Theory* in early 1935? Not because he abandoned his IS-LM approach. Rather, the failure of the *Treatise* taught him to adhere more closely to Marshall's approach to mathematical economics. The more formal approach got him in trouble with the *Treatise*, and it seems he realized that such trouble with the *General Theory* could be avoided with Marshall's approach. Keynes did pull a Marshall as Dimand suggests; but for the reasons Patinkin provides. De-formalization and collaboration were mechanisms he used to protect his work from professional criticism.

The de-formalization of the *General Theory* created definite problems. The book is somewhat obscure, to say the least. Bryce suggested, "The *General Theory* wasn't written to be easy to understand … Anyone who studies that book is going to get

---

[167] Young (1987, 9).

[168] See Keynes (CW 13) for Keynes's collaboration with the General Theory Group.

[169] Patinkin (1982, 226; 1976, 22).

[170] Patinkin (1976, 23; 1982, 27).

[171] Harrod (1951, 57). Even Skidelsky admits, "He was not a remarkable mathematician" (1992, 423).

[172] Moggridge (1976, 19). Austin Robinson writes, "by the exacting standards of Cambridge he was not in that narrow superlative class which alone can hope to achieve fame in the field of pure mathematics" (1947, 9).

[173] Skidelsky (1992, 288, 471). See Keynes (CW 13, 413) for an example of Keynes's mathematical insecurity.

very confused."[174] While it helped shield the work from criticism, de-formalization made the central part of his theory more difficult to understand. Some interpreters, like Klein for example, suggested that "Keynes did not really understand what he had written."[175] Samuelson explained,

> I did not at all understand what it was about. And I think I am giving away no secrets when I solemnly aver—upon the basis of vivid personal recollection—that no one else in Cambridge, Massachusetts, really knew what it was about for some 12 to 18 months after its publication. Indeed, until the appearance of the mathematical [IS-LM] models of Meade, Lange, Hicks, and Harrod there is reason to believe that Keynes himself did not truly understand his own analysis.[176]

Of course, GTE/5/419 proves that Keynes did understand his own analysis. And, as Patinkin stressed, "the revealed preference of the profession is actually for the more formal style of presentation."[177] Keynes's de-formalization meant he has not received proper recognition for originating the influential IS-LM approach. Although he is commonly described as the most influential economist of the twentieth century, his influence might actually be widely underestimated.

Despite the problems it created, de-formalization ended up being a brilliant strategic move. De-formalization catalyzed the more or less mathematically inclined—like Champernowne, Reddaway, Harrod, Meade, Hicks, and later Lange—to provide mathematically based interpretations of the *General Theory*. Indeed, Keynes seemed happy to allow such interpreters due credit for IS-LM. He remained insulated from criticism in the background, while supporting to one degree or another those who published formal IS-LM models. But that is the subject of the next chapter.

References

Alchian, A. A. (1955). The rate of interest, Fisher's rate of return over costs and Keynes' internal rate of return. *The American Economic Review, 45*(5), 938–943.

Backhouse, R. E., & Bateman, B. W. (2010). Whose Keynes? In R. W. Dimand, R. A. Mudell, & V. Vercelli (Eds.), *Keynes's general theory after seventy years* (pp. 8–27). Palgrave Macmillan.

Backhouse, R. E., & Bateman, B. W. (2011). *Capitalist revolutionary: John Maynard Keynes*. Harvard University Press.

Bodie, Z., & Merton, R. C. (2000). *Finance*. Prentice Hall.

Brunner, K. (1996). *Economic analysis and political ideology*. Edward Elgar.

Bryce, R. B. (1977). Keynes as seen by his students in the 1930s. In D. Patinkin & J. C. Leith (Eds.), *Keynes, Cambridge and the general theory* (pp. 39–43). Macmillan.

Bryce, R. B. (1996). Interview with Robert Bryce. In D. C. Colander & H. Landreth (Eds.), *The coming of Keynesianism to America* (pp. 39–48). Edward Elgar.

Carabelli, A. M. (1988). *On Keynes's method*. Macmillan.

[174] Bryce (1996, 44–45).

[175] Klein (1947, 83).

[176] Samuelson (1946, 188).

[177] Patinkin (1976, 76).

Champernowne, D. G. (1964). Expectations and the links between the economic future and present. In R. Lekachman (Ed.), *Keynes's general theory: Reports of three decades* (pp. 174–202). Palgrave Macmillan.
Davidson, P. (1978). *Money and the real world*. Macmillan.
Davidson, P. (1990). The aggregate supply function. In L. Davidson (Ed.), *The collected writings of Paul Davidson* (Vol. 1, pp. 473–477). Macmillan.
Dillard, D. (1948). *Economics of John Maynard Keynes*. Prentice-Hall.
Dimand, R. W. (1988). *The origins of the Keynesian revolution*. Stanford University Press.
Dimand, R. W. (1995). Irving Fisher, JM Keynes, and the transition to modern macroeconomics. *History of Political Economy, 27*(Supplement), 247–266.
Dimand, R. W. (2007). Keynes, IS-LM, and the marshallian tradition. *History of Political Economy, 39*(1), 81–95.
Dostaler, G. (2007). *Keynes and his battles*. Edward Elgar.
Fama, E., & Miller, M. (1972). *The theory of finance*. Rinehart and Winston.
Fibonacci. (1202). *Fibonacci's liber abaci*. Springer 2002.
Fisher, I. (1896). Appreciation and interest. *Publications of the American Economic Association, 11*(4), 1–110[331–442].
Fisher, I. (1907). *The rate of interest: Its nature, determination, and relation to economic phenomena*. The Macmillan Company.
Fisher, I. (1930). *The theory of interest: As determined by impatience to spend income and opportunity to invest it*. Macmillan.
Fitzgibbons, A. (1988). *Keynes's vision: A new political economy*. Clarendon Press.
Fletcher, G. A. (1987). *The Keynesian revolution and its critics*. Macmillan.
Fletcher, G. A. (2008). *Dennis Robertson*. Palgrave Macmillan.
Goetzmann, W. N. (2004). *Fibonacci and the financial revolution*. NBER Working Paper 10352.
Goetzmann, W. N. (2016). *Money changes everything: How finance made civilization possible*. Princeton University Press.
Hansen, A. H. (1953). *A guide to Keynes*. McGraw-Hill.
Harcourt, G. C., & Turnell, S. (2012). On Skidelsky's Keynes. In G. C. Harcourt (Ed.), *On Skidelsky's Keynes and other essays* (pp. 13–55). Palgrave Macmillan.
Harrod, R. F. (1951). *The life of John Maynard Keynes*. Macmillan.
Hirshleifer, J. (1970). *Investment, interest, and capital*. Prentice-Hall.
Johnson, E. S., & Johnson, H. G. (1978). *The shadow of Keynes: Understanding Keynes, Cambridge, and Keynesian economics*. University of Chicago Press.
Kahn, R. F. (1978). Some aspects of the development of Keynes's thought. *Journal of Economic Literature, 16*(2), 545–559.
Kahn, R. F. (1984). *The making of Keynes' General Theory*. Cambridge University Press.
Kent, R.J. (2014). Keynes, Fisher, and the marginal efficiency of capital. *Journal of the History of Economic Thought, 36*(2), 187–192.
Keynes, J. M. (CW) *The collected writings of John Maynard Keynes* (vol. 1–30). Macmillan and Cambridge University Press for the Royal Economic Society.
Keynes, J. M. (1924). Alfred Marshall, 1842–1924. *The Economic Journal, 34*(135), 311–372.
Keynes, J. M. (1932–35). Keynes's lectures, 1932–35: Notes of students. In T. K. Rymes (Ed.), unpublished typescript. Carleton University.
Klein, L. R. (1947). *The Keynesian revolution*. Macmillan.
Laidler, D. E. (1999). *Fabricating the Keynesian revolution*. Cambridge University Press.
Lawlor, M. S. (2006). *The economics of Keynes in historical context: An intellectual history of the General Theory*. Palgrave Macmillan.
Lewin, C. G. (2019). The emergence of compound interest. *British Actuarial Journal, 24*(e34), 1–27.
Marcuzzo, C. (2006). Keynes and Cambridge. In R. Backhouse & B. W. Bateman (Eds.), *The Cambridge companion to Keynes* (pp. 118–135). Cambridge University Press.

Meltzer, A. H. (1981). Keynes's General Theory: A different perspective. *Journal of Economic Literature, 19*(1), 34–64.
Meltzer, A. H. (1988). *Keynes's monetary theory: A different interpretation.* Cambridge University Press.
Meltzer, A. H. (1992). Patinkin on Keynes and Meltzer. *Journal of Monetary Economics, 29*, 151–162.
Meltzer, A. H. (1998). Keynes on the interest rate and redistribution: Reply. *Journal of Post Keynesian Economics, 20*(2), 315–319.
Moggridge, D. E. (1973). From the treatise to the general theory: An exercise in chronology. *History of Political Economy, 5*(1), 72–88.
Moggridge, D. E. (1976). *Keynes.* Macmillan.
Moggridge, D. E. (1992). *Maynard Keynes: An economist's biography.* Routledge.
Muroi, K. (1990). Interest calculation in Babylonian mathematics: New interpretations of VAT 8521 and VAT 8528. *Historia Scientiarum, 39*, 29–34.
Muroi, K. (2015). *The oldest example of compound interest in Sumer: Seventh power of four-thirds.* Working Paper.
Minsky, H. P. (1975). *John Maynard Keynes.* Columbia University Press.
Nevile, J. W. (2000). What Keynes would have thought of the development of IS-LM. In W. Young & B. Z. Zilberfarb (Eds.), *IS-LM and modern macroeconomics* (pp. 133–149). Kluwer Academic Publishers.
O'Donnell, R. M. (1989). *Keynes: Philosophy, economics, and politics.* St. Martin's Press.
O'Donnell, R. M. (1990). Keynes on mathematics: Philosophical foundations and economic applications. *Cambridge Journal of Economics, 14*(1), 29–47.
O'Donnell, R. M. (1997). Keynes and Formalism. In G. C. Harcourt & R. A. Riach (Eds.), *A 'second edition' of the General Theory* (Vol. 2, pp. 95–119). Routledge.
O'Donnell, R. M. (1999a). Keynes's socialism: Conception, strategy, and espousal. In P. Kriesler & C. Sardoni (Eds.), *Keynes, post-Keynesianism and political economy: Essays in honour of Geoff Harcourt* (Vol. 3, pp. 149–175). Routledge.
O'Donnell, R. M. (1999b). The genesis of the only diagram in the General Theory. *Journal of the History of Economic Thought, 21*(1), 27–37.
Patinkin, D. (1976). *Keynes' monetary thought: A study of its development.* Duke University Press.
Patinkin, D. (1982). *Anticipations of the General Theory?* University of Chicago Press.
Patinkin, D. (1987). Keynes, John Maynard (1883–1946). In J. Eatwell, M. Milgate, & P. Newman (Eds.), *The new Palgrave dictionary of economics* (Vol. 3, pp. 19–41). Palgrave Macmillan.
Patinkin, D. (1990). On different interpretations of the general theory. *Journal of Monetary Economics, 26*, 205–243.
Patinkin, D., Leith, J. C. (1977). *Keynes, Cambridge and the General Theory.* Macmillan.
Parker, R. H. (1968). Discounted cash flow in historical perspective. *Journal of Accounting Research, 6*(1), 58–71.
Pasinetti, L. L. (1974). *Growth and income distribution: Essays in economic theory.* Cambridge University Press.
Pasinetti, L. L. (2007). *Keynes and the Cambridge Keynesians: A 'revolution in economics' to be accomplished.* Cambridge University Press.
Plumptre, A. F. W. (1947). Keynes in Cambridge. *The Canadian Journal of Economics and Political Science, 13*(3), 366–371.
Poitras, G. (2000). *The early history of financial economics, 1478–1776: From commercial arithmetic to life annuities and joint stocks.* Edward Elgar.
Presley, J. R. (1979). Robertsonian economics: an examination of the work of Sir D.H. In *Robertson on industrial fluctuation.* Holmes and Meier.
Robertson, D. H. (1931). Mr. Keynes' theory of money. *The Economic Journal, 41*(163), 395–411.
Robinson, J. V. (1937). *Introduction to the theory of employment.* Macmillan.
Robinson, J. V. (1962). Money, trade and economic growth by H.G. Johnson. *The Economic Journal, 72*(287), 690–692.

Robinson, J. V. (1971). *Economic heresies: Some old-fashioned questions in economic theory*. Basic Books.
Robinson, J. V. (1974). What has become of the Keynesian Revolution? *Challenge, 16*(6), 6–11.
Rymes, T. K. (1989). *Keynes's lectures, 1932–35: Notes of a representative student*. Macmillan.
Samuelson, P. A. (1946). Lord Keynes and the general theory. *Econometrica, 14*(3), 187–200.
Schumpeter, J. A. (1954). *A history of economic analysis*. Oxford University Press.
Skidelsky, R. (1992). *John Maynard Keynes: The economist as savior, 1920–1937*. Viking.
Skidelsky, R. (2009). *Keynes: The return of the master*. PublicAffairs.
Stevin, S. (1582). Tables of interest. In D. J. Struik (Ed.), *The principal works of Simon Stevin* (vol. 2, pp. 25–117). C.V. Swets & Zeitlinger.
Tarshis, L. (1977). Keynes as seen by his students in the 1930s. In D. Patinkin, J. C. Leith (Eds.), *Keynes, Cambridge and the General Theory* (pp. 48–89). Macmillan.
Tarshis, L. (1996). Interview with Lorie Tarshis. In D. C. Colander & H. Landreth (Eds.), *The coming of Keynesianism to America* (pp. 49–72). Edward Elgar.
Tobin, J. (1990). Irving Fisher. In J. Eatwell, M. Milgate, & P. Newman (Eds.), *Capital theory: The new palgrave* (pp. 161–177). Macmillan.
Weintraub, S. (1976). Revision and recantation in Hicksian economics: A review article. *Journal of Economic Issues, 10*(3), 618–627.
Weintraub, S. (1977). Hicksian Keynesianism: Dominance and decline. In S. Weintraub (Ed.), *Modern economic thought* (pp. 45–66). University of Pennsylvania Press.
Weintraub, S. (1983). The supply price in the marginal efficiency of capital. *Journal of Post Keynesian Economics, 5*(4), 618–624.
Weston, J. F. (1962). *Managerial finance*. Holt.
Young, W. (1987). *Interpreting Mr. Keynes: The IS-LM enigma*. Polity Press.

Chapter 6
Keynes's Equations and Early Post-General Theory IS-LM Models

The evidence shows Keynes originated the IS-LM equational representation of his *General Theory*. Furthermore, the evidence indicates that there was continuity in his IS-LM approach. He introduced some of the key ideas of the IS-LM model in his *Treatise* of 1930. By late 1932, he had developed formal prototypes of the consumption, investment, and liquidity-preference functions. He introduced the very first formal IS-LM model in late 1933, and he maintained this approach in the mid-1934 drafts of the *General Theory*. He began de-formalizing his theory in late 1934, albeit maintaining his verbal IS-LM approach from GTE/5/419 of late 1933 until his seminal *QJE* article of 1937.

Any history of Keynes's own IS-LM model must address a crucial question: did Keynes himself reject or endorse other early IS-LM-type presentations of his *General Theory*? The first significant point is that opponents of IS-LM have no historical evidence that Keynes ever rejected other IS-LM interpretations of his theory. Although he opposed it, Richard Kahn admits Keynes never publically attacked IS-LM: "the elementary teaching of Keynesian economics has been the victim of IS-LM and related diagrams and algebra. It is tragic that Keynes made no public protest when they began to appear."[1] Similarly, Robert Skidelsky rejects the IS-LM interpretation. Like Kahn, however, he must admit Keynes never objected to it.

> That Keynes never criticized [IS-LM] is perfectly true. My own feeling is that Keynes, although it sounds odd to say this, never grasped the significance of it and never thought it particularly interesting. He never reacted to it, that is the important point. It is not that he said that this is marvelous or awful, he just never reacted and that is puzzling.[2]

[1] Kahn (1984, 160). Opponents of the IS-LM interpretation might point to Robinson (1937, 1947). On Robinson, see Young (1987, 176–177).

[2] Skidelsky (2005, 96). This passage itself is puzzling, for Skidelsky reports Keynes's reactions to Harrod, Meade, and Hicks in an earlier work (1993, 614).

W. Young and E. W. Fuller, *Reinterpreting Mr. Keynes*,
Springer Studies in the History of Economic Thought,
https://doi.org/10.1007/978-3-030-91342-7_6

6.1 Bryce, Champernowne, Reddaway, Harrod, and Meade

Contrary to Skidelsky, Keynes certainly reacted to other IS-LM approaches. His earliest reaction to the IS-LM approach is in a letter to Robert Bryce. On July 3, 1935, Bryce sent Keynes an essay titled *An Introduction to the Monetary Theory of Employment* (1935).[3] This essay played a momentous, albeit underappreciated, role in the history of the Keynesian Revolution. Bryce attended Keynes's lectures from 1932–34, and his lecture notes were the basis of his 1935 essay. He explains,

> Having devoted a couple of years to understanding Keynes's ideas, I decided I'd stay on a third year as a research student and really get the feel of what was happening. During the third year I made expeditions down to the London School of Economics. I was determined to be a missionary for Keynesian ideas. They had sent a missionary up from London to Cambridge to spy on us, by the name of Lerner. I went down and spent half of each week at the London School of Economics. In order to indicate to them what was going on, I had to write Keynes's ideas up without having seen his book—he hadn't finished his book yet. So I had a clandestine publication that I had mimeographed in non-copyright form, and nonpublishable because it was Keynes's ideas. But, anyway, I circulated them. Hayek at the London School was very kind to me and he let me have four consecutive weeks of his seminar to try to explain these ideas to them. The students were very interested.[4]

After introducing Keynes's theory in Hayek's seminar at the London School of Economics in 1935, Bryce went to Harvard in 1936 to do "missionary" work. Joseph Schumpeter was Bryce's supervisor at Harvard and, as he put it, "Keynes was Allah and Bryce was his Prophet."[5] Bryce reported, "I had sufficient encouragement from my episode at LSE that several months later when left Cambridge I went over to Harvard … I used the same notes that I had prepared for use in Hayek's seminar to start the indoctrination of Harvard, before the *General Theory* appeared."[6] Lorie Tarshis explains.

> Bob Bryce introduced Keynes to Harvard. He was there a year earlier with his notes on Keynes's lectures and with his own essay on Keynes's new theory which he'd written to read to the London School. Bob was still at Harvard when I got there and was the center of all information about Keynes.[7]

By way of Bryce's lecture notes, Keynes's own 1933 IS-LM equations were already circulating at Harvard before the *General Theory* was published. Later,

[3] Bryce in Keynes (CW 29, 132–150; Keynes Papers, GTE/1/258–276).

[4] Bryce (1996, 42–43). Hayek adopted a diagrammatic IS-LM approach to Keynes's theory in *The Pure Theory of Capital* (1941, 361–364). In that book, Hayek proceeds with Keynes by "slightly modifying a diagram used by Professor Hicks" (Hayek, 1941, 363). Clearly, Hayek thought Hicks's IS-LM diagram was compatible with Keynes's theory as presented by Bryce, a presentation based on Keynes's lectures. Two of Keynes's other rivals, Dennis H. Robertson and Arthur C. Pigou, had a positive view of Harrod's IS-LM equational approach to Keynes's theory (Young, 1987, 109–111, 172; 1989, 56–62). As will be seen, Harrod's IS-LM equational approach is parallel to that written out by Keynes in his 1933 lectures.

[5] Schumpeter in Galbraith (1996, 137).

[6] Bryce (1977, 40–41).

[7] Tarshis (1996, 63). Klein indicates that he had a copy of Bryce's notes (1944, 55n1; 1947, 42n10).

Tarshis and Salant brought their lecture notes to Harvard. Bryce played a key role in the history of the Keynesian Revolution through his influence at Harvard, for as John Kenneth Galbraith acknowledges, "Keynesian ideas came to the United States and to Washington by way of Harvard."[8]

Bryce's 1935 LSE essay does not contain a formal IS-LM model. Still, he aligns Keynes with the general equilibrium, simultaneous equations approach of IS-LM.

> Now in truth all our quantities,—employment, income, investment, expenditure and our functions—the propensity to spend and the supply curves of consumption and investment as well as others that will be later introduced, are interrelated and hence the actual determination of the quantities must come as the working out these interrelationships. We could only find what they would be by solving a number of simultaneous equations, and could only observe the effect of a change by noting how it worked through or changes these equations. In this respect the problem is like that of the general equilibrium theory of value.[9]

And how did Keynes react to Bryce's general equilibrium, simultaneous equations approach? Keynes wrote to Bryce on July 10, 1935: "Many thanks for sending me a copy of your essay. I think it is excellently done ... [Y]ou have got into it the main elements in my theory."[10] He made this statement in July 1935, when his style of presentation in the proofs of the *General Theory* was most informal. Keynes's July 1935 letter to Bryce shows that he endorsed the general equilibrium, simultaneous equations approach. And through Bryce at Harvard, the endorsed simultaneous equations approach became the mainstream interpretation of the *General Theory* in the USA.

Bryce was a highly successful disseminator of Keynes's theory in influential academic circles, albeit not publishing his essay. The earliest IS-LM equations were published by those in Keynes's own circle: David Champernowne, W. Brian Reddaway, Roy Harrod, and James Meade. John R. Hicks and Oskar Lange also published influential IS-LM papers. Table 6.1 summarizes the IS-LM equations from the earliest IS-LM papers, and it shows they all contain the same basic set of equations.[11] Contrary to Skidelsky, Keynes reacted to these expositions, explicitly, or implicitly.

David G. Champernowne published the first IS-LM paper, entitled "Unemployment, Basic and Monetary: The Classical Analysis and the Keynesian" (1936), in

---

[8] Galbraith (1987, 20; 1998, 12). Skidelsky writes that Harvard was "the centre for the diffusion of Keynes's ideas through the profession and government.... Most of the leading American names associated with the Keynesian Revolution—Samuelson, Galbraith, James Tobin, Robert Solow, Seymour Harris—passed through Skidelsky" (1992, 580). Also see Samuelson (1988, 32; 1996, 158–159).

[9] Bryce in Keynes (CW 29, 136; Keynes Papers, GTE/1/263).

[10] Keynes (CW 29, 150).

[11] Robert Solow wrote, "there were three papers that tried to extract a model from the *General Theory*, not just one. Roy Harrod's was published before J.R.'s, in the January issue of *Econometrica*, and James Meade's appeared shortly afterward in the detailed Report of the Oxford meeting. It is not too far-fetched to say that the same basic equations could be detected in all three versions. At some celestial level of abstraction, they could be described as identical products" (1984, 14; 1991, 971). Also see Young (1987, 28–29), Rymes (1989, 19), Patinkin (1990, 213), Moggridge (1992, 594), Samuelson (1996, 164), Laidler (1999, 304), and Dimand (2007, 88).

Table 6.1 Early post *General Theory* IS-LM Models

Author	Date	Goods market equilibrium	Consumption/saving function	Investment function	Money market equilibrium
Champernowne	June 1936	$S_s = S_d$	$S_s(N, r)$	$S_d(N, r, Q)$	$M_s = M_d(r, Q)$
Reddaway	June 1936	$S = Y - C$	$S = f(Y)$	$I = h(Y, r)$	$M = L_1(Y) + L_2(r)$
Harrod	Jan 1937	$i = \psi(x, y)$	$x = \phi(y, i)$	$x = \phi_1(MPK, y)$	$y = \chi(m, i)$
Meade	Feb 1937	$I = xp_x + yp_y$	$yp_y = (1-s)I$	$i = E(P)/p_x$	$p_x K/(M-kI) = L(i)$
Hicks	April 1937	$I = N_x + N_y$	$I_x = S(I, i)$	$I_x = C(I, i)$	$M = L(I, i)$
Lange	Feb 1938	$Y \equiv C + I$	$C = \phi(Y, i)$	$I = F(i, C)$ $\therefore I = F(Y, i)$	$M = L(i, Y)$

Champernowne: S_s = saving, S_d = investment, N = employment, r = interest rate, Q = state of the news, M_s = quantity of money, M_d = demand for money (liquidity preference)
Reddaway: S = saving, Y = income, C = consumption, I = investment, r = interest rate, M = quantity of money, L = liquidity preference
Harrod: i = income, x = (saving = investment), y = interest rate, MPK = marginal productivity of capital, m = quantity of money
Meade: I = income, x = investment, p_x = price of a unit of capital goods, y = consumption, p_y = price of a unit of consumption goods, s = propensity to save, i = interest rate, E(P) = expected annual yield on unit of capital goods, K = stock of capital, M = quantity of money, k = proportion of money for transactions, L = liquidity preference
Hicks: I = income, I_x = investment, S = saving, i = interest rate, C = marginal efficiency of capital, M = quantity of money, L = liquidity preference
Lange: Y = income, C = consumption, I = investment, i = interest rate, M = quantity of money, L = liquidity preference

the form of a review of Keynes's book. It must be stressed that Champernowne was Keynes's student, and he attended Keynes's lecture on December 4, 1933.[12] Keynes was Champernowne's supervisor (tutor) and he was a member of Keynes's selective Political Economy Club. The serious teaching at Cambridge during this time was done by supervision, while the Political Economy Club was Keynes's forum for influencing students and colleagues.[13] Finally, Champernowne was a member of Keynes's Cambridge Apostles. Champernowne submitted his IS-LM paper before publication of the *General Theory*, and he acknowledged the paper "was based on Keynes' lectures and supervisions … [O]ne can derive IS-LM from the equations."[14]

W. Brian Reddaway published the second IS-LM paper, "The General Theory of Employment, Interest and Money" (1936). Like Champernowne, Keynes was

[12] Dimand (2007, 82; 2019, 182).

[13] See Johnson and Johnson (1978, 88) and Moggridge (1992, 190).

[14] Champernowne in Young (1987, 83–84). Rymes agrees, "Champernowne's published diagrams and equations can easily be cast in IS-LM terms" (1989, 19). Young (1987, 96) shows how to derive the IS and LM curves from Champernowne's diagrams.

Reddaway's supervisor at Cambridge, he was a member of the Political Economy Club, and he attended Keynes's lecture on December 4, 1933.[15] Keynes secured Reddaway a post in the Bank of England and, later, the University of Melbourne.[16] Keynes wrote to Reddaway on August 17, 1936, "I enjoyed your review of my book in the *Economic Record*, and thought it very well done."[17] In short, the two earliest IS-LM papers were produced by students who worked directly under Keynes, and he explicitly endorsed Reddaway's IS-LM approach to the *General Theory*.

Roy Harrod was the author of the third IS-LM paper, "Mr. Keynes and Traditional Theory" (1937).[18] Harrod studied economics under Keynes for two terms during 1922–23, and they remained close colleagues until Keynes's death in April 1946. Harrod was a member of the General Theory Group—consisting of Kahn, Joan and Austin Robinson, Harrod, and Meade.[19] These young economists helped Keynes refine the *General Theory*. Harrod had a significant impact on the *General Theory*, as evidenced by the Harrod–Keynes diagram.[20] As noted, this diagram is logically equivalent to the IS curve. Later, the Keynes family commissioned Harrod to write the official biography, *The Life of John Maynard Keynes* (1951).

Keynes wrote Harrod on August 30, 1936, "I like your paper (may I keep the copy you have sent me?) more than I can say. I have found it instructive and illuminating, I really have no criticisms. I think that you have reorientated the argument beautifully."[21] Harrod viewed Keynes's reply as an endorsement of his IS-LM interpretation: "I am delighted that you approve of the form into which I have cast your theories."[22] It cannot be argued that Keynes was only politely encouraging a younger supporter of his ideas. Keynes wrote to Dennis Robertson on September 20, "Roy has written for the Econometric Meeting at Oxford an elucidation of my book which I think extraordinarily good."[23] Harrod worked closely with Keynes, and Keynes warmly endorsed his IS-LM interpretation of the theory.

James Meade authored the fourth IS-LM paper, "A Simplified Model of Mr. Keynes' System" (1937). Like Harrod, Meade was a member of the General Theory

---

[15] Dimand (2007, 82).

[16] Reddaway's father was the Cambridge historian William Fiddian Reddaway. In 1903, Keynes and Fiddian were cofounders of the Social Work Committee (Moggridge 1992, 67).

[17] Keynes (CW 14, 70; Keynes Papers, GTE/2/1/72). Laidler notes that "Reddaway [used] what is nowadays almost standard notation" (1999, 305). Also see Young (1987, 74), Patinkin (1990, 219), Cord (2012, 100), and Harcourt (2012, 35, 295).

[18] For the original copy of the paper, see Keynes (Keynes Papers, GTE/2/2/41). As Young (1989, 58) shows, Harrod was contemplating this paper as early as November 1935.

[19] See Young (1987, 9).

[20] Moggridge writes, "The correspondence with Roy Harrod was particularly fruitful in producing changes to the manuscript" (1992, 568).

[21] Keynes (CW 14, 84; Keynes Papers, GTE/2/2/64).

[22] Harrod in Keynes (CW 14, 86; Keynes Papers, GTE/2/2/68).

[23] Keynes (CW 14, 88).

Group. In collaboration with Kahn, he played an important role in the development of the Keynesian multiplier.[24] Later, Meade worked closely with Keynes in the British Treasury during the Second World War.[25] Keynes penned Meade on September 14, 1936: "Thanks for the copy of your paper. It's excellent. I have no criticisms to suggest."[26] Keynes told Meade, "it was a true representation of the *General Theory*."[27]

6.2 Hicks and Lange

That John R. Hicks introduced the IS-LM model is one of the great myths in modern economics. Hicks introduced the IS-LM diagram. But as GTE/5/419 shows, Keynes originated the IS-LM equational approach to his theory approximately three years before Hicks. And Hicks admitted that he had seen student notes from Keynes's lectures. Keynes wrote to Hicks in June 1935,

> The channels through which my ideas are reaching you sound rather alarming! Probably you will gather the tendency, but do not take the details too seriously! My book is a fairly fat one and I try to cover the whole ground of the fundamentals. But in my own view it is merely a beginning. I agree with you that very large vistas are opening up. I deliberately refrain in my forthcoming book from pursuing anything very far, my object being to press home as forcefully as possible certain fundamental opinions—and no more.[28]

Hicks writes in the accompanying footnote, "These no doubt were notes on the lectures that Keynes had been giving at Cambridge—notes which were beginning to circulate at LSE."[29]

In addition to seeing notes from Keynes's lectures, Hicks read Harrod's paper and Meade's paper before he started writing his own. Hicks wrote to Meade on September 6, 1936:

> Harrod has asked me to send his paper on to you, and I take the opportunity of returning your own paper at the same time. I am sorry not to have returned your paper before, but I was waiting till I saw Harrod's before I decided what to write myself, and I didn't know how much of yours I should want until then. Now I have got a good deal of my paper done, and can manage without that from now on. I am taking up a number of Harrod's points, but

[24] See Kahn (1931, 188; 1984, 98–99) and Meade (1933, 1993). Dimand writes, "The first in Keynes's circle to publish a multiplier analysis incorporating personal saving was James Meade, in a Fabian Society pamphlet on *Public Works in Their International Aspect* in January 1933" (1988, 158; 1994, 1140).

[25] See Howson and Moggridge (1990).

[26] See Young (1987, 34).

[27] Keynes in Young (1987, 37). Solow recalled that the IS-LM papers by Meade, Reddaway, and Lange "really taught us [at Harvard] Keynesian economics" (in Harcourt, 1986, 18).

[28] Keynes in Hicks (1973, 8).

[29] Hicks (1973, 8n1).

> making my paper on the whole rather critical of Keynes. I have got some maths in my paper, and have been careful to use your symbols, so as not to cause unnecessary confusion.[30]

Keynes did not receive Hicks's IS-LM paper until October 16, 1936, and he did not respond until March 31, 1937. Keynes replied, "I found it very interesting and really have next to nothing to say by way of criticism."[31] At the time, Hicks viewed Keynes's letter as an endorsement of the IS-LM diagram. Hicks wrote to Keynes on April 9, 1937, "I had hardly hoped that you would be so much in agreement with it; but I am delighted to find that you are."[32] Hicks maintained four decades later, "I think I may conclude from this letter (as I have always done) that Keynes accepted the SILL diagram as a fair statement of his position—of the nucleus, that is, of his position."[33]

Keynes's March 1937 letter to Hicks has taken on a central role in the controversy over the IS-LM interpretation. Like Hicks, many scholars view Keynes's comments as an endorsement of Hicks's paper. Still, some commenters argue Keynes objected to Hick's IS-LM interpretation. For example, Joan Robinson wrote in 1978: "Hicks used to be fond of quoting a letter from Keynes which, because of its friendly tone, seemed to approve of but it contained a clear objection to a system that leaves out expectations of the future from the inducement to invest."[34]

It is true that Keynes objected to several points in Hicks's IS-LM paper. But his criticisms do not constitute a rejection of Hicks's IS-LM interpretation. First, he criticizes Hicks's notation:

> On one point of detail. I regret that you use the symbol *I* for income. One has to choose, of course, between using it for income or investment. But, after trying both, I believe it is easier to use *Y* for income and *I* for investment. Anyhow we ought to try and keep uniform in usage.[35]

It should be noted that Hicks used Meade's notation, and Keynes did not criticize Meade on this point. Thus it seems Keynes did not view this as a serious problem. Also, Hicks did not appear to view this as a major issue. He replied to Keynes, "I am sorry about using *I* for Income.... Other people, I find, are in the same care; so that I doubt if there is much chance of getting consistency in notation."[36]

More importantly, Keynes objects to certain Parameters in Hicks's IS-LM equations. He explicitly states that he tried Hicks's IS-LM equations before Hicks.

> At one time I tried the equations, as you have done, with *I* [income] in all of them. The objection to this is that it overemphasizes current income. In the case of the inducement to invest, expected income for the period of the investment is the relevant variable. This I have attempted to take account of in the definition of the marginal efficiency of capital. As soon as

---

[30] See Young (1987, 33, 35).

[31] Keynes (CW 14, 79; Keynes Papers, GTE/2/2/310). Also see Hicks (1973, 9).

[32] Hicks in Keynes (CW 14, 81; Keynes Papers, GTE/2/2/314).

[33] Hicks (1973, 10; 1977, 146).

[34] Robinson (1978, 13). A similar position is taken by Skidelsky (1992, 614–615).

[35] Keynes (CW 14, 80; Keynes Papers, GTE/2/2/311).

[36] Hicks in Keynes (CW 14, 81; Keynes Papers, GTE/2/2/314).

Table 6.2 Keynes's summer-1934 IS-LM model—long form

Component	Equation	Source
Consumption function	$C_w = Q_1(N, r, e)$	CW 13, 483
Investment function	$I_w = Q_2(N, r, e)$	CW 13, 483
Liquidity preference	$r = L(M)$	GTE/6/1/129
Effective demand	$N = f_1(N, r, e) + f_2(N, r, e)$	CW 13, 483

Note 1 C_w = consumption, N = employment (income), r = interest rate, e = marginal efficiency of capital, I_w = investment, L = liquidity preference, M = quantity of money
Note 2 On Keynes's 1934 liquidity preference equation, also see Keynes (1932–35, C47, F15, H34, O27)

Table 6.3 Keynes's summer-1934 IS-LM model—short form

Component	Equation	Source
Consumption function	$C_w = f_1(N)$	CW 13, 483
Investment function	$I_w = f_2(r, e)$	CW 13, 484
Liquidity preference	$r = L(M)$	GTE/6/1/129
Effective demand	$N = f_1(N) + f_2(r, e)$	CW 13, 484

Note 1 C_w = consumption, N = employment (income), I_w = investment, r = interest rate, e = marginal efficiency of capital, L = liquidity preference, M = quantity of money
Note 2 The investment function is derived from Keynes's effective demand equation
Note 3 On Keynes's 1934 liquidity preference equation, also see Keynes (1932–35, C47, F15, H34, O27)

> the prospective yields have been determined, account has been implicitly taken of income, actual and expected.... My own feeling is that present income has a predominant effect in determining liquidity preference and saving which it does not possess in its influence over the inducement to invest.[37]

Here Keynes is referring to the equations in the mid-1934 drafts. As Table 6.2 confirms, in Summer 1934, Keynes did include current income (employment) in the consumption function and investment function.

However, Keynes promptly removes income (N) from the investment function. He wrote, "We shall argue subsequently that both r and e are comparatively unimportant to C_w, so that $N_1 = f_1(N)$ approximately; also that N has not much bearing on I_w."[38] Table 6.3 shows Keynes's Summer-1934 model in short form.

Thus, Keynes did try Hicks's equations approximately two years before Hicks. Significantly, Keynes did not object to Hicks's IS-LM approach to the *General*

[37] Keynes (CW 14, 80–81; Keynes Papers, GTE/2/2/312–13). Meltzer agrees, "Keynes was willing to accept the IS-LM model with some qualifications, principally about expectations" (1988, 255).
[38] Keynes (CW 13, 483–484).

Theory; he merely raised concerns about which parameters to include in each function. Nevertheless, Keynes was correct to insist, "At one time I tried the equations, as you have done." And this represents an explicit statement by Keynes that he developed his own IS-LM approach before Hicks.

Hicks's replied to Keynes on April 9, 1937. He did not discount the importance of expectations in the investment function. Quite the contrary.

> I remain impenitent about including income in the marginal efficiency of capital equation. Of course I agree that it is expected income that logically matters; but the influence of current events on expectations (admittedly a loose and unreliable connection) seems to me potentially so important, that I feel much happier if it is put in and marked unreliable.[39]

In 1981, Hicks published a paper titled "IS-LM: An Explanation." It has come into the literature that Hicks recanted on the IS-LM interpretation in this paper. For example, Paul Davidson writes, "John Hicks (1981), more than two decades ago, in an article published in the *Journal of Post Keynesian Economics*, specifically noted that he (Hicks) was wrong when, in 1937 he interpreted Keynes in terms of his IS-LM framework."[40] He elaborates,

> By the mid-1970s, Hicks (1976, pp. 140–1) was ready to admit that his IS-LM model was a "potted version" of Keynes. By 1979, Hicks (1979, p. 38) was arguing that economics is embedded in calendar time and a relationship that held in the past could not be assumed to hold in the future. In an article in the *Journal of Post Keynesian Economics* entitled "ISLM: An Explanation", Hicks (1981, p. 139) recanted his IS-LM model when he wrote: "As time has gone on, I have myself become dissatisfied with it [the IS-LM apparatus]". In this article, Hicks admitted that the IS-LM formulation did not describe Keynes's general theory approach at all.[41]

First, Hicks did not reject the IS-LM interpretation by labeling it "a potted version of the central argument of the General Theory."[42] Hicks wrote in that same work, "It is not a bad representation of Keynes; but it does not get his predecessors (the 'classics' as he called them) at all right."[43] Furthermore, Hicks never claimed that his IS-LM diagram was the *General Theory* in its entirety: "it was never intended as more than a representation of what appeared to be a central part of the Keynes theory. As such, I think it is still defensible. But I have never regarded it as complete in

[39] Hicks in Keynes (CW 14, 82; Keynes Papers, GTE/2/2/314). This seems consistent with certain statements in the *General Theory*: "the level of employment at any time depends, in a sense, not merely on the existing state of expectation but on the states of expectation which have existed over a certain past period" (CW 7, 50).

[40] Davidson (2005, 398). Indeed, Davidson takes credit for being "someone who had some influence in inducing John Hicks (1982) to recant the IS-LM model as being only a 'potted version' of Keynes's *General Theory* and not a proper representation of Keynes's analytical model" (2003, 247).

[41] Davidson (2007, 186).

[42] Hicks (1967, vii).

[43] Hicks (1967, 143). Laidler agrees, "Hick's version of classical economics was … every bit as much of caricature as was Keynes's version" (1999, 309).

itself."[44] His phrase "potted version" indicates that Hicks thought IS-LM did capture the central part of Keynes's system.

Second, a careful reading of Hicks's 1981 paper shows that Hicks never criticizes IS-LM as an interpretation of Keynes's *General Theory*.[45] He writes, "I have, however, not concealed that, as time has gone on, I have myself become dissatisfied with it."[46] Then he cites a passage from an earlier work in truncated form. The full passage reads,

> The letter which Keynes wrote me about that paper has now been published. I think I am justified in concluding from that letter that Keynes did not wholly disapprove of what I had made of him. All the same, I must say that that diagram is now much less popular with me than I think it still is with many other people.[47]

As he indicates, Hicks used the IS-LM diagram in his book *The Trade Cycle*: "I also made use of it in some chapters (11-12) of my book the *Trade Cycle* (1950)."[48] In his 1981 essay on IS-LM, he is recanting on his own use of the diagram in his earlier works. Hicks came to believe the IS-LM diagram does not reflect the economic reality in which human beings live. He thought there were "divergences between reality and the theoretical model."[49] A crucial problem, as Hicks saw it, is that IS-LM mistreats time.[50] Although he abandoned it as a tool of economic analysis, Hicks never recanted on the IS-LM diagram as an interpretation of the central core of Keynes's theory.

Oskar Lange wrote the last of the early IS-LM papers, "The Rate of Interest and the Optimum Propensity to Consume" (1938). Lange's paper was more frequently cited than Hicks's in the early phase of the Keynesian Revolution.[51] Indeed, Paul Samuelson dubbed the IS-LM model the "Keynes–Lange system."[52] Although Lange's paper appeared after Hicks's, Keynes's reaction to the paper is especially significant because it appeared in print. Keynes wrote in the *Quarterly Journal of Economics*, "The analysis which I gave in my *General Theory of Employment* is the same as the 'general theory' explained by Dr. Lange."[53] Clearly, Keynes himself did not believe Lange bastardized the *General Theory*. Beyond that, Lange acknowledged that his IS-LM equations correspond to those of Reddaway and Hicks: "A similar

---

[44] Hicks (1974, 6). He writes in the accompanying footnote, "It would appear that Keynes himself accepted it as such" (1974, 6n5).

[45] This point was made by Patinkin (1990, 224).

[46] Hicks (1981, 139).

[47] Hicks (1976, 140–141; 1984, 270).

[48] Hicks (1981, 139).

[49] Hicks (1981, 153).

[50] See Hicks (1976, 1984).

[51] As Goulven Rubin writes, "Lange (1938) was influential, probably as influential as Hicks (1937), during the takeoff of the Keynesian revolution. A beta-search on JSTOR for the period from 1938 to 1950 gave us sixteen citations for 'Mr Keynes and the Classics a Suggested Interpretation,' against twenty-five for 'The Rate of Interest and the Optimum Propensity to Consume'" (2016, 301).

[52] Samuelson (1947, 354). Also, Mabel Timlin refers to IS-LM as the Keynes–Lange system (1942, 10). Also see Young (1987, 121).

[53] Keynes (CW 14, 232n1).

system of equations has been given for the first time by Reddaway ... [Dr. Hicks] treats the subject in a similar and very elegant way."[54] Lange also refers readers to Harrod's IS-LM paper. Keynes's direct endorsement of Lange's IS-LM paper can also be viewed as an indirect endorsement of the IS-LM papers by Reddaway and Hicks.

In summary, the evidence shows it is inaccurate to suggest that "Keynes never accepted the IS-LM framework."[55] Rather, Donald Moggridge is justified to write:

> Keynes read many of them [IS-LM papers] and 'approved' of all where we know of no adverse comments.... Many of these expositions attempted to formulate the model and did so on remarkably similar lines, as Oscar Lange, and early user of such models, point out in 1938. All worked in terms of a simple three equation, two identity model that was to become the mainstay undergraduate expositions of the theory—and still is.[56]

6.3 Other Early IS-LM Models

Keynes explicitly endorsed at least five IS-LM papers between 1936 and 1938. However, he did not respond to all the IS-LM representations of his theory published during his lifetime. He died in April 1946, and there were at least ten authors who took an IS-LM approach to his theory before his death. Tables 6.4 and 6.5 show the relation between Keynes's own IS-LM approach and later interpreters. Table 6.4 summarizes the earliest IS-LM equations in Keynes's notation, whereas Table 6.5 summarizes the earliest IS-LM equations in the standard notation popularized by Hansen (1949). As these tables illustrate, all these works contain the same basic set of equations.

Kei Shibata authored the first of the early IS-LM papers to which Keynes did not respond. This neglected paper, "Some Questions on Mr. Keynes' General Theory of Employment, Interest and Money," was published in July 1937, meaning it is was sixth by publication date. Shibata was the first to publish IS-LM type equations with a consumption function. However, having read Lange's paper in manuscript, it is not surprising that Shibata used a consumption function, as Lange did, rather than a saving function.[57]

Chapter 8 of Paul Samuelson's 1940 doctoral dissertation *Foundations of Analytical Economics* was entitled "The Stability of Equilibrium: Comparative Statics and Dynamics." This chapter was subsequently published in *Econometrica* in April 1941, and as Chapter 9 in his enormously influential 1947 work *Foundations of Economic*

---

[54] Lange (1938, 12n1). Also see Patinkin (1990, 214).

[55] Davidson (2003, 247).

[56] Moggridge (1992, 594). Also see Presley (1979, 200), Fletcher (1987, 55, 79, 126; 2008, 190), Patinkin (1990, 214), Meltzer (1992, 160), Samuelson (1996, 164), Barens (1999, 85), King (2002, 31), and Cord (2012, 106).

[57] Shibata (1937, 95).

Table 6.4 Early IS-LM models—standard notation based on Keynes 1933

Author	Date	Goods market equilibrium	Consumption/ saving function	Investment function	Money market equilibrium
Keynes	December 1933	$Y = C + I$	$C = \phi_1(w, Y)$	$I = \phi_2(w, \rho)$	$M = A(w, \rho)$
Keynes	Spring 1934	$Y = C + I$	$C = \phi_1(Y)$	$I = \phi_2(w, \rho)$	$M = A(\rho)$
Keynes	Summer 1934	$Y = C + I$	$C = \phi_1(Y)$	$I = \phi_2(\rho, MEC)$	$M = A(\rho)$
Champernowne	June 1936	$S = I$	$S = \phi_1(Y, \rho)$	$I = \phi_2(Y, w, \rho)$	$M = A(Y, \rho)$
Reddaway	June 1936	$S = Y - C$	$S = \phi_1(Y)$	$I = \phi_2(Y, \rho, MEC)$	$M = A(Y, \rho)$
Harrod	January1937	$Y = C + I$	$S = \phi_1(Y, \rho)$	$I = \phi_2(\rho, MEC)$	$M = A(Y, \rho)$
Meade	February 1937	$Y = C + I$	$S = \phi_1(Y, \rho)$	$I = \phi_2(\rho, MEC)$	$M = A(Y, \rho)$
Hicks	April 1937	$Y = C + I$	$S = \phi_1(Y, \rho)$	$I = \phi_2(\rho, MEC)$	$M = A(Y, \rho)$
Shibata	July 1937	$Y = C + I$	$C = \phi_1(Y)$	$I = \phi_2(\rho, MEC)$	$M = A(\rho)$
Lange	February 1938	$Y \equiv C + I$	$C = \phi_1(Y, \rho)$	$I = \phi_2(\rho, MEC, C)$	$M = A(Y, \rho)$
Samuelson	1940	$Y = C + I$	$C = \phi_1(Y, \rho)$	$I = \phi_2(Y, \rho, MEC)$	$M = A(Y, \rho)$
Timlin	1942	$Y = C + I$	$C = \phi_1(Y, \rho)$	$I = \phi_2(\rho, MEC, C)$	$M = A(Y, \rho)$
Modigliani	1944	$S = I$	$S = \phi_1(Y, \rho)$	$I = \phi_2(Y, \rho, MEC)$	$M = A(Y, \rho)$
Klein	1944	$Y = C + I$	$C = \phi_1(Y)$	$I = \phi_2(\rho, MEC)$	$M = A(Y, \rho)$
Hansen	1949	$Y = C + I$	$C = \phi_1(Y)$	$I = \phi_2(\rho, MEC)$	$M = A(Y, \rho)$

Note 1 Y = income, C = consumption, I = investment, w = state of news (expectations or confidence), ρ = interest rate, M = quantity of money, A = liquidity preference (money demand), MEC = marginal efficiency of capital

Note 2 Keynes was first to arrive at $M = A(Y, \rho)$. This appears in the mid-1935 draft (GTE/6/3/29), the 1935 lectures (1932–35, L29), and the *General Theory* (1936, 199)

Note 3 Y and ρ are in real terms for Lange, Timlin, Modigliani, Klein, and Hansen. Since IS-LM is a fixed-price model, however, real income equals nominal income and the real interest rate equals the nominal interest rate

Note 4 For Lange and Timlin, since $C = C(Y, \rho)$, the investment equation $I = I(\rho, MEC, C)$ can be recast as $I = I(Y, \rho, MEC)$

Sources Samuelson (1940, 217; 1941, 114; 1947, 276),Timlin (1942, 8), Modigliani (1944,46), Klein (1944, 74, 80–82), and Hansen (1949, 61, 72)

Analysis.[58] In the 1941 paper and 1947 book, Samuelson aligns his IS-LM equations with "Meade, Hicks, and Lange."[59] Again, Keynes endorsed these papers. A cursory look at Tables 6.4 and 6.5 might suggest the investment function in Samuelson's paper is slightly different than Lange's, for it includes income rather than consumption. But as noted in Table 6.1, income is implicit in Lange's investment function, since consumption is a function of income. Therefore, Keynes's direct endorsement

[58] For example, Robert E. Lucas recalled, "Samuelson's *Foundations* was a big influence when I started graduate school. His book was just a bible for my generation of economists" (2005, 274; 2014, 215).

[59] Samuelson (1940, 216; 1941, 113; 1947, 276).

Table 6.5 Early IS-LM models—standard notation based on Hansen 1949

Author	Date	Goods market equilibrium	Consumption/ saving function	Investment function	Money market equilibrium
Keynes	December 1933	Y = C + I	C = C(Y, E)	I = I(i, E)	M = L(i, E)
Keynes	Spring 1934	Y = C + I	C = C(Y)	I = I(i, E)	M = L(i)
Keynes	Summer 1934	Y = C + I	C = C(Y)	I = I(i, MEC)	M = L(i)
Champernowne	June 1936	S = I	S = S(Y, i)	I = I (Y, i, E)	M = L(i, E)
Reddaway	June 1936	S = Y − C	S = S(Y)	I = I(Y, i, MEC)	M = L(i, Y)
Harrod	January1937	Y = C + I	S = S(Y, i)	I = I(i, MEC)	M = L(i, Y)
Meade	February 1937	Y = C + I	S = S(Y, i)	I = I(i, MEC)	M = L(i, Y)
Hicks	April 1937	Y = C + I	S = S(Y, i)	I = I(i, MEC)	M = L(i, Y)
Shibata	July 1937	Y = C + I	C = C(Y)	I = I(i, MEC)	M = L(i)
Lange	February 1938	Y ≡ C + I	C = C(Y, i)	I = I(i, MEC, C)	M = L(i, Y)
Samuelson	1940	Y = C + I	C = C(Y, i)	I = I(Y, i, MEC)	M = L(i, Y)
Timlin	1942	Y = C + I	C = C(Y, i)	I = I(i, MEC, C)	M = L(i, Y)
Modigliani	1944	S = I	S = S(Y, i)	I = I(Y, i, MEC)	M = L(i, Y)
Klein	1944	Y = C + I	C = C(Y)	I = I(i, MEC)	M = L(i, Y)
Hansen	1949	Y = C + I	C = C(Y)	I = I(i, MEC)	M = L(i, Y)

Note 1 Y = income, C = consumption, I = investment, E = expectations (state of news or confidence), i = interest rate, M = quantity of money, L = liquidity preference (money demand), MEC = marginal efficiency of capital
Note 2 Keynes was first to arrive at M = L(i, Y). This appears in the mid-1935 draft (GTE/6/3/29), the 1935 lectures (1932–35, L29), and the *General Theory* (1936, 199)
Note 3 Y and i are in real terms for Lange, Timlin, Modigliani, Klein, and Hansen. Since IS-LM is a fixed-price model, however, real income equals nominal income and the real interest rate equals the nominal interest rate
Note 4 For Lange and Timlin, since C = C(Y, i), the investment equation I = I(i, MEC, C) can be recast as I = I(Y, i, MEC)
Sources Samuelson (1940, 217; 1941, 114; 1947,276), Timlin (1942, 8), Modigliani (1944, 46), Klein (1944, 74, 80–82), and Hansen (1949, 61, 72)

of Lange's paper might also be viewed as an indirect endorsement of Samuelson's influential IS-LM equational approach to the *General Theory*.

Like Shibata, Mabel Timlin's work *The Keynesian Revolution* (1941) is neglected. As Tables 6.4 and 6.5 indicate, however, Timlin provides the same set of IS-LM equations found in Lange. And she defends her interpretation by noting "Mr. Keynes's

Table 6.6 Shibata (1937)

Component	Equation
Consumption function	$D_1 = \psi(N)$
Investment function	$D_2 = F(E, r)$
Liquidity preference	$M = L(r)$
Effective demand	$D_1 + D_2 = \phi(N)$

Note D_1 = consumption, D_2 = investment, N = employment, E = marginal efficiency of capital, r = interest rate, M = quantity of money, L = liquidity preference

approval of Dr. Lange's 'general system' as an analysis of his own."[60] Thus Keynes indirectly endorsed Timlin via Lange. Furthermore, Benjamin Higgins reports that he had a copy of Bryce's notes from Keynes's lectures, and he shared the notes with Timlin.[61] Hence Timlin was well positioned to confirm Lange's equational approach is not a bastardization of Keynes's theory.

Franco Modigliani's "Liquidity Preference and the Theory of Interest and Money" (1944) is one of the most influential papers in the history of the Keynesian Revolution and the Neoclassical Synthesis.[62] The paper opens with references to Hicks and Lange, and he later refers readers to Timlin.[63] Indeed, Modigliani was a member of Lange's seminar in 1939-40, and he learned Keynesian economics from Lange: "[Jacob] Marschak invited me to take part in a seminar organized in New York by Oskar Lange, the noted Polish economist at that time."[64] Although he uses a saving function rather than a consumption function, Modigliani's basic IS-LM equational system closely parallels Samuelson's and, by extension, Lange's. Therefore, Keynes's direct endorsement of Lange might be seen as an indirect endorsement of Modigliani's basic IS-LM system.

Lawrence Klein wrote his doctoral dissertation *The Keynesian Revolution* (1944) under Paul Samuelson. In a footnote, Klein mentions that he had a copy of Bryce's notes from Keynes's lectures: "A copy of some unpublished notes by R.B. Bryce, who was then at Cambridge, has been provided to me."[65] Beyond that, he praised Reddaway's IS-LM approach: "Reddaway's article, on the other hand, was one of the best reviews of the book. This writer saw quite clearly the fundamental contributions

---

[60] Timlin (1942, 8n2).

[61] Higgins (1992, 9).

[62] Patinkin refers to the IS-LM model as the "Hicks-Modigliani IS-LM model" (1976, 76). Luigi Pasinetti writes, "Franco Modigliani's 1944 *Econometrica* formulations, jointly with J.R. Hicks IS-LM model (Hicks, 1937), set the pattern for the way Keynes's *General Theory* has been adapted and taught to a whole generation of post-war economics students" (2005, 36).

[63] Modigliani (1944, 45, 50n9).

[64] Modigliani (2001, 19, 165). Marschak hosted the famous September 1936 Econometric Society meeting in Oxford where Harrod, Meade, and Hicks presented their IS-LM papers. Modigliani and Patinkin were Marschak's doctoral students. See Hagemann (2017), Dimand and Hagemann (2020 and Dimand (2020) for more on Modigliani's association with Marschak and Lange.

[65] Klein (1944, 55n1; 1947, 42n10).

of the new economics and was one of the first to be able to formulate a mathematical model of the skeleton system."[66] All this shows that Klein's IS-LM equational system has links to Keynes's lectures. Finally, Klein lists Lange as one of the "friends and colleagues [who] have read the manuscript and have made important suggestions and criticisms."[67]

In his book *Monetary Theory and Fiscal Policy* (1949), Alvin Hansen provides the IS-LM equations that are now the standard representation of the *General Theory*. Although certainly a misnomer, the IS-LM model is now commonly referred to as the "Hicks–Hansen model." As Tables 6.4 and 6.5 show, Hansen's IS-LM equations are identical to Klein's, and Klein's equational system has definite links to Keynes's lectures and the officially endorsed IS-LM papers of Reddaway, Hicks, and Lange. In summary, the IS-LM equations standardized by Hansen can be traced directly to Keynes's own December 1933 IS-LM approach and the early IS-LM papers Keynes explicitly endorsed.

To conclude, Keynes consistently endorsed the IS-LM interpretation after the *General Theory* was published, and his endorsements are interrelated. Tables 6.4 and 6.5 show that Lange's equational system was basically the same as Keynes's 1933 system. As Lange recognized, however, Reddaway, Hicks, and Harrod provided very similar IS-LM equational systems. Tables 6.4 and 6.5 confirm this. Thus Keynes's direct endorsement of one IS-LM paper can be viewed as an indirect endorsement of every other. In fact, given the Lange–Keynes nexus, Keynes was in effect reaffirming his own December 1933 IS-LM approach each time he endorsed an IS-LM paper. His forceful public endorsement of Lange's article was key, though, for this paper played an immense role with key figures of the Neoclassical Synthesis: Samuelson, Modigliani, and Klein.

References

Barens, I. (1999). From Keynes to Hicks—an aberration? IS-LM and the analytical nucleus of the General Theory. In P. Howitt, E. de Antoni, A. Leijonhufvud (Eds.), *Money, markets, and method: essays in honour of Robert W* (pp. 85–120). *Clower*. Edward Elgar.

Bryce, R. B. (1996). Interview with Robert Bryce. In D. C. Colander, H. Landreth (Eds.), *The coming of Keynesianism to America* (pp. 39–48). Edward Elgar.

Champernowne, D. G. (1936). Unemployment, basic and monetary: The classical analysis and the Keynesian. *The Review of Economic Studies, 3*(3), 201–216.

Cord, R. (2012). *Reinterpreting the Keynesian revolution*. Routledge.

Davidson, P. (2003). Setting the record straight on a history of post Keynesian economics. *Journal of Post Keynesian Economics, 26*(2), 245–272.

Davidson, P. (2005). Responses to Lavoie, King, and Dow on what post Keynesianism is and who is a post Keynesian. *Journal of Post Keynesian Economics, 27*(3), 393–408.

Davidson, P. (2007). *John Maynard Keynes*. Palgrave Macmillan.

Dimand, R. W. (1988). *The origins of the Keynesian revolution*. Stanford University Press.

---

[66] Klein (1944, 115; 1947, 92).

[67] Klein (1947, ix).

Dimand, R. W. (1994). Mr Meade's relation, Kahn's multiplier, and the chronology of the general theory. *The Economic Journal, 104*(426), 1138–1142.

Dimand, R. W. (2007). Keynes, IS-LM, and the Marshallian tradition. *History of Political Economy, 39*(1), 81–95.

Dimand, R. W. (2019). Lectures on the monetary theory of production and the general theory of employment. In R. W. Dimand & H. Hagemann (Eds.), *The elgar companion to John Maynard Keynes* (pp. 181–185). Edward Elgar.

Dimand, R. W. (2020). Keynesian economics at the cowles commission. *The Review of Keynesian Studies, 2*, 22–45.

Dimand, R. W., & Hagemann, H. (2020). Jacob Marschak and the cowles approaches to the theory of money and assets. *The European Journal of the History of Economic Thought, 27*(6), 901–918.

Fletcher, G. A. (1987). *The Keynesian revolution and its critics*. Macmillan.

Fletcher, G. A. (2008). *Dennis Robertson*. Palgrave Macmillan.

Galbraith, J. K. (1987). Keynes, Roosevelt, and the complementary revolutions. *Challenge, 30*(6), 19–23.

Galbraith, J. K. (1996). Interview with John Kenneth Galbraith. In D. C. Colander & H. Landreth (Eds.), *The coming of Keynesianism to America* (pp. 131–143). Edward Elgar.

Galbraith, J. K. (1998). John Maynard Keynes: From retrospect to prospect. *Journal of Post Keynesian Economics, 21*(1), 11–13.

Hagemann, H. (2017). Franco Modigliani as American Keynesian: How the university in exile economists influenced economics. *Social Research, 4*(40), 955–985.

Hansen, A. H. (1949). *Monetary theory and fiscal policy*. McGraw Hill.

Harcourt, G. C. (1986). *Controversies in political economy: Selected essays of G.C. Harcourt*. New York University Press.

Harcourt, G. C. (2012). *On Skidelsky's Keynes and other essays: Selected essays of G.C.* Harcourt. Palgrave Macmillan.

Harrod, R. F. (1937). *Mr. Keynes and Traditional Theory. Econometrica, 5*(1), 74–86.

Harrod, R. F. (1951). *The life of John Maynard Keynes*. Macmillan.

Hayek, F. A. (1941). *The pure theory of capital*. Chicago University Press.

Hicks, J. R. (1937). Mr. Keynes and the 'Classics': A suggested interpretation. *Econometrica, 5*(2), 147–159.

Hicks, J. R. (1950). *A contribution to the theory of the trade cycle*. Oxford University Press.

Hicks, J. R. (1967). *Critical essays in monetary theory*. Oxford University Press.

Hicks, J. R. (1973). Recollections and documents. *Economica, 40*(157), 2–11.

Hicks, J. R. (1974). *The crisis in Keynesian Economics*. Basil Blackwell.

Hicks, J. R. (1976). Some questions of time in economics. In A. M. Tang, F. M. Westerfield, & J. S. Worley (Eds.), *Evolution, welfare and time in economics* (pp. 135–151). Lexington Books.

Hicks, J. R. (1977). *Economic perspectives: Further essays on money and growth*. Clarendon Press.

Hicks, J. R. (1979). *Causality in economics*. Basic Books.

Hicks, J. R. (1981). IS-LM: An explanation. *Journal of Post Keynesian Economics, 3*(2), 139–154.

Hicks, J. R. (1984). Time in economics. In D. Helm (Ed.), *The economics of John Hicks* (pp. 263–280). Basil Blackwell.

Higgins, B. (1992). *All the difference: A development economist's quest*. McGill-Queen's University Press.

Howson, S., & Moggridge, D. E. (1990). *The wartime diaries of Lionel Robbins and James Meade, 1943–45*. St. Martin's Press.

Johnson, E. S., & Johnson, H. G. (1978). *The shadow of Keynes: Understanding Keynes, Cambridge, and Keynesian economics*. University of Chicago Press.

Keynes, J. M. (CW). *The collected writings of John Maynard Keynes* (vol. 1–30). Macmillan and Cambridge University Press for the Royal Economic Society.

Keynes, J. M. (1932–35). Keynes's lectures, 1932–35: Notes of students. In T. K. Rymes (Ed.), unpublished typescript. Carleton University (1988).

Kahn, R. F. (1931). The relation of home investment to unemployment. *The Economic Journal, 41*(162), 173–198.

Kahn, R. F. (1984). *The making of Keynes' general theory*. Cambridge University Press.

King, J. E. (2002). *A history of post Keynesian economics since 1936*. Edward Elgar.

Klein, L. R. (1944). *The Keynesian revolution*. Dissertation, Massachusetts Institute of Technology.

Klein, L. R. (1947). *The Keynesian revolution*. Macmillan.

Laidler, D. E. (1999). *Fabricating the Keynesian revolution*. Cambridge University Press.

Lange, O. R. (1938). The rate of interest and the optimum propensity to consume. *Economica, 5*(17), 12–32.

Lucas, R. E. (2005). Interview with Robert E. Lucas Jr. In B. Snowdon & H. R. Vane (Eds.), *Modern macroeconomics: Its origins, development and current state* (pp. 272–293). Edward Elgar.

Lucas, R. E. (2014). Robert E. Lucas, Jr. In R. W. Spencer & D. A. Macpherson (Eds.), *Lives of the laureates: Twenty-three Nobel economists* (pp. 208–232). The MIT Press.

Meade, J. E. (1933). *Public works in their international aspect*. The New Fabian Research Bureau.

Meade, J. E. (1937). A simplified model of Mr. Keynes' system. *The Review of Economic Studies, 4*(2), 98–107.

Meade, J. E. (1993). The relation of Mr Meade's relation to Kahn's multiplier. *The Economic Journal, 103*(418), 664–665.

Meltzer, A. H. (1988). *Keynes's monetary theory: A different interpretation*. Cambridge University Press.

Meltzer, A. H. (1992). Patinkin on Keynes and Meltzer. *Journal of Monetary Economics, 29*, 151–162.

Modigliani, F. (1944). Liquidity preference and the theory of interest and money. *Econometrica, 12*(1), 45–88.

Modigliani, F. (2001). *Adventures of an economist*. Texere.

Moggridge, D. E. (1992). *Maynard Keynes: An economist's biography*. Routledge.

Patinkin, D. (1990). On different interpretations of the general theory. *Journal of Monetary Economics, 26*, 205–243.

Presley, J. R. (1979). *Robertsonian economics: An examination of the work of Sir D.H. Robertson on industrial fluctuation*. Holmes and Meier.

Reddaway, W. B. (1936). The general theory of employment, interest and money. *Economic Record, 12*, 28–36.

Robinson, J. V. (1937). *Introduction to the theory of employment*. Macmillan.

Robinson, J. V. (1947). *Essays in the theory of employment*. Macmillan.

Robinson, J. V. (1978). Keynes and Ricardo. *Journal of Post Keynesian Economics, 1*(1), 12–18.

Rubin, G. (2016). Oskar Lange and the Walrasian interpretation of IS-LM. *Journal of the History of Economic Thought, 38*(3), 285–309.

Rymes, T. K. (1989). *Keynes's lectures, 1932–35: Notes of a representative student*. Macmillan.

Samuelson, P. A. (1940). *Foundations of analytical economics*. Dissertation, Harvard University.

Samuelson, P. A. (1941). The stability of equilibrium: Comparative statics and dynamics. *Econometrica, 9*(2), 97–120.

Samuelson, P. A. (1947). *Foundations of economic analysis*. Harvard University Press.

Samuelson, P. A. (1988). In the beginning. *Challenge, 31*(4), 32–34.

Samuelson, P. A. (1996). Interview with Paul Samuelson. In D. C. In Colander & H. Landreth (Eds.), *The coming of Keynesianism to America* (pp. 145–178). Edward Elgar.

Shibata, K. (1937). Some questions on Mr. Keynes' general theory of employment, interest and money. *Kyoto University Economic Review, 12*(1), 83–96.

Skidelsky, R. (1992). *John Maynard Keynes: The economist as savior, 1920–1937*. Viking.

Skidelsky, R. (2005). Interview with Robert Skidelsky. In B. Snowdon & H. R. Vane (Eds.), *Modern macroeconomics: Its origins, development and current state* (pp. 91–100). Edward Elgar.

Solow, R. M. (1984). Mr Hicks and the classics. *Oxford Economic Papers, 36*, 13–25.

Solow, R. M. (1991). Keynes's lectures. *The Economic Journal, 101*(407), 971–972.

Tarshis, L. (1996). Interview with Lorie Tarshis. In D. C. Colander & H. Landreth (Eds.), *The coming of Keynesianism to America* (pp. 49–72). Edward Elgar.
Timlin, M. (1942). *Keynesian economics.* The University of Toronto Press.
Young, W. (1987). *Interpreting Mr. Keynes: The IS-LM enigma.* Polity Press.
Young, W. (1989). *Harrod and his trade cycle group.* Palgrave Macmillan.

Chapter 7
The Legacy of December 1933: Re-interpreting Mr. Keynes

Up to now, our narrative, for the most part, has been concerned with an overlooked page of equations and scribbled text by perhaps the best-known economist of the modern era: John Maynard Keynes. Indeed, when put in the context of the outcome of a misfiled letter from one future Nobel laureate in Economics to another, Hicks to Meade, regarding interpretational exposition of Keynes's approach to the economy—as dealt with by Young in *Interpreting Mr Keynes*—this overlooked document acquires cardinal importance. It was the basis for Keynes own December 1933 IS-LM approach and thus requires a re-interpretation of Keynes.[1]

But what was the impact, or legacy, of Keynes's simple equational approach of December 1933? When viewed in the retrospect of almost a century of analysis regarding both national and international economic processes from the theoretical and policy perspective, it becomes clear just how important the IS-LM framework set out by Keynes in December 1933 was to be. It was the foundation stone for much that became, and still is, macroeconomics, albeit, after its extension, augmentation, and transformation. The metamorphosis from Keynes's own December 1933 equation system to more sophisticated expositions occurred in stages, via alternate routes, with some being less and others more successful in sustaining their central messages.

Two papers stand out as best reflecting what we call the "Legacy of December 1933." The first is a paper by Hicks published in French in *Revue d'Economie Politique*, and it has never been translated to our knowledge.[2] This 1945 paper, entitled "The *General Theory* after Nine Years," served as a retrospective and prospective for Hicks, as it looked back at his changing views regarding Keynes's system, evolving from "depression economics" to that of near "full employment." Here, he presented his own new "dynamic" approach to Keynes's system, as will be seen in Table 7.1.[3]

[1] On Hicks's misfiled letter to Meade, see Young (1987, 35).

[2] Hicks (1945).

[3] Hicks (1945, 2).

W. Young and E. W. Fuller, *Reinterpreting Mr. Keynes*,
Springer Studies in the History of Economic Thought,
https://doi.org/10.1007/978-3-030-91342-7_7

Table 7.1 Early dynamic IS-LM models

Author	Date	Goods market equilibrium	Consumption/ saving function	Investment function	Money market equilibrium
Samuelson	1940	$Y_t = C_t + I_t$	$C_t = C(i_t, Y_{t-1})$	$I_t = F(Y_t, i_t)$	$M = L(Y_t, i_t)$
Klein	1944	$Y_t = C_t + I_t$	$C_t = C(r_t, Y_{t-1})$	$I_t = I(Y_t, r_t)$	$M = L(Y_t, r_t)$
Modigliani	1944	$Y_t = Y_{t-1} - S_t + I_t$	$S_t = S(Y_{t-1}, r_t)$	$I_t = I(Y_{t-1}, r_t)$	$M = L(r_t, Y_{t-1})$
Hicks	1945	$Y_{n+1} = C_{n+1} + In$	$C_{n+1} = C(Y_n)$	$I_n = I(Y_n, i_n)$	$M = L(Y_n, i_n)$

Note Y = income, C = consumption, I = investment, i and r = interest rate, M = quantity of money, L = liquidity preference (money demand), S = savings. In Samuelson, i_t is constant (1940, 223)
Sources Samuelson (1940, 224–226), Klein (1944, 141), Modigliani (1944, 25), Hicks (1945, 6–7)

The second paper is Patinkin's "In Defense of IS-LM."[4] Here, as in Hicks's 1945 paper, Patinkin set out a retrospective and prospective for the IS-LM approach to Keynes. It encompassed areas where IS-LM was applied to "prices and inflation"—that is, the debate in the 1970s between Friedman and Tobin conducted in IS-LM term.[5] Additionally, Patinkin addressed "international economics," where the IS-LM system was applied to the open economy by Fleming and Mundell.[6] Finally, Patinkin mentioned "aggregate supply and demand" (AS-AD) as manifest in the metamorphosis of IS-LM into this type of analysis.

Interestingly enough, only a decade or so after IS-LM type approaches became popular, an early development of AS-AD by Marschak and Brownlee occurred. It is worth noting, however, that these early works on AS-AD did not impact the textbooks or theorists, as in the case of IS-LM.[7]

When the IS-LM/AS-AD approach gained traction, it became the focus for the cleavage between the Old Keynesian approaches and the developing New Classical Model (NCM) based upon the work of Lucas, Sargent, and Wallace, among others.[8] Thus, a temporary displacement of IS-LM from the core of macroeconomics occurred.[9] A New Keynesian Model (NMK) emerged from the late 1970s to the early 1990s, and all of these works were essentially extensions of IS-LM.[10] Indeed, as King put it, "New Keynesian macroeconomics has pushed the idea that traditional IS-LM analysis remains the best way to think about the determination of aggregate demand."[11] With the cross-cutting cleavage of rational expectations, however,

---

[4] Patinkin (1987).

[5] See Friedman (1970, 1972) and Tobin (1972). Gordon (1974) prepared a useful volume on the debate.

[6] See Fleming (1962) and Mundell (1963).

[7] See Brownlee (1950) and Marschak (1951). Although second by publication date, Marschak presented his analysis earlier in his 1948 and 1949 lectures at the University of Chicago.

[8] See Lucas (1972) and Sargent and Wallace (1975, 1976).

[9] Lucas declared in 1980, "Keynesian economics is dead" (2013, 500).

[10] See Fischer (1977), Phelps and Taylor (1977), Gordon (1978, 1990), Fischer and Dornbusch (1978), Taylor (1980), Mankiw (1985, 1990, 1992) and Mankiw and Romer (1991).

[11] King (1993, 80).

a convergence of NCM and NKM started to emerge. This convergence, and IS-LM, became the core of the "New Neoclassical Synthesis," or "New IS-LM Model," as attested to by King, Goodfriend, and others.[12]

On the other hand, Romer proposed doing away with LM and proposed a monetary policy function in its place.[13] Krugman, for his part, defended the IS-LM framework at this time.[14] Romer's position gained traction with the publication of Woodford's 2003 work *Interest and Prices*.[15] This position advocated what could be termed an IS/Interest-Rate-Rule/AS framework, where the financial markets are cleared via price rather than LM. Woodford contended this model approach had been adopted by Central Banks, although it did not appear as of then in undergraduate or graduate textbooks. This was ostensibly "corrected" at the undergraduate and graduate levels by the IS/Phillips-Curve/Monetary-Policy-Rule approach of Carlin and Soskice, among others.[16]

Be this as it may, thus far we have been discussing the static approach to the IS-LM equations of Keynes's December 1933 document. But what of the dynamic approach? This originated, again, as seen in Table 7.1, with Samuelson and proceeded through Klein, Modigliani, and Hicks, to Blanchard and Fischer.[17] The dynamic approach to IS-LM continued in the NKM via the "dynamic IS-LM equation" (including actual and expected output gaps and inflation rates) at its core, as expressed in Woodford and Galí.[18]

One final element regarding the legacy of Keynes's December 1933 IS-LM equations remains: their application as the basis for the development of what Klein called "Statistical Models," or econometric models of the macroeconomy. Now, following on from his 1944 thesis, in January 1946, a decade after the publication of Keynes's *General Theory*, Klein presented "A Macroeconomic System, USA, 1921–1941" at the Cleveland meeting of the Econometric Society. As he put it, "a statistical model of the structure of the US economy can be developed from the established theories of household and firm behavior and fitted to the data of the interwar period." He then proposed what he called "a plausible model" consisting of twelve equations and four definitions, including consumption ("demand for consumer goods"), investment and inventory ("demand for private plant and equipment," "demand for inventory"), labor ("demand for labor"), and money demand and supply, among other equations.[19]

---

[12] See Goodfriend and King (1997) and King (2000).

[13] Romer (2000).

[14] Krugman (2000).

[15] Woodford (2003).

[16] Carlin and Soskice (2005).

[17] See Samuelson (1940), Klein (1944), Modigliani (1944), Hicks (1945), Blanchard (1981), and Blanchard and Fischer (1989).

[18] Woodford (2003) and Galí (2015, 2018).

[19] Klein (1946, 159–162).

A year later, Klein published a paper in the *Journal of Political Economy* entitled "Theories of Effective Demand and Unemployment," an explicit extension of "the ideas on Keynesian economics."[20] This would appear in his "forthcoming book" on the Keynesian revolution, a book based upon his 1944 MIT PhD dissertation supervised by Samuelson. In his influential 1947 book *The Keynesian Revolution*, he fleshed out his "statistical modeling" (econometric) approach to "Keynesian economics."[21] In 1950, in his Cowles research monograph *Economic Fluctuations in the United States, 1921–1941*, Klein finally published what he called "the complete system" in the chapter entitled "Statistical Models."[22]

Thus, less than two decades after Keynes developed his December 1933 IS-LM equation system, it had metamorphasized—not only by expansion and amendment, but also by means of parameterization and estimation—into the "statistical models" set out by Klein. It eventually developed into Old Keynesian macroeconometric models of the 1960s and 1970s, which were supplanted by DSGE models of NKM vintage later on—albeit DSGE with the core of the "New IS-LM." But that is another story. Keynes's own December 1933 IS-LM equations, therefore, are the key to understanding the history of both the Old and the New Macroeconomics.

References

Blanchard, O. (1981). Output, the stock market, and interest rates. *The American Economic Review, 71*(1), 132–143.

Blanchard, O., & Fischer, S. (1989). *Lectures on macroeconomics*. MIT Press.

Brownlee, O. (1950). The theory of employment and stabilization policy. *Journal of Political Economy, 58*(5), 412–424.

Carlin, W., & Soskice, D. W. (2005). *Macroeconomics: Imperfections, institutions, and policies*. Oxford University Press.

Dornbusch, R., & Fischer, S. (1978). *Macroeconomics*. McGraw-Hill.

Fischer, S. (1977). Long-term contracts, rational expectations, and the optimal money supply rule. *Journal of Political Economy, 85*(1), 191–205.

Fleming, J. M. (1962). Domestic financial policies under fixed and floating exchange rates. *Staff Papers, International Monetary Fund, 9*, 369–379.

Friedman, M. (1970). A theoretical framework for monetary analysis. *Journal of Political Economy, 78*(2), 193–238.

Friedman, M. (1972). Comments on the critics. *Journal of Political Economy, 80*(5), 906–950.

Galí, J. (2015). *Monetary policy, inflation, and the business cycle: An introduction to the new Keynesian framework*. Princeton University Press.

Galí, J. (2018). The state of new Keynesian economics: A partial assessment. *Journal of Economic Perspectives, 32*(3), 87–112.

---

[20] Klein (1947a, 108).

[21] Klein (1947b). Lucas describes Klein's *The Keynesian Revolution* as "a pretty nice little book" and reports: "So, when I think of Keynesian economics or at least the Keynesian economics I signed on for, it was part of this econometric model-building tradition" (2004, 15, 22).

[22] Klein (1950, 101–105).

Goodfriend, M., & King, R. G. (1997). The new neoclassical synthesis and the role of monetary policy. In B. S. Bernanke & J. J. Rotemberg (Eds.), *NBER macroeconomics annual 1997* (pp. 182–231). MIT Press.

Gordon, R. J. (1974). *Milton Friedman's monetary framework: A debate with his critics*. The University of Chicago Press.

Gordon, R. J. (1978). What can stabilization policy achieve? *American Economic Review, 68*(2), 335–341.

Gordon, R. J. (1990). What is New-Keynesian economics? *Journal of Economic Literature, 28*(3), 1115–1171.

Hicks, J. R. (1945). La théorie de Keynes aprés neuf ans. *Revue D'économie Politique, 55*, 1–11.

King, R. G. (1993). Will the new Keynesian macroeconomics resurrect the IS-LM model? *The Journal of Economic Perspectives, 7*(1), 67–82.

King, R. G. (2000). The new IS-LM model: Language, logic, and limits. *Federal Reserve Bank of Richmond Economic Quarterly, 86*(3), 45–103.

Klein, L. R. (1944). *The Keynesian revolution*. Dissertation, Massachusetts Institute of Technology.

Klein, L. R. (1946). A macroeconomic system, USA, 1921–1941. *Econometrica, 14*(2), 159–162.

Klein, L. R. (1947a). Theories of effective demand and employment. *Journal of Political Economy, 55*(2), 108–131.

Klein, L. R. (1947b). *The Keynesian revolution*. Macmillan.

Klein, L. R. (1950). *Economic fluctuations in the United States, 1921–1941*. John Wiley & Sons.

Krugman, P. (2000). How complicated does the model have to be? *Oxford Review of Economic Policy, 16*(4), 33–42.

Lucas, R. E. (1972). Expectations and the neutrality of money. *Journal of Economic Theory, 4*(2), 103–124.

Lucas, R. E. (2004). My Keynesian education. In M. De Vroey & K. D. Hoover (Eds.), *The IS-LM model: Its rise, fall, and strange persistence* (pp. 12–24). Duke University Press.

Lucas, R. E. (2013). The death of Keynesian economics. In M. Gillman (Ed.), *Collected papers on monetary theory* (pp. 500–503). Harvard University Press.

Mankiw, N. G. (1985). Small menu costs and large business cycles: A macroeconomic model of monopoly. *The Quarterly Journal of Economics, 100*(2), 529–537.

Mankiw, N. G. (1990). A quick refresher course in macroeconomics. *Journal of Economic Literature, 28*(4), 1645–1660.

Mankiw, N. G. (1992). The reincarnation of Keynesian Economics. *European Economic Review, 36*(2–3), 559–565.

Mankiw, N. G., & Romer, D. (1991). *New Keynesian economics*. MIT Press.

Marschak, J. (1951). *Income, employment, and the price level: Notes on lectures given at the University of Chicago, Autumn 1948 and 1949*. Augustus M. Kelley.

Modigliani, F. (1944). Liquidity preference and the theory of interest and money. *Econometrica, 12*(1), 45–88.

Mundell, R. A. (1963). Capital mobility and stabilization policy under fixed and flexible exchange rates. *The Canadian Journal of Economics and Political Science, 29*(4), 475–485.

Patinkin, D. (1987). *In defense of IS-LM*. UCLA Economics Working Papers 537.

Phelps, E. S., & Taylor, J. B. (1977). Stabilizing powers of monetary policy under rational expectations. *Journal of Political Economy, 85*(1), 163–190.

Romer, D. (2000). Keynesian macroeconomics without the LM curve. *The Journal of Economic Perspectives, 14*(2), 149–169.

Samuelson, P. A. (1940). *Foundations of analytical economics*. Dissertation, Harvard University.

Sargent, T. J., & Wallace, N. (1975). Rational expectations, the optimal monetary instrument and the optimal money supply rule. *Journal of Political Economy, 83*(2), 241–254.

Sargent, T. J., & Wallace, N. (1976). Rational expectations and the theory of economic policy. *Journal of Monetary Economics, 2*(2), 169–183.

Taylor, J. B. (1980). Aggregate dynamics and staggered contracts. *Journal of Political Economy, 88*(1), 1–23.

Tobin, J. (1972). Friedman's theoretical framework. *Journal of Political Economy, 80*(5), 852–863.
Woodford, M. D. (2003). *Interest and prices: Foundations of a theory of monetary policy*. Princeton University Press.
Young, W. (1987). *Interpreting Mr Keynes: The IS-LM enigma.* Polity Press.

Appendix

Robert B. Bryce Notes: December 4, 1933

In the last lecture we covered determinants of investment.

But rate of interest now to be discussed.

Last concept—liquidity preference really "the demand for money"—the way of summing up the eagerness of people to hold their wealth in the form of money rather than other forms.

The decision as to how accumulated savings will be held is a different decision from the volume of saving

Similar apparent freedom of choice—just as the total savings has to add up to the amount of saving—so does the amount of money have to add up to what the banks will give—a man cannot increase his stock of money without influencing others

So in hoarding—the total stock of money cannot increase from one side

"Misguided attempt to carry over the economy of the individual to the economy of the aggregate"

Motives for holding money—as in the *Treatise* income business and savings—but it is really all one pool—better Keynes thinks now not to earmark the money—but to consider the demand to hold money as a net result due to a complex of motives.

The desire to hold money is net result of the income, business, precautionary and speculative motives

1. Income motives depend on usual consideration—length of receipt and disposal interval

2. Business motive is analogous for the businessman—to bridge the gap.

3. Precautionary motive—to provide for contingencies and unforeseen opportunities (should this not come under 4, i.e., speculative motive?)—also against future fixed money payments.

Strength of these three depend not only on business "konjunctur" cycle but also on the facility of overdrawing (borrowing)—important in normal times—also the rate of deposit interest

W. Young and E. W. Fuller, *Reinterpreting Mr. Keynes*, Springer Studies in the History of Economic Thought, https://doi.org/10.1007/978-3-030-91342-7

4. Speculative motive—depends on what Keynes called "state of bearishness"—influenced by estimates of future changes in money value of other forms of wealth

Under these motives individuals and corporations decide how much cash to hold

What is the method by which all those are reconciled with the amount of cash supplied?

(a) When cash held constant (i.e., M is constant) an individual can only increase cash by holding income or selling an asset—either of these affects someone else's cash—hence somebody or another faced with a price [?] decision to reconcile cash desires of the two

The result is that prices must conform to level where those who will give cash are equal to those who take cash

The level of prices influences persons' desire to hold cash. Prices will fall or rise to level where the amount of cash is in conformity with supply and desires.

Where all members of the community are alike—the change of price will occur and no movement of cash holdings—but in fact this does not happen—there is a change in cash distribution due to differences between people.

Change in price is the important thing—the movement in cash is less important—in both theory and observed fact—effect of change in news causes more price change than change in volume of sales—"people are more alike than different."

In the main it is prices which change—changes in distribution of cash even out.

Prices cover three things—commodities, equities and debts

We can lump together commodities and equities—the first being an equity with one quasi-rent only. The value of the equity is composed of the prospective quasi-rent and the rate of interest—the value of debts only of the rate of interest

Both can be affected by the state of the news

In assuming the quantity of money is fixed and to say price levels are decided is to say there is definite scale of quasi-rents and rate of interest

This can all happen if banks regulate interest to keep money constant

But is just as reasonable to assume rate of interest is fixed and money varies—"or it can do a bit of both"

This enables our schedules of liquidity preference to be expressed in three dimensions.

rate of interest—state of news, etc.—then, a determined M quantity of money

$M = A(w, \rho)$

A is the state of liquidity preference

That is, a potentiality of the mind of the public towards holding of cash.

It is the rate of interest which brings the quantity of money into alignment with the state of liquidity preference having regard to the state of the news

We now have the essential determinants of the rate of interest: M, w and A

Hence causes of the rate of interest are from outside

Two former theories—intersecting supply and demand curves of capital—another abortive method is to get it "out of" the marginal productivity of capital

This is Keynes's "quantity equation" parallel with $M = kR$.

From a formal point of view, there is no reason to choose between them

The only reason for preference is that Keynes thinks it is best to relate M to ρ—one can relate M to the magnitude of the national debt or the price of a first folio of Shakespeare—but why would we?

– no formal superiority but Keynes's terms are more relevant to the subsequent analysis

He will omit the elaborations of this.

He will now consider

We have

$Y = C + I$

in given w (In a given state of the news), C is a function of Y [i.e., $C = \phi_1(w, Y)$]

I is a function of w [$I = \phi_2(w, \rho)$]

i.e., $Y = \phi_1(Y) + \phi_2(\rho)$ when w is given

Hence it is largely ρ that is important

Assumption Given w

Definition Suppose N total number of men employed

N_1 producing for consumption

N_2 producing for investment

Assumption propensity to spend and to consume is given

Then $N_1 = f_1(N) \quad N_2 = f_2(\rho)$

$N = f_1(N) + f_2(\rho)$

Given liquidity preference and quantity of money

$f_2(\rho) = f_3(M/W)$ which Keynes can't elaborate

W = money wage rates

In any given w (state of the news), N within the maximum set by the marginal disutility of labour (i.e., under optimum employment) and amount of employment depends on the propensity to consume, liquidity preference and the ratio of money supply to the rate of money wages.

The state of the news is somewhat like the state of confidence.

Keynes thinks he has isolated the relevant things now

It is only by altering one of these things that we can regulate the amount of employment. Full employment is the limiting value given by other considerations.

The equations are only illustrations and are n.g. (no good?). The real tool is a method of thought.

– many other things

An illustration. In the long run, capital must be kept scarce enough to yield quasi-rents by enough to pay (rate of interest). Let one imagine a society well enough equipped that marginal productivity of capital is zero or negative but has a banking system and a ρ (rate of interest) not negative.

As soon as anyone saves entrepreneurs make losses and capital will not be replaced—stock of capital becomes less—stock must fall till prospective quasi-rent becomes equal to rate of interest—roughly.

If all capital alike—it won't begin to be replaced until it is all earning ρ—Hence an oscillation—a cyclical movement in the stationary society—can keep this perpetual oscillation consistent with psychological conditions

The same thing can happen if the rate of interest cannot fall below a given figure—when it is unprofitable to lend below this

Hence oscillatory movement when ρ cannot fall below a given figure and where capital is abundant

(But why would it be necessarily oscillatory—dangers of prolonged unemployment)

In such a community where capital is such that marginal productivity is knocking hard against the minimum rate of interest there is an upper limit to N (employment) and to general prosperity—and an oscillation below that

Keynes belief is we have reached some such thing

The minimum rate of interest is set by doubt as to whether lender will be eventually repaid

If we can reduce this minimum to zero then bank (Central Bank?) can regulate optimum output

Keynes wants to see this gradual reduction of the minimum profitable rate of interest

Hence get rid of troubles of capitalist system

It is even permissible to play with the idea that in past history it is the inability of ρ to fall that has brought down civilization as community gets richer etc.—good

This trouble causes more discontent, of course, than a natural poverty—(full stop)

Alec Cairncross Notes: December 4, 1933

Liquidity preference sums up demand for money. Individual choice must square with provision of money by banking authority (cf., saving).

Instead of splitting up money into various forms of deposits we do better to take aggregate preference for money according to complex of motives whose various strengths determine people's holdings.

(1) Income motive: size and intervals

(2) Business motive: bridging time of receipts/incurring of expenses, general activity of dealing, etc.

(3) Precautionary motive: contingencies/emergencies, unforeseen opportunities for advantageous purchases

Holding of money to meet subsequent liability fixed in terms of money

Cheapness/reliability of obtaining cash by short term borrowing, briskness of business, etc. determine willingness to hold cash. Facilities for getting accommodation very important in abnormal times. Rate of deposit interest as against possible interest elsewhere.

(4) Speculative motive: state of bearishness. Expectations as to future course of prices of securities/goods.

Suppose monetary authority holds money constant. Individual can increase cash (a) by selling some asset or (b) by not spending his income. Whatever course he takes someone is faced with problem: what reduction in price he must make to induce someone to purchase assets/sell (part with) cash. Prices fall to point at which those who wish to increase their cash are as influential as those who wish to diminish theirs. Buyers = sellers. If everyone is similar, change in expectations will simply lead to change in price. As a rule however there will be some displacement of cash as well. This however is incidental to different circumstances of different individuals. (Evens up inequality of response). Commodities: equities (ownership of prospective quasi-rent—commodity is equity whose quasi-rents have only one term): debts. In case of debts only rate of interest enters.

Banking authority can fix quantity of money/let rate of interest adjust itself or vice versa or both in part

$$M = A(w, \rho)$$

w = state of news, ρ = rate of interest,

M = demand for money, A = state of liquidity preference

ρ is determined by other factors

$$Y = C + I$$

$$= \phi 1(w, Y) + \phi 2(w, \rho)$$

$$= \phi 1(Y) + \phi 2(\rho)$$

or level of income depends on the rate of interest

N (total men employed) = N_1 (consumption) + N_2 (investment)

$= f_1(N) + f_2(\rho)$ (Given state of news or of confidence)

and $f_2(\rho) = f_3(M/W)$

(W = rate of wages)

f_1 indicates propensity to consume f_3 indicates liquidity preference

Marvin Fallgatter Notes: December 4, 1933

Last time I completed an analysis of the determinants of the rate of interest, without however showing what determined the interest-rate itself, because the factors themselves depended on the rate, and the circularity was not then avoided. To complete the analysis I must introduce the last of my special concepts, that which I will call the Liquiditive Preference of people, that is, the demand which exists for money rather than another form of wealth. A man may decide, as we saw before, whether to devote his income to purchases for consumption, or to Savings, and in what proportions to divide it between them. Now he has a further decision to make, if he is devoting some to Savings. He is to decide whether to hold his savings in the form of cash or in some form of investment, and in what proportion to divide his Savings between these two.

"As in the previous instance, here too he appears to exercise free choice in this alternative. But here also it is a two-sided question. In the community as a whole, the total money holdings of individuals must be equal to the total quantity of money which the banks have created." In my *Theory of Money* I divided money holdings into three classes, Income Deposits, Business Deposits, and Savings Deposits. Critics have pointed out, and I think justly, that the fund of money is one undivided one, and there is no counterpart in actuality to this division. I am inclined to agree with this criticism. There is no earmarking of money as between these different purposes on the part of the holder. It is better to consider it from the point of view of the motives back of individual desires to hold money. These are four as follows.

1. The income motive. This corresponds with the similar item in the *Treatise on Money*. individuals hold money for the purpose of smoothing out irregularities or intervals in the receipt of income as compared to the routine uses for it. (It is the thing which i would term the flywheel effect.)

2. The Business motive. This is the similar motive in the case of the business man. It is the working capital held for the purpose of tiding over intervals between the receipt of income from sales and operations.

3. The Precautionary motive. One keeps money to provide for contingencies of an unforseen kind; and, one mustn't forget, to take advantage of unforseen opportunities for advantageous purchases; and in order to meet a future fixed obligation.

The strength of each of these three motives depends not only upon the state of trade, but also upon the ease and cheapness of credit; and the rate of deposit interest, and all such matters, in a way which is quite evident.

4. The Speculative motive. This depends upon the state of expectation with regard to the trends of trade, and also upon the expectation as to the trend of the price level. If it is anticipated that prices will fall, one has a motive for holding money, while if it is expected that prices will rise, one will rather tend to hold equities.

Now consider what are the mechanisms by which the aggregate decisions to hold money are made equal to the sum of the money which the banks have created. There are two ways by which an individual can increase his cash holdings: (1) by not spending all of his income, but withholding a part of it. (2) by selling some of his fixed assets which are in the form of some other kind of wealth. Either one of these operations will affect the cash holdings of someone else. For if he fails to spend what he otherwise might have, then the persons from whom he might have bought will have less money; while if he sells some asset, then there must be a buyer who will part with an equal sum of money. So in either case there will be a second party, who will be motivated in the matter of the proposed or consummated transaction, by price considerations. So if people wish to increase their cash holding prices must fall to such a level that the aggregate wishes of the sellers and non-consumers to follow this motive at the lower price, is balanced by the aggregate wishes on the part of others to buy their offerings or to fail to not-buy following their customers' non-consumption.

So it can be said that prices are determined by the Quantity of Money and the Liquidity Preference of the Community.

Consider the simplest case, of a community all of whose members are identical in this respect. Then a change in the state of expectations will cause a change in the price level, but not a redistribution of cash holdings. Actually, since people are not all alike in respect to the effect of the news upon their propensity to hold cash, a displacement of cash holdings will occur. It will require both this displacement, and a change of prices, to bring about a new equilibrium. But the redistribution of cash holdings is accidental, one might say, or incidental; it is the change in price-level which is the important effect.

By "news" or state of expectation, we mean the influence on people's economic actions of such things as the reported developments in such a things as President Roosevelt's unpredictable character. It is becoming quite a stereotyped phrase in the financial columns to say that "the effect on prices was al 1 out of proportion to the justification in the news-item". So the first case is more approximately realized than the other, that is people do, in effect, behave more similarly in respect to their propensity to hold cash than would be expected.

Price levels are made up of three things, altho the first two may be taken together:

1. Commodities. i.e., Q_1
2. Equities. i.e., $\Sigma Q_1 + Q_2 + \ldots$
3. Debts.

Commodities may be regarded as a special case of Equities, those with but a single quasi-rent term. The $d_1, d_2 \ldots$ factors should really be indicated here, of course, and thus both Equities and Debts are concerned with the interest rate, and both of them may be affected by the news. So every state of the news has an Expectation-value and an interest-rate appropriate to it. Suppose that the quantity of money is fixed, as by having the authorities acquiesce in accepting any interest rate ρ such as it will take with the quantity of money remaining constant. Or alternatively, let the interest-rate p be fixed by the authorities, and let the quantity of money adjust itself to this value. Or, the authorities can do a little of both.

Schedules of the Liquidity Propensity can be stated in a three-dimensional form then, a relation between the state of the news and the interest-rate, the Quantity of

Money being taken as the dependent variable. The relation can be written in symbols

$$M = f(w, \rho)$$

where M is the demand for money, f the Liquidity Propensity functional relation, w the state of the news, and ρ the interest rate. We can consider that the potentiality towards holding cash will, in a given condition of monetary supply, bring the rate of interest into conformity with the state of expectation, or that it will, under a prevailing interest-rate, bring the quantity of money into conformity with the state of expectation, or that it will influence the amount of money which the banking system creates, and also the rate of interest.

This is how the rate of interest is determined, according to our present analysis. This is the alternative to the two classical views already discussed and seen to be abortive.

1. The rate of interest is given by the intersection of two curves, the supply of Savings, and the Demand for Capital.

2. The other attempted to get it out of the Marginal Efficiency of Capital, i.e., the Q's. In Marshall's half-hearted attempt, he saw that he was becoming circular. But there are plenty of others who have adopted this view without seeing that it is circular. In the present view we avoid this circularity.

In the *Treatise on Money*, there was an equation on this subject, which I called the Cambridge Equation, which was written

$$M = kR$$

This is a permissible analysis in agreement with the present one, which lumps together Δw and $\Delta \rho$. But then, w lumps together many things, which could perhaps be disentangled if desired. There is always an arbitrariness about such things. You choose an analysis which will disintegrate the things you wish to call attention to. Here the reason for preferring the analysis given, is that there is point to bringing out the fact that $M = f(\rho)$, because this is a fact upon which our monetary system of managing currency is based.

Now with all the materials at hand, let us pursue the analysis. We have that

	$Y = C + I$
We found that	$C = \phi 1(w, Y)$
And	$I = \phi 2(w, \rho)$
So	$Y = \phi 1(Y) + \phi 2(\rho)$

showing that the rate of interest is the determining factor as to the volume of employment or the income of the community in an entrepreneur economy. But a better analysis is this one: Let N be the total employment, N_1 being the number employed in producing consumers goods, and N_2 the number employed in producing investment goods. Then in a given state of the news,

$$N = N_1 + N_2 = f_1(N) + f_2(\rho) + f_3(M/W)$$

for a reason which I cannot go into now, tho I give it to you to think over. This is on the assumption of not full employment. It shows that the quantity of employment is a function of four things:

1. The State of Confidence
2. Previous Consumption
3. The Liquidity Preference
4. The Quantity of Money

This may be called the General Law of Employment, in contrast to the Particular Law of Employment previously given, which tells you how much employment there will be, i.e., the national income under a state of full employment.

These equations are merely a means of exposition, and not a productive tool. The real tool is thought, and they are not a substitute for it, but at most a guide, or embodiment.

In the long run capital must earn interest equal to the prevailing rate of the monetary system and the established habits and customs for fixed returns. To consider this take limiting cases:

Consider that there is such an abundance of capital that its marginal efficiency is zero, and that the rate of interest is not negative, i.e., it costs nothing to keep money on hand. Consider that people save. Not all the national income is spent on production of consumers goods and capital replacements. Then entrepreneurs must lose, and so capital will be allowed to deteriorate, it being not worth while to replace it. The amount of capital must fall until it earns the prevailing rate of interest. Thus you will have cycles of diminishing capital and increasing capital, with a period which is a function of the life of capital goods and of peoples propensity to save.

If there is a minimum rate of interest fixed by institutions, again, under abundant capital you will get these oscillations. So a minimum interest rate sets limits to the prosperity and employment of the country. Even if it sank to zero you would get them, unless saving were discouraged.

It is my judgment that we are near such a stage of set minimum interest, at the present time.

Here is a suggestion that the evils of capitalism could be gradually and effectively eliminated by this process of the evaporation of the rate of interest. In pioneering times capital is scarce and highly productive so that it will earn large rates. As capitalization approaches completion, its productivity approaches zero as just shown. The ownership of capital then ceases to confer wealth and power and inequality of income, and the entrepreneur's motive of business as a game of skill, already evident as a notable one, would stand out as the governing one. The tendency for this to occur is offset by the presence of conventions as to (1) interest and (2) saving.

We might play with the idea that the inability of the interest rate to fall has brought down empires. In the building up process, the population was in a condition of "natural" poverty to which they were adjusted, and which is steadily being mitigated. There is ample employment, and the abundance of both capital goods and consumption goods increases. With the increase in capital goods toward the saturation point, the risk increases that the interest rate will not fall fast enough, unemployment will appear and rapidly rise. The rapid rise of riches falters. All classes suffer. Social discontent is much greater than under the "natural" poverty, and there is destructive social disorder.

Thus it is of overwhelming importance that the optimum interest rate be determined by institutions and banking practice. And the bad effect of saving must be recognised. All past teaching has (if my view here given is correct) been either irrelevant, or else positively injurious. We have not only failed to understand the economic order under which we live, but we have misunderstood it to the extent of adopting practices which operate most harshly to our detriment, so that we are tempted to cure the ills arising out of our misunderstanding, by resort to further destruction in the form of revolutions.

This instead of the sensible procedure of understanding the remarkably efficient machine which we have built up, whose smooth workings will yield in the course of a relatively few years an optimum of material prosperity; understanding it to keep it in running order and letting it serve our purposes instead of defeating them. At the rate we were going before the last dislocation, 30 years would have sufficed to build up our capital to the optimum level.

Walter Salant Notes: December 4, 1933

Liquidity preference—hold savings in cash or in some other claim to wealth. Man cannot increase his stock of money without inducing others to act in certain way—net result must be zero.

People's desire to hold money determined by complex of (1) Income motive—bridging interval between receipts and disbursements. Also certainty of interval. (2) Business motive—bridge interval of sale proceeds and incurring of expenses. (3) Precautionary motive—provision for contingencies—emergencies and unforeseen bargains. Amount needed for this depends on facilities for getting cash—must hold more cash if we cannot get overdrafts. Also rate of deposit interest compared with interest paid by other ways of using cash. (4) Speculative motive—"state of bearishness" as to future changes in value of goods and securities.

A can increase cash only by persuading or forcing somebody else to lower his cash holdings. B can only maintain cash by selling an asset to C. Prices must fall to a level at which aggregate desire to hold cash equals amount of cash released. Where everyone similar, everyone would have same amount of cash but with change in price level. The change in cash exists only where there is difference in responses of people to change in expectations.

Both expected quasi-rent and rate of interest can be affected by news. Banking authority can fix either rate of interest or quantity of money and let other one adjust itself. Functional relationship between demand for money (M); state of liquidity preferences (A); (w) state of news

$$M = A(w, \rho) \qquad \rho = \text{rate of interest}$$

Given w and A banking system can fix M and therefore rate of interest is determined; or can fix rate of interest and therefore quantity of money is determined. This at least associates the rate of interest with the quantity of money.

$$Y = C + I = \phi 1(w, Y) + \phi 2(w, \rho) \quad \text{Level of income depends on interest}$$

N = total number of employed; N_1 = on consumption goods; N_2 = on investment goods

$$N_1 = fN \qquad N = N_1 + N_2$$
$$= f_1(N) + f_2(\rho) + f_3(M/W)$$

W = rate of wages

f_1 = propensity to consume

f_3 =

Actual rate of interest has falled enough to get down to lowered marginal efficiency of capital—because of institutional factors. It is within the power of the banking system to lower it.

Lorie Tarshis Notes: December 4, 1933

In last lecture covered determinants of investment. But rate of interest now. Last concept—"liquidity preference"—really, the demand for money—the way of summing up the eagerness of people to hold their wealth in money rather than in other forms.

Decision as to how accumulated savings will be held a different decision from that giving volume of saving.

Similar apparent freedom of choice: just as total savings must add up to amount of savings—so does amount of money add up to what the bank will give. Man cannot increase his stock of money without influencing others.

So in hoarding, total stock cannot increase from one side. Watch "misguided attempts to carry over the economics of the individual to the economics of the aggregate."

Motives for holding money, as in *Treatise*—income business and savings, but it so really all one pool. Better, Keynes, thinks now, not to earmark the money—but consider as a net result due to complex of motives.

Desire to hold money is net result of the income, business, precautionary and speculative motives.

1 Income motives depend on—usual considerations—length of receipt–disbursement interval.

2 Business—analogous for the businessman to bridge the gap.

3 Precautionary motive—to provide for contingencies and unforeseen opportunities (why not under 4)—also against future fixed money payments.

Strength of these three factors depend not only on business "conjuncture" but on facility of overdrawing (borrowing)—important in normal times, also rate of deposit interest.

4 Speculative motive—depends on what Keynes called "State of Bearishness"—influenced by estimates of future changes in value of other forms of wealth …

Under influence of these motives, individuals and corporations decide how much cash to hold.

What is method by which effects of all these are reconciled with amount of cash supplied?

(a) When cash held is constant—i.e. M = a constant

A can only increase cash by holding income or selling assets—either of these plans affects someone else's cash. Hence somebody or other faced with a price decision to reconcile cash desires of the two.

Result is that prices must conform to level where those who will give cash are equal to those who will take it.

The level of prices influence the desires of persons to hold cash. Prices will rise or fall to the level where the amount of cash is in conformity with supply and desires.

Where all members of community are alike change of price will occur and no movement of cash holdings—but in fact this does not happen. There is a change in cash due to differences between people.

Change in price is the important thing—the movement in cash is less important—in both theory and observed fact. Effect of change in news causes more price change than volume of sales—"people are more alike than different." In the main it is prices—changes in cash even out.

Prices cover three things—commodities, equities and debts.

We can lump together commodities and equities—commodities being an equity with one quasi-rent only. The value of the equities is dependent on the prospective quasi-rents and the rate of interest—the price of debts is the rate of interest.

Both can be affected by news.

In assuming the quantity of money constant, to say price levels are decided is to say there is definite scale of quasi-rents and rates of interest.

This can all happen if banks regulate rate of interest to keep M constant.

But it is just as reasonable to assume rate of interest fixed and M varying—"or it can do a bit of both."

This enables our schedules of liquidity preference to be expressed in three dimensions—rate of interest, state of news, etc.—then a determined M (quantity of money),

$M = A(w, \rho)$: A is state of liquidity preference. That is a propensity of mind of public toward holding of cash.

It is the rate of interest (ρ) which brings the quantity of money into line with the state of liquidity preference having regard to the state of the news.

We now have the essential determinants of the rate of interest—A (Liquidity Preference)—w (State of News)—M (Quantity of Money). Hence causes of rate of interest from outside.

Two former theories—intersecting supply and demand curves of capital—other abortive method—to get it "out of" the marginal productivity of capital.

This is Keynes "quantity equation" parallel with $M = kR$.

From formal point of view no reason to choose between them.

The only reason for preference is that Keynes thinks it best to relate M to ρ.

One can relate M to the magnitude of the National Debt or the price of a first folio of Shakespeare—but why would we? No formal superiority but Keynes terms more relevant to subsequent analysis.

We have $Y = C + I$

In a given w (state of news): C = function of $Y = \phi_1(w, Y)$

I is a function of w: $\phi_2(w, \rho)$

i.e., $Y = \phi_1(Y) + \phi_2(\rho)$ when w (given)

Hence largely ρ that is important.

Given w suppose N – total employed

N_1 producing for consumption and N_2 producing for investment

Given propensity to spend and consume, then

$N_1 = f_1(N)$: $N_2 = f_2(\rho)$

$N = f_1(N) + f_2(\rho)$

Given liquidity preference $f_2(\rho) = f_3(M/W)$

In any given w (state of the news), within the maximum set by the margin disutility of labour (i.e., under optimum employment), the amount of employment depends on propensity to consume, liquidity preference, and the ratio of M to rate of money wages.

State of the news is something like state of confidence.

Thinks he has isolated the relevant changes now.

It is only by altering one of these things that we can regulate the amount of employment. Full employment is limiting value given by other considerations. The equations are only illustrations and are no good. The real tool is a method of thought. Many other things? Illustration: In long run, capital must be kept scarce enough to yield quasi-rents big enough to pay rate of interest but one can imagine a society so well equipped with capital that marginal productivity of capital is zero or negative (seemingly answers question of its E_s) but which also has a banking system and a rate of interest, not negative.

As soon as anyone saves, entrepreneurs make losses and capital will not be replaced—stock of capital becomes less. Stock must fall until prospective quasi-rents become equal to rate of interest (roughly). If all capital alike it won't begin to be replaced until all capital is earning ρ. Hence an oscillation, a cyclical movement in the stationary society—can keep this perpetual oscillation consistent with (psychological?) conditions.

The same thing can happen if the rate of interest cannot fall below a given figure—when it is unprofitable to lend below this.

Hence oscillating movement when ρ cannot fall below a given figure and where capital is abundant.

In such a community is such that marginal productivity is knocking hard against the minimum rate of interest there is an upper limit to N and to general prosperity—and an oscillation below that.

Keynes' belief is that we have reached some such thing.

Minimum set by doubt as to whether lender will be eventually repaid.

If we can reduce this minimum to zero, then banks can regulate optimum output.

Keynes wants to see this gradual reduction of the minimum profitable rate of interest. –hence get rid of troubles of capitalist system.

Even permissible to play with idea that in past history it is the inability of ρ to fall that has brought down civilizations (effect of organized moratoriums, etc. today?—L.T.).

As community gets richer, etc.—good—

This trouble causes more discontent of course than a natural poverty.

Bryn Thring Notes: December 4, 1933

Liquidity preference. proportion of assets which a man likes to hold in form of cash & deposits.

Income deposits, business deposits, savings deposits—all in one deposit, nor earmarked. or income motive (bridging interval between receipt & disbursal of income depending on how often it comes in, its size (certainty) the business motive—interest between receipt of sale proceeds and incurring of costs—the precautionary motive—for unforeseen accidents or opportunities of good bargains, or to meet a future liability, amount held also depends on facilities for borrowing.

Commodities & equities (= ownership of prospective quasi rents), and debts

Every state of the news, quantity of money being fixed, has its appropriate expectation of quasi rents, & rate of interest, & the banks may fix rate of interest & let appropriate quantity of money to the state of the news, find itself,

$$M = A(w, \rho)$$

w – state of news
ρ – rate of interest
A – state of liquidity preference

therefore neither 2 curves, nor marginal efficiency of capital explain the rate of interest

Keynes says rate of interest comes from the policy of the banking authority about quantity of money, and the state of liquidity preference of the public. (prices) $M = kR$ just as true, but not much point, not relevant.

Summary $Y = C + I$

State of news being given, this function of Y or $= \phi 1(w, Y)$

$I = \phi 2(w, \rho)$

If state of news & expectation is given

$Y = \phi 1(Y) + \phi 2(\rho)$ i.e. other things given, income depends on rate of interest

N_1 – employed on consumption production

N_2 – employed on investment goods

N = total $= N_1 + N_2$

$N_1 = f_1(N)$ – amount of consumption is fixed if employment is fixed

$N = f_1(N) + f_2(\rho)$ i.e. investment depends on rate of interest

$= f_1(N) + f_3(M/W)$ wage

In any given state of news (or state of confidence) employment depends on propensity to consume f_1, state of liquidity preference & quantity of money related to quantity of wages.

= how much employment there will be, so long as less than full employment.

equations are a means of exposition, not a tool—this is the method of thought the equations may help us to comprehend,

are we knocking against point where minimum rate of interest is set by institutional practices, optimum quantity of capital where rate of interest is 0 (zero).

Index

W. Young and E. W. Fuller, *Reinterpreting Mr. Keynes*, Springer Studies in the History of Economic Thought, https://doi.org/10.1007/978-3-030-91342-7

E

F

G

H

I

CPSIA information can be obtained
at www.ICGtesting.com
Printed in the USA
LVHW080850070322
712805LV00004B/257

9 783030 913410